Creating a Life
Worth Living

Creating a Life Worth Living

A PRACTICAL COURSE IN CAREER DESIGN FOR ASPIRING WRITERS, ARTISTS, FILMMAKERS, MUSICIANS, AND OTHERS WHO WANT TO MAKE A LIVING FROM THEIR CREATIVE WORK

Carol Lloyd

HarperPerennial

A Division of HarperCollins*Publishers*

HarperCollins books may be purchased for educational, business, or sales promotional use. For information please write: Special Markets Department, HarperCollins Publishers, Inc., 10 East 53rd Street, New York, NY 10022.

FIRST EDITION

Designed by Alma Hochhauser Orenstein

Library of Congress Cataloging-in-Publication Data
Lloyd, Carol, 1963–
   Creating a life worth living / by Carol Lloyd. — 1st ed.
     p. cm.
   Includes bibliographical references.
   ISBN 0-06-095243-1
   1. Vocational guidance. 2. Creative ability.   I. Title.
HF5381.L56   1997
650.1—dc21   97-6822

01 ❖/RRD 15 14 13

For my mother and father

There is a vitality, a life force, a quickening that is translated through you into action, and because there is only one of you in all time, this expression is unique. If you block it, it will never exist through any other medium. It will be lost. The world will not have it. It is not your business to determine how good it is, nor how valuable it is, nor how it compares with other expressions. It is your business to keep it yours clearly and directly, to keep the channel open.

You do not even have to believe in yourself or your work. You have to keep open and aware directly to the urges that motivate *you*. Keep the channel open. There is no satisfaction whatever at any time. There is only a queer, divine dissatisfaction, a blessed unrest that keeps us marching and makes us more alive.

—MARTHA GRAHAM TO AGNES DE MILLE

Contents

Acknowledgments

My love and thanks to Hank Hyena for feeding the cat, brutal editing, and providing me with a living example of creative commitment, and to Rebecca Wink, my friend and editor. Thanks to Britt Aagesson and Tanya Shaffer for reading the manuscript and sharing their enthusiasm; to Alair MacLean, Jody Suden, Fufkin Vollmeyer, Hope Windle, Elisheva Hart, Laura Nilsen, Adriana Marchione, Lory Anderson, and Galen Newman for their nudging, ideas, and support. To Franny Nudelman for dragging me to dance class; Laura Miller for encouraging me without cause; and to my friends—you know who you are.

Thanks to the long-distance angels who helped bring this book to the world: Julia Cameron for her phone call from New Mexico; my editor, Megan Newman; and my agent, Richard Parks; to all the artists and innovators I interviewed who generously shared their insights and stories; and finally, to all my students, who poured out their quandaries and their dreams, their revelations and their questions, which eventually became the substance of this book.

Introduction

> When I dare to be powerful, to use my strength in the service of my
> vision, then it becomes less and less important whether I am afraid.
>
> —AUDRE LORDE

You are actively searching for two things: the creative life you want to lead and the way to create and maintain that life so that you are as sane and as happy and as financially solvent as you want to be. . . .

I began writing the first words of this book ten years ago, long before I had ever professed any interest in career counseling. The words, directed at my secret self, were scribbled in the pages of my journal. It was a brilliant Sunday afternoon the summer after my supposed graduation from college. I say supposed because I had two Incompletes—one of which was my senior thesis. In those days, I felt that as long as I still had a project owed to some institution greater than myself, my life held purpose. When people asked what I was doing, I could say, "Finishing my degree." Perfectly respectable and vague. I knew that the day I finished school, the geography of my life would transform from a small but fertile ecosystem into a desert stretching out in all directions—full of choices and, at the same time, so damned empty.

That particular Sunday I was visiting my parents and trying desperately to avoid the topic of what I was going to do with my life. My mother, in her gentle, persistent way, managed to insinuate my future into our every conversation.

ME: These peaches are great. Are they organic?
HER: I hear the horticultural program at State is wonderfully innovative.
    You always did like fresh fruit.
ME: Do you mind if I do a load of laundry?

HER: Jack Miller's son just started a rock 'n' roll Laundromat. Have you ever thought something like that would be fun?

I was there to eke out the last drops of childhood oblivion, but she kept interrupting with her cheerful inquiries. Finally she asked me directly, "Have you thought about what you really want? Not just the job, the *life*."

Although I was tempted to respond with the adolescent mantra, "*Mo*-om, gimme a break," I knew I shouldn't let the opportunity slip by. I was well aware that many people were not so lucky as to have someone ask them what they really wanted to do. My mother didn't really care what career I chose as long as I didn't short-sheet my own desires. She knew what it was like to sleep in a mismade bed. Like many women of her generation, she had delayed her real ambitions to conform to an ideal of the suburban housewife. While I had not been subjected to the same sociopolitical forces, I think she intuited that my tendency might be to choose something I wasn't really excited about just because it seemed "safer."

I decided to take advantage of my mother's interest in my future. Besides, if I could prove that I was really grappling with these questions, then at least she'd leave me alone for the rest of the weekend and I could revert to my natural vegetable state.

I outlined what I saw to be my three main options: academia, social work, and art. Although all the choices were rather murky, each represented a distinct facet of my identity. I wrote a narrative describing my sense of what each of these lives would look like—one, five, ten, and twenty years down the road. I listed the pros and cons of each life. I tried to imagine how I would feel on my deathbed with each particular choice.

I showed the papers to my mother. Trying my best to impress her with my diligence and maturity, I informed her that I was vacillating between social work and academia. One was "socially responsible," I explained, the other "intellectually challenging."

"But what do you really want to do?" my mother asked, raising one sharpened eyebrow at the pages marked ART.

"I don't think that's really the point," I said peevishly.

"Heck it isn't!"

My mother encouraged me to pick the realm I felt most passionately about, *not* the one I felt I should or even could do—thereby setting me loose on the path of an artist and entrepreneur. For an eager-to-please gal like me, the notion of not answering to an overriding institution or organization was pretty disorienting. No corporate ladders to climb, no ivory towers to scale, no bureaucratic jungles to bushwhack? There was no clear path to success but, it seemed, so many ways to fail. At the same time, I was also exhilarated. From the fanatical age of six I had been telling people that I wanted to be a writer, but by the time I reached college, I had decided that the dream was little more than a self-indulgent cliché that I simply needed to outgrow. Writing down the three primary avenues of my future was the first step in a process that would allow me to choose what I really wanted to do and to construct a life leading toward that place.

Not that I didn't swerve and veer wildly around trying to discover my place in the artistic and employment universe. In the years just after college, my sense of self catapulted from black hole to rising star to lunar eclipse on a daily basis. I moved to San Francisco, where, with several thousand other art-damaged, interdisciplinary bohemians, I juggled a handful of part-time jobs ranging from fascinating to annoying— teaching at a home for unwed mothers, running a theater arts camp for children, working as an editorial assistant at an academic publishing house, catering for a cookie store. I also ran myself ragged pursuing a plethora of art forms—acting, writing, dancing, choreographing, directing. I wrote theater criticism, started four businesses, and, of course, returned to graduate school for the all-important M.F.A. degree. I felt like a hawk circling a mouse that kept disappearing into a hole. I was always moving, swooping, searching, but at the end of the day, I was still hungry!

Sometimes I looked on enviously as friends who had chosen more conventional careers earned good livings and always seemed to know what they were supposed to do next. My passion for many things combined with my stubborn unwillingness to go out and "get a real job" created a different set of obstacles than those facing my more career-minded friends. Every day there were a million things I could do. A million things I wanted to do. And nobody but me to make sure I did any of them. I felt like I was reinventing the wheel every day of my life.

At the same time, the little career counseling session I gave myself provided me with a determination and faith that allowed me to take risks and build a creative life. My long-term commitment to following my passion was the single gift I would fall back on when all the other gifts—luck, discipline, inspiration—seemed to let me down.

This clarity of direction distinguished me from many of the other struggling artists I knew. These smart, talented, independent individuals had begun abandoning the things they had professed they most wanted to do. Shrugging off their madcap creative dreams, they talked in hushed monotones about professional degrees. Shuffling from temp job to temp job, they worried about whether to go permanent, loathing the idea while at the same time yearning for stability. Even when their creative careers were on the rise, they admitted that they didn't have an overall plan. I was convinced that if they clarified their desires and created a plan of action in a creative, open-minded context, they wouldn't be so quick to leave their dreams behind.

One hot night in a little hut in Bali, I got the chance to try out my career counseling system. I was traveling and studying dance with a choreographer who had been my friend, business partner, and artistic collaborator for years. We were in one of the most beautiful, creative spots on earth and she couldn't enjoy it. She was worrying about her future—her mind a hot pot of imagined dance companies, medical school applications, and M.F.A. programs all stewing in the bitter broth of doubt. I whipped out my pen. "Okay, Samantha," I cried with game-show vigor, "We're going to give you . . . A Life Worth Living." That night, as monkeys howled from the nearby forest, we mapped out her options, brainstormed new ideas, and systematically tried to find new solutions. As the sun spilled into the tropical sky and we fell into sleep, Samantha was not the only one who had found a new career direction.

I began applying my brand of creative career counseling to my friends' career problems. With no small grain of salt, I kept calling it "A Life Worth Living." After all, who was I to preach the path to career nirvana? At dinner parties friends would tease me, "Hey, Carol, pass me a life worth living." And I'd willingly oblige. I discovered that creative people were hungry to discuss these issues and that I instinctively knew how to help them clarify what they wanted, navigate the vague terrain between vision and real life, and arrive at practical solutions.

It went on like that for years, this spontaneous thing I did for my friends.

Gradually, this "thing" evolved into a formalized process. I began to work with friends of friends, then strangers. I began seeing patterns among different personalities and different creative forms. Based on the wildly enthusiastic response, I realized that I had tapped into a need for a career process designed specifically for creative people. Some of my students had already gone to traditional career counselors and had been disappointed. As one young filmmaker put it:

They gave me a two-hour multiple choice test with questions like, "Which would you rather be for Halloween: a) a fireman, b) a monster, c) a famous politician, or d) a kitten? Then they asked me about my job history—which amounted to a lot of word processing and office work. Then they told me I was artistic and should think about pursuing a career in arts administration. Then I went home and ate a whole roll of Pillsbury cookie dough.

Artists and other innovators face substantially different obstacles in creating a career. Old-fashioned career advice is largely irrelevant. People who want to live a creative life must create their lives in entirely their own way. They can't depend on anybody to tell them how. At the urging of friends, I created a workshop that guided artistic people through the process of discovering their own life worth living.

The demand for the workshops surpassed my expectations. I watched people's lives transform in miraculous ways and I watched the pile of handouts and scribbled lecture notes burst the corners of my old Peachy folder.

Then one day I got a call from a woman whose book on creativity I had admired. In a moment of "inspired procrastination" (an important technique I will discuss in detail later), I had written her a letter a few days before—telling her about my workshop and my writing.

"Have you written about your workshop?" she asked me.

"Uh, not really."

"You should write a book."

"Excuse me?"

She spoke slowly and gently, as if to a child. "This is a call, telling you, you should write a book."

"Oh." I swallowed. "Sure."

Just as it took an unfamiliar hand to push me gently off the cliff and into the ether of a new project, I hope this book can do the same for you.

What It Is and What It Ain't

First of all, let me assure you that there are no career tests in this book. This is a process for reinventing your life. You are the inventor, not me. The project of the self-help book has always seemed a paradoxical one. While the author is madly positing abstract principles about life, the book's real purpose lies in creating a space for processing the reader's very personal, individual experience. For this reason I use the image of the scaffolding to remind you that my process is only a temporary structure to help you build your own dream house. The scaffolding may be generic, but your house will be unique. My scaffolding may help you to climb high enough to see some spectacular views, but you'll want a custom-designed home to keep you there, safe and strong. When the house is ready for you to live in, you will remove the scaffolding because it's no longer useful.

From the ample techniques, ideas, and opinions scattered throughout these pages, you can build your own creative structure, your own house of dreams. By "structure," I mean everything from your daily habits to your belief system, the particulars of your artistic vision to your relationships with people and places—in other words, all those elements of your life that together propel you to your chosen future.

Though I have tried to avoid lifestyle prescriptions, I do finally advocate some kind of self-imposed creative structure—outside of the demands of a day job or the biological demands for food and sleep. Without this structure, we too easily fall prey to entropy. Time dances by us. Freedom becomes a kind of prison; we fly in so many directions we can't go anywhere.

There are reams written on the extraordinary powers of the human imagination, the healing forces of creativity, the mysteries of the artistic process. This book draws from such writings but attempts a very different task: *to apply the artistic process to building a career*. It doesn't assume much about you or your beliefs. It doesn't assume you need a dose of rah-rah, go-get-'em positive thinking or, on the other hand, a rigid authoritative diet of tasks and laws. It also doesn't assume you buy into therapeutic definitions or religious doctrines. It is with the utmost respect for my readers that I embark on this book with a solemn vow to avoid psychobabble, prescriptive bromides, and sacrosanct euphemisms. Except when necessary, that is. Sometimes the prophetic voice of sweeping generalizations works wonders, and then I don't hesitate to use it. So now that I've totally reneged on my solemn vow, I hope you can see how untrustworthy I am. Don't take my word for it. Do it, use it, critique it. Experience it yourself.

As in all teaching relationships, both parties participate in the consensual hallucination that the teacher has the answers. In this process, which offers techniques but not solutions, possibilities but not imperatives, it is more important than ever to be clear about the limits of the teacher's understanding. Not because I am a fraud and have nothing to offer but because, for creative people, living by an internal system is the only way.

Borrowed ideas about being creative can inspire and work for a while, but their power won't last unless you adapt them to your particular chemistry, desire, ambition, culture, and values. That said, we can learn a lot from other people; artists are not grown in vacuums but in the fecundity of social influences. So learn, borrow, and steal what you can, but, as you move through this process of finding a new direction, make sure you listen to yourself. To this end, I have included an exercise in most chapters asking you to articulate what you learned and what you still need to explore.

The only thing this book does assume is that you are an artist.

"Hey, wait a minute, I'm not an artist."

Well, maybe not in the limited sense. I define artist in the broadest possible terms—not only the literary, visual, and performing arts, but also all those careers and personalities that demand that you create your own life. Some of my students didn't consider themselves "artists" even within this broader definition. At a certain point, however, they realized that they needed to approach their lives and career problems in a creative way. Even signing up for the class was, on some level, an acknowledgment of the fact that they had an artist inside them waiting to burst forth.

Every life can benefit from the brilliance and thrill of unleashed creativity, but there are some professions that cannot survive without it. Scientific invention, journalism, events planning, teaching, scholarship, electronic media, consulting, organizational development, bodywork, counseling, and entrepreneurial work are just a few of the careers that require the creative process. While this may seem like a weird collection, all these jobs involve creation, self-reliance, and synthesizing a complexity of elements into a single whole.

Many careers in embryonic fields are both unhampered and unaided by institutional structure. Because of this absence of structure, these careers demand a more inventive and multifaceted approach than they will a hundred years hence. For example, when Freud was doing "talk therapy," he was also inventing it. The creative demands in his evolving field were far greater than those imposed upon a conventional psychologist today.

If you don't see yourself as an artist or involved in any pioneering career, but just have lots of competing interests, then the Life Worth Living process can help you sort out and synthesize your desires. If you want to shift your life toward creativity but you're not sure how, then this book can help you discover your path and embark on that journey.

For many, the most difficult challenge is discovering what they really want to do. For others the challenge lies in planning the life and committing to it. Others have no trouble dreaming or planning the dream, but giant, tentacled obstacles impede their everyday progress and prevent them from reaching their goals. Still others have accomplished a lot in their lives, but their careers no longer fulfill their needs—be they money, creativity, or intellectual challenge.

So if your desired career demands creativity, if your life begs for unification and balance, if your mind craves an as-yet-uninvented path, you are undergoing an artistic process: a mix of alchemy and common sense, magic and action. This duality of dreaming big and acting small forms the core philosophy from which this process springs.

This book will guide you through a creative planning process with a moment-to-moment attention to your life as you live it *now*. On the one hand, you will be exercising your imagination to build a clearer vision of the future through long-term imagining. I call this "eagle vision" or "stretching the dream muscle." At the other end of the spectrum, you will be creating those daily habits that allow you to work systematically, regardless of the weather, your mood, your successes or failures. This daily effort I call "squirrel work" or "flexing the action muscle." I have found that most people struggling with creating their careers either have cramped dream muscles or weak action muscles.

How the Book Is Organized

Part 1, "The Dive," engages you in the process of strengthening your relationship to your dreams with rigorous daily habits.

Chapter 1, "Ecstatic Task," introduces the daily action, a technique you will use to set in motion the transformation of your daily life. Through "listening to the voices of the day," you'll begin to understand how your own internal soundscape supports or undermines your dreams.

Chapter 2, "Stoking the Coals," leads you through a series of conceptual, visual, and verbal exercises to ignite the idea-generating part of your brain and train your imagination to rise from the mired realm of worry to the inspired world of play.

In Part 2, "The Dig," you will engage in a process of search and research—churning up all your ancient desires, present needs, and timeless inclinations.

Chapter 3, "Excavating the Future," leads you through an archaeological dig through your memories for forgotten career paths, creative catalysts, and buried desires.

Chapter 4, "The Kaleidoscope of Creativity," examines ten distinct creative types, their employment challenges, special talents, and particular needs. You'll explore your unique blend of creativity and the ways that you can create a work life to support it.

Chapter 5, "Neglected Needs," will help you rethink your relationship to time, money, and desire. Through clarifying your nonartistic needs, you'll gain a clearer picture of the parameters of your creative well-being.

Chapter 6, "The Drudge We Do for Dollars," explores the paradigm of the day job. It describes the various kinds of day jobs and how they can support or undermine your long-term creative goals.

Part 3, "The Design," guides you through an in-depth planning process, thereby developing your "eagle vision." These chapters will lead you deep into your own ideas and dreams, compelling you to give them life through concrete detail.

Chapter 7, "The Long and Winding Roads," addresses the problem of indecision and competing interests. You'll be invited to walk down three possible paths into three distinct futures. Through this exercise you'll gain a clearer idea of your true desires, your urgent interests, and your long-term commitments.

Chapter 8, "Goals," redefines goals and then guides you through the process of conceiving a single, long-term goal, reflecting your most important creative aspiration.

Chapter 9, "A Map to the Moon," provides a series of techniques from fiction, film, visual art, architecture, and theater to draw a map to your newly defined goal—from today's bite-size actions to the dream's culminating event.

Part 4, "The Doing," plunges you back into the power of "squirrel work." Through specific exercises and techniques, you will work toward making today a vehicle that can transport you into your chosen future.

Chapter 10, "Magic at Work," reinvents your workday. You'll be asked to analyze your current lifestyle and build a new model for your everyday creative process.

Chapter 11, "Building a Bridge You Can Jump On," guides you in building an emotional and practical support system through friendships and creative alliances. These relationships will help you follow through on your plan and ensure you an ongoing creative community.

Chapter 12, "Swimming in the Darkness," helps you see your new life as a balance of long-term creative projects, practical transitional situations, and regenerating daily life. Through the Five-Arena Calendar, you will organize the whole of your new artistic, self-directed life. The chapter also offers some parting thoughts on perseverance, faith, and curiosity.

About the Interviews

Between chapters you'll find interviews with individuals who have successfully carved out careers for themselves based on their creative impulses. Through their stories, these artists, inventors, and entrepreneurs offer inspiration, valuable practical advice, and fascinating examples of how ordinary people invent extraordinary lives.

When I first began my interviews for this book, I worried that the people who had already fully manifested their careers would have very little to say about their observations on the creative process or pursuing an uncharted career. Despite all my intellectual ideas to the contrary, part of my brain still believed that Hollywood claptrap that creative geniuses were born and not made. To my surprise, however, the more creatively fulfilled and successful the person was, the more he or she had to say on the issues of creativity, self-direction, and the struggle of the journey.

In fact, nearly all of the artists and innovators I interviewed described intensely self-reflective periods in which they figured out what creative attitudes and daily rituals they needed in order to continue working. Many seemed to be in an ongoing cycle of soul-searching. When I described my book, they surprised me by saying, "Hey, I would definitely buy a book like that—I'm always looking for new ways to think through these things." It wasn't something they had gotten over just because they had achieved success. The constant search for self-knowledge was an essential part of replenishing their creativity and keeping their work interesting.

A Note on Using This Book

Since this book has grown out of a workshop, it is designed to be read and practiced in weekly portions. Let yourself read through the chapter first, work through the exercises during the rest of the week, and then treat yourself with the interview. Working through the book in weekly segments will reinforce the lesson that all creative work takes place in real time and that if you want to make a change, you may as well begin now.

Here are a few suggestions for making this process fun:

- Give yourself time to work on it consistently, no matter what your mood is.
- Let these next few weeks be a time when you allow yourself to break old habits and try new things. One woman who took the workshop said that for the first time since her childhood, she began remembering her dreams. Other people have discussed a sensation of seeing their friends in a new light, falling in love with a new art form, breaking ties with a person who dampened their creative flame. Embrace these inner earthquakes; take pleasure in these new sensations. Let these next few weeks offer you safe passage to a strange new place in your life.
- Career and long-term planning? How horrifyingly dull. This process is about how you can infuse these ugly, prosaic words with the charged intensity of a child's password. For instance, I like to think of "work" as a password for play and "long-term planning" as a password for casting my imagination into the future on an invisible fishing line miles and miles long.

Right now, before you begin, free associate with the words listed below. Redefine the words in your own way. Let the definitions be wild, irrational, contradictory, optimistic, and foul. Just write whatever you feel. We will return to them at the end of the process and see if any of your perspectives have shifted.

Career:

Job:

Work:

Art:

Plan:

Goal:

PART I

The Dive

Begin it now . . .

> Until one is committed, there is hesitancy, that chance to draw back, always ineffectiveness. Concerning all acts of initiative (and creation), there is one elemental truth the ignorance of which kills countless ideas and splendid plans: that the moment one definitively commits oneself, then providence moves too. All sorts of things occur to help one that would never otherwise have occurred. A whole stream of events issues from the decision, raising in one's favor all manner of unforeseen incidents and meetings and material assistance, which no person could have dreamed would have come one's way.
>
> —W. H. MURRAY

> Whatever you can do or dream you can, begin it. Boldness has genius, power, and magic in it.
>
> —GOETHE

Begin it now . . . In this part you will take the first step in committing to a long-term creative life by diving into the present with a new awareness and a new habit.

Ecstatic Task

The Daily Action

You need not leave your room. Remain sitting at your table and listen. You need not even listen, simply wait. You need not even wait, just learn to become quiet, and still, and solitary. The world will freely offer itself to you to be unmasked. It has no choice; it will roll in ecstasy at your feet.

—FRANZ KAFKA

In a dark corner of her childhood house, her father sometimes set up a makeshift laboratory. She used to sneak in and play there, watching the bubbling liquids, measuring the weight of her little hands on the scale. Officially, she wasn't allowed to touch the instruments, but her curiosity often got the better of her. When her sisters were outside playing, she escaped to the laboratory, a sanctuary of quiet, concentration, and potential.

Marie Curie's mystical attitude toward the laboratory never changed. Later, when her laboratory was no more than a drafty basement, and the work of isolating radioactive metals became arduous and frustrating, this private place of work remained a pleasurable retreat from a world of chatter and opinion. The conception of the laboratory as a place of serious play, a continuous present moment that could hold her captive with eternity's questions, was born in her childhood through a simple ritual. It is this dark corner of the basement reserved for private play that most often gets disregarded as we grow up. We peek into the stairway from time to time, but are too busy with the rooms above and their many inhabitants to descend. We forget that it was this secret haven that fueled our curiosity and imagination in the first place. In this world of information overload and constant communication, it is easy to lose touch with the habit of making time for curiosity.

This book seeks to help you build the private laboratory in which you will reinvent your life. But the grand experiment will not be over when, in eleven weeks, you read the last page of this book. You'll have a box of new tools you can continue to use to hammer out your future. Specifically, there are three things I hope you will take away from this book: first, a clearer vision of what you really want and a commitment to that vision; second, a step-by-step plan for achieving that vision; and third, a daily process that develops strong, healthy work habits and keeps your vision in sharp focus. Of all of these, the daily process is by far the most crucial. For it is in the present moment that creative work happens, and without a rigorous relationship to today, the power of tomorrow is no more than a shadow puppet casting elaborate darkness over all our endeavors. You may use this book to get an inspirational shot in the arm, but the only way for it to have lasting value is by committing to a daily process that will live beyond these pages.

To help you begin the building of your personal laboratory, I'm giving you mine to borrow—just as Marie Curie's father unwittingly lent his laboratory to his youngest daughter. Use the tools in this chapter as your working laboratory for the next few weeks. When you reach the eighth chapter, you will be asked to assess how this laboratory is working for you and to begin reshaping it into a new process tailored to your creative chemistry.

The Daily Action

The daily action is fifteen minutes of a focused activity performed every day at the same time of day. Choose an activity that creates an empty space where your creativity can reassert itself. Let the action be solitary and process oriented. You are giving yourself fifteen minutes of emptiness within the blur of living. Some examples of daily actions are dancing alone in your living room, meditating, walking, writing in a journal, drawing without purpose, singing improvisational melodies, doing yoga, and gardening.

Don't limit your imagination: Invent your own daily action if you feel the impulse. One of my students, Tracy, set up a little altar to her grand-mother who had recently died and whom she missed terribly. Her grandmother had always been a great source of inspiration and good advice, and Tracy didn't want to sever this connection to her wisdom. Every morning before she began work on her novel, she sat down and had a conversation with her grandmother. Without making any claims to supernatural communication, Tracy used these conversations to tap into the part of herself that carried her grandmother's spirit and wis-dom. Tracy claimed the action filled her with hope and energy.

Nellie, a jewelry designer and sound producer, dragged herself every morning up her fire escape to sit on her roof and watch the sun come up. Though she lived on a busy urban street, her rooftop musings gave her time with nature and a sense of quiet before she began her day.

Victor played his bongo drums—not complicated rhythms but a sin-gle meditative beat. Anne kept a journal that she wasn't allowed to write sentences in—only drawings, doodles, and lists and charts. Michael walked around his neighborhood watching people and appreciating architecture. Bob stretched to his favorite music. Rita kept a stream-of-consciousness dream journal.

During my interviews with established artists, I found that many of them had their own form of daily action. Mary Gaitskill, the novelist and short-story writer, engages in a type of meditation. Standing qui-etly, she focuses on her breathing and observes her thoughts and feel-ings.

"Imagery comes into my mind and I follow it," she explained. "It's like dreaming, only you're conscious. You can manipulate the dream to see where it goes. It's not only calming but it reminds me of the part of me that's always creating stories and images." Her particular style of meditation doesn't function to empty her mind or fill her with positive thoughts; rather, it is a method of quieting her mind and letting her imagination run wild.

In choosing a daily action for yourself, avoid activities that require you to respond to stimuli or follow a formula too closely. Activities like organizing papers, exploring the Internet, writing letters to old friends, reading, or reciting prayers can be extremely useful, calming, and life affirming, but they don't create the simple, empty space necessary to bring your mind *and your mind alone* to the fore. Also, beware of actions that can become too product oriented and therefore tarnished by anxiety about success or failure. Sometimes people try to make the daily action do double duty for them: They try to finish an old project and disguise it as a daily action. The clearer, simpler, and more enjoyable the daily action, the more useful and edifying it will be in the long run. It should be fun and above all *easy in its actual execution.* If you have difficulty convincing yourself to do an easy action, you will learn that you have issues with discipline, time, concentration, and solitude in their purest form. But if you give yourself a daily action that is burdened by ambition or complexity, you will always be able to say, "Well, I quit my daily action because standing on my head and writing poetry in iambic pentameter really *is* tough. It's not like I have problems with discipline or concentration."

I like to think of the action as an empty receptacle that my imagination inhabits for a few minutes a day. Conversely, when I begin viewing it as a path to progress, I immediately start limiting my playfulness, my enjoyment of the moment. For a while my daily action was playing guitar. I couldn't play at all, so it was just making noise with the strings and singing weird melodies. Then I began taking lessons and got really excited about the possibility of playing real songs. I had assignments from my teacher, exercises, and a feeling that I "should" practice for the lesson. The daily action fell apart; it wasn't easy anymore—it was another pursuit. It was just too charged with meaning. The wonderful thing about your daily action is that you should be able to do it as well today as you can ten years from now.

Unlike some forms of meditation, the goal of the daily action is not an empty mind. Blank time is enough. Let your mind go where it wants to that day. In this empty place, allow yourself to brainstorm, make wild plans, imagine the impossible, worry about silly things. Let yourself stretch your dream muscle and express your inner whiner. Space out, tune in, rev up, calm down. Let your mind do whatever it wants to do, while your body does the action.

How Does the Daily Action Work?

> Don't say you're going to stop biting your fingernails, say you're going to stop biting *one* fingernail.
>
> —SONNY KRASNER

As you begin the process of reorienting your life, you'll probably be asking yourself to build some new habits and to take certain calculated risks. That means change. And change, as we all know, isn't always comfortable. Maybe you don't know what the changes are yet. But in the meantime you can begin to prepare yourself. Don't try to change everything about your life at once; first practice with the equivalent of one unbitten fingernail, in tiny fifteen-minute windows. You can look into these windows every day and see yourself working, creating, changing, and getting used to change itself. Since fifteen minutes is such an insignificant amount of time, you will have a hard time convincing yourself you just can't squeeze it in. It will set you in motion, even if you are not yet sure of your direction.

Inspiration grows into full-scale creation through persistence and imagination. The daily action exercises both. Doing your daily action every day (seven days a week), at the same time of day, will make self-discipline a habit. In this way, the daily action reinforces the truth that tiny steps can scale giant mountains. Once your action becomes incorporated into your life, it will become a ritual imbued with its own power—the power of your own energy, focus, and joy. The ritual will become an invaluable tool for sustaining and replenishing your creative energy during hard times.

In addition to providing you with structure and self-discipline, the daily action strengthens your imagination by instituting emptiness into your day. Like a loyal animal, the imagination will come when it knows the door is open. Having an empty time for imaginative wanderings will help you create clearer visions of your future and a more intense experiencing of your desires. Maintaining clarity of vision is an essential difference between those who conceive *and realize* great ideas and those who simply conceive great ideas. The people who make it happen take time to make their ideas clear. As entrepreneur/designer Loretta Staples says, "If you are clear about what you want, the world responds with clarity."

Perhaps the most important gift from the daily action is time to watch your mind at work. If every day when you sit down to draw or do yoga, you can only think about everything else you should be doing, consider whether you're habitually telling yourself that you should be somewhere else, doing something else. If your inner voices chatter on and on about what your life is going to be like ten years from now, you may learn that you have a tendency to leap into the future without a handle on the present. If you sit down to write in your journal and your mind is a jumble of urges and feelings about loved ones, you might ask yourself if you are resisting attention to your own life.

If you're in a state of intense uncertainty about your desires and your direction, be patient with the daily action. Because more than likely, during this brief respite from productivity, you will be besieged with those annoyingly profound questions: Who am I? How do I do this? Why am I in debt? What is to be done?

You may think, Shouldn't I know already? Why should I be subjected to these thoughts, over and over? Do the action anyway, making it fun and playful for yourself. While worrying and hand-wringing very rarely yield new perspectives, the daily action can work like magic. It is not my intention to keep you in a state of continual navel-gazing. It will, however, give you the opportunity to think through these old questions about career and creativity in the broad light of day.

Here are some common questions about the daily action.

I can't imagine just putting my work aside and saying, Okay, now I'm doing my daily action. What if the phone rings?

If you're working you're not doing your daily action, and vice versa. You can't do your daily action in your work space. Even if you have the most lackadaisical temp job or the most flexible home-employment situation, you still may be interrupted by a request, a phone call, a fax. And, of course, that's as it should be. You're working! If you work at home where the boundaries between work and life are utterly muddy, then create a daily action like walking or gardening that gets you out of your house.

You said the daily action should be fun, but I don't think I have a problem with indulging myself. How is it different from going out for a fancy lunch?

At its absolute core, I do think that the daily action is wonderfully indulgent, but in its form it is pure and rather ascetic. You are not following your daily whim as to what you want to eat. You are not taking time off. You are staying present with yourself to do one thing and only one thing, simply and cleanly, every day, at the same time of day. This demands focus and energy as well as self-love.

I just fell in love so my sleeping schedule's kinda . . . unpredictable. Sometimes I don't sleep at home. My work schedule is different every day, the whole idea of doing it the same time of day every day seems impossible.

Well, you don't have to do your action at the same time, but if you do, the technique is both easier and more effective. Ideally, you should do your action as soon as you wake up. Try attaching it in time and place to your morning shower or brushing your teeth. I imagine you make time for personal hygiene in your life and don't think that's such a big deal. That's because it's a habit. That's what your daily action must become: a healthy fifteen-minute habit.

You also might choose an action that you can do without embarrassment or hassle (sketching, writing in a journal?) anywhere, no matter whose bed you wake up in.

I'm not a morning person. Can I do it at night?

I have a prejudice for morning daily actions because I think they establish your priorities for the day. Each day has a symbolic meaning. If you do your daily action every morning at the beginning of the day, you will silently teach your mind and soul that your creative life comes first. Not your day job, not your new lover's sleeping habits, and not the demands of the phone. If you leave your action until the end of the day when you're tired and craving free time, you may begin to resent the daily action. On the other hand, there are some people who wake up and become fiercely creative at night. They don't mind shutting themselves away from their social life to funnel their energy into something quiet and solitary.

I barely have enough time to do the things I need to do now. How am I supposed to add another thing to my list that is totally unproductive?

It's definitely a challenge for some people's schedules. But for the most part, the struggle to find time in the day for yourself alone is going to show you just how much time you give away to other people or projects that you really don't want or need. Understanding how you use or abuse your own time offers great insights and is likely to give you enormous motivation to change your patterns and carve out some time for this very important transition that you're undertaking.

Embarking on a Career Change: Emotions and Resistance

Any time you undertake a project as large and important as changing the focus of your life or your work, deep psychological issues can arise that exacerbate an already fragile process. One of the best ways we can protect ourselves in advance is to know that these emotions may surface and be prepared for them to work themselves through our minds the way a cold virus works itself through our bodies—ultimately leaving us stronger and immune to this particular strain of affliction.

These feelings may not express themselves through common symptoms. You may not consciously think, Gee, I'm angry at my friends for making fun of my new project, but you may suddenly feel a great aversion to answering your phone or listening to messages. (This may be a reasonable way of dealing with obnoxious friends, but you could undermine yourself by not returning the calls from those people who *do* give you support.) You may find yourself eating strangely or your sleeping patterns altered. You may not consciously feel fear, for instance, but suddenly you won't want to get out of your bed in the morning. You may actually think you're coming down with something physical. You may suddenly need ten hours' sleep a night or suffer from insomnia.

Hal, who had just managed to reorganize his schedule to rehearse for three hours every morning for his upcoming solo performance, suddenly felt the urge to sleep nine hours a night, even though for his entire life he had been happy with seven.

"Why am I sleeping so much? It's ridiculous," he exclaimed.

"What's the first thing you do every morning?" I asked.

"I get up, and I rehearse; I memorize lines."

For many years he had managed to create solo performance that didn't require rehearsal. He hated to rehearse because it heightened his fears about the quality of the work and his lack of acting training. Now this show—which involved a lot of character monologues—was forcing him to change his daily habits. Though he was being "disciplined" and productive, the fear remained and was being expressed through his overwhelming desire to sleep. While his mind had triumphed, his body didn't really want to get up and begin this newly forming habit. When we spoke after a month, he had accustomed himself to the new schedule and was actually enjoying the rehearsal process. He also had returned to his typical sleeping patterns. If he had given too much meaning to his pseudodepressive symptoms, he might have been tempted to quit, which is just what the fear-driven part of his brain and body wanted him to do.

Some fear is healthy. It keeps us from jumping off buildings and saying smug things to violent drunks. But fear also works against us. Fear colludes with our most conservative self and allows us to stop before we try, dismiss before we think, mock before we imagine. We've all seen it in others; it is so easy to perceive when you watch a friend refuse to take advantage of some remarkable opportunity, simply out of fear. But they don't often say, "I'm too afraid." They say, "I don't know if I'm ready," or "I'm just too busy right now." At the heart of their fear is the message, "If I try to get something really wonderful, I'll have to screw up everything that is already just okay."

Everyone has this voice inside them; it's a voice of survival and ancient necessity. Beware its power. The voice will arise when it is totally inappropriate and you are simply *thinking through* ideas, not threatening your livelihood or future stability in any way. Whether you are a relentlessly spontaneous artiste who has never thought of making a long-term plan or a terminally responsible professional for whom the idea of refocusing your life toward creative interests is really scary, the voice of fear can wreak havoc on your dreams before you ever take the slightest risk.

If unmanageable feelings of fear arise while working through this process, try the following:

1. Write the feelings down. All of them. Now ask each of them, Who are you? Listen to the tone of the feelings; note the vocabulary from which they are made. Is this internal voice reinforced by any external forces, people, memories? Watch them as displays of theatricality—watch them build to a climax and fade on the page. Write out the fears until *they bore you to death* and, for the time being, have lost some of their power.

2. Sit down and do your daily action or some other fifteen minutes of endeavor on your creative work. Work against your impulse to run away. Watch the tug of war between will and whim. Just as it is a natural response to pull back when skiing down a steep hill, we often want to pull away from the vertigo of creativity. Yet both on the slopes and in the creative process, pulling back makes us speed up and run out of control. When this happens, don't try to think it through. Do something. One small, tiny, teeny creative action. Only for fifteen minutes. Don't do any more than that little tiny action (unless you are having too much fun). Often after the doing begins, even the most daunting projects become fun, and no matter how many hundreds of times we experience this, some strange, sinister amnesia descends upon us and wipes away our memory of the pure pleasure found in concentration.

3. Know that this cycle of learning and relearning is part of a creative life. It is not a linear, predictable process. If you are feeling fear, the adventure has already begun. Rejoice in knowing that every artist or innovator experiences this dizzying uncertainty. Some learn to enjoy it, others to tolerate it, others continue to believe that the inner turmoil and instability is a sign that their creative aspirations are "wrong."

4. When you are feeling fear of some project or idea or dream, ask yourself, What am I still curious enough about to override my fear? Follow your curiosity like a delicious scent leading you to a kitchen. Let your curiosity peel back the dry, bitter skin of drudgery to find the sweet fruit of fun at the core. *Focus on what you love rather than fixating on the feelings of discomfort that sometimes accompany desire.*

5. Remember: Doing is significantly different than not doing. Doing not only "gets things done," it teaches lessons you cannot possibly learn theoretically and can loosen even the most stubbornly entrenched feelings. My emphasis on experimentation and action comes from the belief that feelings—while important—can also play tricks on us. In this therapeutically minded culture, feelings are often equated with reality. An overemphasis on feelings can lead to passivity and paralysis in the areas that demand great discipline. To this end, resolve that this month be a month of dabbling and doing in concert with contemplation. Know that when you are feeling bad or unmotivated, you can still do good things for yourself. Just because you have an onslaught of negative feelings when you undertake to reinvent your life, doesn't mean the project is a bad idea. Bad feelings are not necessarily bad omens, symptoms of mental or physical illness, or indicators that you're "not ready." They're just feelings, and very natural ones at that.

DENNIS DUN, ACTOR

Dennis Dun sometimes worried that he was doomed to be a dabbler. After studying marketing in college because he thought it was "practical," he sought help from a string of career counselors. "They told me I should be in toys because it was off-beat." Knowing only that he didn't want a "regular job," he embarked on a sprawling career search—working as a clerk in a store, tutoring children at the YWCA, supervising underprivileged teens in cleaning up a mall. At the same time, he took painting and photography classes and pursued a variety of sports. "I didn't know what I was doing. I just had all this energy," he explained. When he applied to Macy's as a stockperson, they saw his degree in marketing and convinced him to enter their management training program.

"It was hell. I was really depressed. I was surrounded by all these upper-middle-class white kids whose parents were probably in retail too and they were so psyched about it. I just felt like such a geek. I knew I had to do something else."

Distraught and disgruntled, he signed up for an acting class at the San Francisco–based Asian-American Theater. "It was like a light shined on me. A revelation. All the things I had been taking in—sound and rhythm from athletics and images from visual art. From the get-go I was involved six days a week."

Eventually he veered off his career track at Macy's. He cobbled together a living from odd jobs and pursued acting seriously. Acting was not only a career choice but an exploration of Dun's cultural identity. "I grew up first in a black/Latino neighborhood and then a white neighborhood so I never really thought about what it meant to be Chinese-American. Theater was a real journey, because I was excited about developing work that was specifically Asian-American. It was never about fame or going to Hollywood."

Motivated by this personal journey, he tapped into the "obsessed" part of himself that allowed him to work happily day and night to hone his acting skills. "When I woke up in the morning the first thing I did was reach for the script I was working on. I would spend hours and hours studying my lines, every motivation. I was so obsessed, I wondered if I could ever have a relationship."

In addition to acting class and plays, Dun participated in all aspects of the Asian-American theater community. He did administrative work, served on various committees, stage-managed, and built sets. Yet perhaps because of this purity of intention, it wasn't long before he was getting good roles in local theater and then film. He landed a series of jobs in major motion pictures like *The Last Emperor, Year of the Dragon,* and *1,000 Pieces of Gold* as well as a regular role on the television drama *Midnight Caller* for three years. Twenty years later, he looks back on his early years of intense creativity and financial struggle as a time to which he would like to return artistically. "I think I was a better actor then and it was clear that the work I was doing was important to me. I want to get back to that. Sometimes Hollywood can distract you from the real work."

His story of reluctant success is not uncommon. While it's easy to covet the accolades and rewards that accompany mainstream acceptance, it's not necessarily easy to enjoy them and remain true to your artistic intention. Recently, to remedy his longing for a simpler, more personal kind of art, Dun has begun writing solo shows for himself with his wife and collaborator Cynthia Leung. Now every morning he leaves the house by eight o'clock and goes to a café to write for two hours. Only later does he go home and return calls to his agent and take care of the business of being a professional actor. This daily ritual has helped him reorder his life so he puts his most important creative work first.

Listening to the Voices

For most of us, working toward ou   wn intuition, and respecting our own auth   e. Our
society, for all the chatter about Ame   ality,
consistently discourages self-directed   ch
us to be independent and self-motivate   e
teacher's assignments, not make up our
ask us to redefine our jobs in order to reali_
to conform to the already established syste
with precision. So there's every reason in the
But don't let the alien sensation of taking you_
seriously deter you from what you really want _
love.

Before you can create anything—a film, a da   a sculpture, a
life—you must allow your vision of it to grow into something clear and
vivid and, above all, seductive. The first task at hand is getting to know
the materials from which you will build that vision. Of all of the building
blocks that go into the making of a creative life—place, people, energy,
talent—one of the most essential is what I call the internal soundscape.
This collage of memory, desire, and logic comprises the voices that
direct you moment by moment through your day. These voices are not
expressions of your talent or your intelligence, but they do regulate
your response to them.

If great art is made of 98 percent perspiration and 2 percent inspiration, then inspiration must be 98 percent listening and 2 percent
expression. Alice Walker, when asked how she begins the process of
writing a novel, replied, "There is just something that never goes away.
It is always with me no matter what I'm doing; I literally cannot lose it."
Alice Walker speaks as if the subject chooses her and slowly begins to
possess her. Finally, she gives in to the possession—sets aside time to
write about it. Thus Walker's process is about listening—actively paying attention to the tides of her consciousness. Hearing Alice Walker
talk about her process reminded me of an old Sufi tale:

A seeker once asked a guru, "What are the three secrets to enlight-
enment?"

The guru said, "One, pay attention. Two, pay attention. Three, pay
attention."

Listening to the voices of the day can allow you to see your own patterns in high relief. What are your cycles of hope and ideas and frustra-

tion? When do you overestimate your ability to get things done? When do you give up before you've tried? When do you concentrate best? The following scenario narrates the voices of the day as I have had them described to me by many a frustrated student. Do you recognize anything in this internal soundscape that reminds you of your own?

Morning's Call to Action

- Maybe you are unemployed or it's your day off. The day stretches before you like a vast dry plain dotted with bits of paperwork, phone calls, and career paths extending out in different directions, fading into a shimmering heat wave.

  In the morning, the voice says, "So much I could do, I will do, no matter what. The day is giant and I will fill it with my energies."

- Maybe you're off to a job you consider an unhappy distraction from your true purpose, your real life. And as you're rushing toward a place you'd rather not go, there's the voice of morning whispering:

  This is what I really want to do: at lunchtime, I'll make those phone calls, I'll sketch or write that poem. If I just do everything right, if I don't get distracted—tonight I will practice my guitar, plan my next business, look for new work and fill in those graduate applications.

- Maybe you're partially employed. From your morning's perspective, you have a few hours of work, but also a lot of free time, time that you can structure and fully exploit for all its opportunities. Oh yes, you do need to take the cat to the vet and buy your mother a birthday present, but none of that will take long; there's so much you can get done.

Whether you have days upon days to yourself or are scheduled into a hole, the voice of morning speaks full of tremulous hope and ambition. It scoffs at your past failures and defiantly lays claim to your present as if the person you were yesterday was just a sorry impostor for the person you will prove yourself to be by nightfall.

The voice of morning speaks from the source of your potential, not from your reality. It is the voice of desire, not of action. It is your greatest friend if you can harness its energy, and your greatest enemy if you let it run amuck without a scaffolding to climb.

The beautiful thing about artistic people is that they think big. Real big. The problem can be that the bigness of their imagination or desire can get in the way of their seeing and appreciating the present moment.

If reality arrives—more complex than the imagination had conceived—the big idea collapses and in comes the voice that states matter-of-factly, "I can't do this: I need this and this and this or I can't do anything."

Enter afternoon: the voice of survival.

Stoic Sigh of Afternoon

If morning cries, calls, and cackles with glee and hunger, the afternoon speaks in well-modulated tones, all reason and explanations. The morning voice speaks in a childish first person, while the afternoon voice uses the second person like a disappointed but "practical" authority figure:

> You can't do it all today. You're tired, blood sugar is low, boredom high. You need time and focused energy. Perhaps today isn't the appropriate day . . . maybe next Saturday, or after you pay off your debts, or reorganize your desk, then maybe you can start on all these ambitious projects. I'm not undermining you, I'm just using plain common sense.

Suddenly, the afternoon voice sees the obstacles, the prerequisites, the needs. There's an hour and a half till dinner and how in the world did you ever think you could get all this done? *And* rest, *and* eat. Suddenly, that's really all you want to do.

"After dinner," afternoon remarks, "you'll get some work done—not read that thriller, not watch television, not hang out with family or friends, not catch up on phone calls."

There is still a little hope left in afternoon, but it wants evening to take the responsibility for doing the work.

Night Purrs

After dinner the voice becomes a lethargic, well-fed lioness. The voice says, "I've tried all day, now I want some fun or luxury or laughter." There are a few unpaid bills piled up on your desk. You make a deal with the night creature who is licking your face with its warm tongue and wrapping you in soft, husky whispers:

> Come to bed, forget it. Or go out, don't you want to have a good time? Give it up. You deserve a little something sweet.

You make a deal with the pleasure-seeking beast. Do the bills and you're free.

"Free! Whatever you want for the rest of the night," the indulgent voice of night coos:

Don't worry, tomorrow is a new day, tomorrow will be different, you'll plan better, have more control of your time, you need some fun and sleep to refresh you for tomorrow!"

As you fall asleep the luxury-and-laughter voice of night begins to melt into morning. Your imagination goes wild dreaming up new realities in hairy neon vividness. The creative urge, the one you've been putting off all day, breaks through and takes over, in the only time when you let it, during sleep. Finally, it has free rein to do and think whatever it pleases. It spins universes, rouses revolutions, composes symphonies, invents languages. Upon waking, the imagination shrinks into a subtle neglected creature in your menagerie of selves; it creeps back into a dark hole waiting to be coaxed from the darkness.

Fresh but restless, you awake from your creative romp in dream time. Your morning voice rises up high and hungry. As you wipe the sleep from your eyes, the manic ambitious child boils up in your blood, and you wonder, just for a split second, how you're going to make today any different from yesterday.

They say tomorrow is a new day. Yes and no. Only if we let it be. The Vedic saying "I will use my memories but I will not let my memories use me" springs to mind. How can we plumb the depths of our past and not be imprisoned by them? Let a new awareness of your inner soundscape begin to pave a road to a future you will be proud to remember.

EXERCISES IN INHABITING YOUR PRESENT

1. Choose and do your daily action for the next seven days. Commit to a single action for this week.

Action:
Time:
Place:

   Check a circle every day you do your action:

○   ○   ○   ○   ○   ○   ○

2. What do the voices of the day say to you? Listen through the course of a weekday, then transcribe them.

3. According to your inner voices of the day, create your ideal schedule in which you take maximum opportunities from each voice. For instance, if your afternoon voice says, "I want to feel free to daydream in the afternoon," then create a schedule with an afternoon nap. It doesn't matter what the reality of your daily schedule is *now*. This is an ideal schedule. Once you have created it, look at where you might make changes in your current day.

4. Individual homework: Every week you will give yourself personal homework on the stuff of life that is most passionate for you. If you're not sure about what direction you're going in, then pick any area and strike out with abandon. Give yourself homework that you would *not* normally do otherwise and that expresses the very essence of your ambitions. Make the task so small that you cannot *not* do it. The tasks might be creative, logistical or research oriented.

5. What did you learn from this chapter? What didn't you learn that you wish you had? Where can you seek out that learning?

DAVID LLOYD, PAINTER

David Lloyd grew up obsessed with animals, surfing, and art. With his visceral, kinetic, nonintellectual approach to life, Lloyd exemplifies the physical creativity typical of a maker.* At the age of twenty-five, after a slew of low-wage jobs and a decade spent in the idyllic, relentlessly ephemeral pursuits of a surfer, Lloyd devoted himself to his painting. After a year at a community college and three years at Cal Arts, he was signed onto Margo Levin's gallery in Los Angeles, catapulting him into the heady, seductive art world of the 1980s.

From his home and studio in Los Angeles, he lives a monocled monk's[†] life. From time to time he teaches at an art college or summer intensive program, but for the most part he depends on selling paintings and sculptures to make a living. Innocent curiosity, the principle that he carries each day into his studio, has kept his creative work alive regardless of moods or misfortunes.

Q: What does your workday and week look like now?

A: I don't have specific hours I work in the studio, but I go in every day and work at least four hours, sometimes more. But I'm not somebody who works long stretches at a time. I get tired and my mind gets dulled, so I find if I eat something or go somewhere, when I come back, I'm clearer. It's not to say I don't get obsessed with the work. I work on one piece at a time until it's done. That's unlike a lot of artists that I know who work on a number of different works because it makes them feel like there's no one work that they're overly invested in. But for me, I just feel like I'm postponing the inevitable, because at some point I gotta make the damn thing work so I might as well stay with it.

Q: What does your week look like? Do you work every day?

A: Probably five days a week on average. I make art whenever I want to make art. I don't say, Oh, gee, it's Sunday, I shouldn't go into the studio. It's fun. It's a pain in the ass but it's still interesting. So if the mood strikes you on a Sunday afternoon when you're supposed to be reading the paper at the beach, then you go to the studio.

---

*For a definition of the maker, see page 65.
[†]For a definition of the monocled monk, see page 178.

Q: How did you develop your creative process?

A: Adults have a hard time making art, and kids don't. You give a kid a bunch of coloring books, construction paper, all that crap kids love to screw around with, and they just start making things. It's a pure creative impulse. Adults go in their studio and they have all this horse-shit in their heads about what it's like to be an artist, whether artists have a big skylight and a fancy studio or whether they live in a little crummy place; whether it's okay to have a cappuccino in the middle of the day or they should be smoking cigarettes and drinking beer; whether they should have a show or shouldn't have a show . . . it just piles on so thick it's no wonder so many people get stuck. I constantly try to peel back that stuff and say I don't give a damn what goes on today, I can go in and screw around. When kids play, they play for the pure pleasure of playing. And sometimes it's very creative, but there's no reward at the end of it. You just do it for the sake of doing it. And if you get in the right frame of mind you can treat your art like that. When you get rid of all that stuff, this weird creative process starts happening. It's just a matter of getting away from all the baggage—the exterior stuff.

So in my creative process I start by just screwing around. I'll have some thought about where I want a piece to go, but I'm not too attached because I know it might take a turn that I'll have to follow. Or I might just draw, or make little things—take bits and pieces and collage them together. I do whatever I feel like at the moment to get past all the expectations. Because I've watched too many artists try to intellectualize their way through art-making, and for me that doesn't work.

I was not good in school, and wasn't good at traditional things a lot of kids were good at. So I had a rebellious quality that artists have to have. Artists have to accept the fact that you can't first please society and then please yourself as an artist because it won't work. You have to go in saying, "What's interesting to me is the process of making art and I'm not gonna worry about the other stuff."

I guess that I've had an easier time than most people because I've always had the urge to create visual things. Some people think, Gee, I want to become a painter, but there's nothing about painting that they really like, it's just something that they've decided they should be doing. One of the secrets to being a good artist is doing what comes naturally. You have to follow the path of least resistance. People think that because something comes easily to them it's not as important. I've known so many artists who are bound and determined to do a certain kind of work, and yet they're brilliant in another kind of work—but they don't value it, because it's easy for them. But that ease is where their brilliance lies. Too often artists forget to follow their own sensibility, and get too caught up in what they think is hot or not hot, or political or not political.

Q: Do you have any role models or mentors in terms of process, in terms of seeing how people work in a healthy, productive way?

A: Picasso. One of the first things I noticed about him was that he didn't make distinctions between art forms. Everything he did was art. He would paint or draw or make things. He would move from style to style. I remember as a little kid looking at a book of his masks made out of cardboard. Or his famous piece that put a bicycle seat and handlebars together to make a bull. He was just making things, and for me that was so exciting because it took the pressure off.

The institution of Cal Arts was also very influential. It was this strange place where you walked in and all the rules of society just ceased to exist. You want to walk around naked? Have at it. You want to live in a refrigerator and talk to people through the ventilator holes? Fine. You want to make a painting? Fine. Everything's fine. In that environment, the creativity that most people have buried in them naturally rises to the surface.

Q: Where did you learn self-discipline?

A: I don't know if I have self-discipline in the traditional sense: paying your bills, doing the dishes, going to the studio every day and working a certain amount, doing everything you're supposed to do because you're responsible. I don't know that I am. A lot of artists aren't that self-disciplined. It's kind of bullshit. What happens is an artist gets interested in something and then they get very selfish about it and they're willing to push other things aside in their life just to follow something that they find interesting. It's more of an obsessive quality where you want to see what happens with something. You just keep doing it and everyone says, "Oh, gee, you're so disciplined." Forget the fact that you have no money or the landlord's p.o.'d. It's a matter of following what you're interested in. Because it doesn't take any discipline to do what you're interested in. It's a funny thing. It takes a lot of discipline to do what you don't want to do. And that goes back to doing what you like, doing what's fun. That's one of the secrets to making art. It's this weird paradox that people seem to think it's supposed to be hard and not fun and then they don't do it and they wonder why. Well, who ever does anything they don't want to do? Unless they have to.

Q: What kind of human support system do you have?

A: My family and a few friends. Probably my parents have been the most important support system. Because I think that in the visual arts, artists are like everybody else in business. They're competitive and they will only turn you on to something when they've already gotten it and exploited it as far as they can get something out of it. Of course there are exceptions but because the art world is so competitive, artists don't tend to be a very altruistic bunch. It's the people around you who want to see you succeed, whether they're artists or not. If you find someone who thinks it's really great you're an artist and says, "Hang in there, keep making art," even if they don't know anything about art, they can be very important. Artists need somebody to tell them that what they're doing is good and they should keep it up, keep going. "Well, I don't think it's good"—keep trying. "I don't know if anybody will like it"—who cares? Keep on doing it. Just do what you're interested in. Pure positive reinforcement. Even if you know somebody's bullshitting you, it's important. You don't need someone to come in and critique you all the time. That doesn't do any good for most people unless it's someone who you trust and has the capacity for truly constructive criticism. It's such a strange thing to be an artist in the first place, because you're always wondering if what you're doing is worth anything. It's not like being a doctor where you can see what you've done. You're doing something that's very subjective. So all it takes is two or three people to walk into your studio and say, "What the hell are you doing?" Most artists don't react well to that. Psychologically you need to have people who pat you on the back and say you're doing great. It's amazing what that will do. Having some smart-ass critic tell you something . . . you think you're gonna learn a lot from it but you don't. You have to find your own way.

Q: Do you have any tricks you play on yourself when you don't feel like working, to get yourself to work?

A: There's a number of things I do. Number one, I go look at art books, and art. I say, Today it's okay that I won't make anything. I don't have to produce. Today I'm just going to look at stuff. Go to a thrift store, go to a bookstore, walk around, it doesn't matter. And if you give yourself that, you might get to a point where you want to go back in the studio, because there's something you've seen that excites you, that you want to apply to your art.

If you're really not in the mood to make serious art, figure out what's the most fun thing to do. Like make a geeky watercolor, throw paint around, or make a charcoal painting of a dog—it doesn't matter, you just go and start doing things. Because sure enough . . . it's just the act of doing anything. A lot of people have said to me, "Oh, you're so productive. How do you do this? God, you've made so much work." I don't put pressure on myself to be a genius every time I go into the studio. And not every painting is going to be great. Sometimes you make a painting and it isn't so good, and you just have to say, Okay, well, the next one will be better. It's a process, a long process.

Q: How did you support yourself before you made a living off your art?

A: I worked in art galleries: schlepping art, moving art, hanging art.

Q: Why did you choose this?

A: Because it's in the art world, and you meet people.

Q: And even before that, before you were in art school?

A: I lived at home, mooching off Mom and Dad, working in the back bedroom making paintings. One of the secrets of supporting yourself as an artist, whether you're young or old or anytime, is don't get too involved in a day job. It's a rare artist that can work forty or fifty hours a week at a demanding job and then go make art. Most people are just too burnt. I say live as cheap as you can. Time is better than money. If you can figure out a way to get by, work part-time. And most people don't believe they can do that. They say, "Oh, you have to work forty hours a week plus benefits and stuff . . ." Maybe, maybe not. I know a lot of artists who have gotten by.

Q: Talk about some of your failures and how you moved past them.

A: I would say that a quarter of the work I make is a complete failure, and a quarter is semifailure, is just okay. And maybe another quarter is good, and a quarter is really good. You have to understand that failure is built in. That's true for every artist—even the most famous ones. What happens is that society believes that somebody is a genius so everything they do is genius, but they make as much crap as everybody else. There's no artist on earth that produces everything perfectly, because that's inhuman; human beings don't work like machines, they don't pump out perfection all the time. They make really great things and then they make stuff that's mediocre. So let yourself off the hook for making a shitty painting or something. Failures are what make artists good. No two ways about it. If you're never making bad art, then you're not progressing, I guarantee it.

Q: Can you talk about times when you experienced failures publicly or in your process?

A: My very first show got a horrible review. Right out of art school, first one-man show, got a terrible review in the *Los Angeles Times*. The way I dealt with it is that I decided that the critic was a moron. Literally. Because had I bought into his rap about my work, I would have been buying into what he thought I should be. What I wanted to be and what he wanted me to be were two separate things. So I got my feelings hurt, I got scared, and then I got pissed. And I vowed that I was not gonna buy into his rap.

Q: Have your thoughts of success changed since you began?

A: Yes. As a younger artist I wanted fame more; that was about wanting acceptance, public recognition, good reviews. You want all this stuff because it's about seeking validation from the outside. As you get older as an artist, the outside validation seems less and less important. I've become far more interested in the process of making art, and things I want to do before I die, than getting all this adulation from the outside. It's a really funny shift. You see it with artists who move out of the cities because they want to be the hell away from it all. They don't want to deal with openings and curators and dealers and critics and all that stuff. What they want to do is have their heads clear so they can get to the essence of what they were trying to do in the first place. And it's not about pleasing everybody and getting your name in a magazine.

Q: What was the most frustrating period of your development as an artist?

A: When I felt like I was, for a long time, emulating other artists. I was very easily influenced. It was frustrating because I'd make a painting or a piece of art and I would say, Oh no, that looks just like so and so. Now, looking back on it, I realize that was essential to my development. I was exorcising these things out of my system, refining down to my own voice. I believe it's a part of younger artists' development to emulate things they see, and in doing that, if they don't worry about it and they just keep moving, they wake up one day and they realize that this piece of art they made doesn't look like anyone else's. And it's not like you can force yourself—"Okay, this looks like so and so, forget it, I won't deal with that kind of art anymore." It takes a long time. That's why I have such a problem with the idea that the art world is so youth-oriented. If you're twenty-five you're somehow hotter than if you're thirty-five, and if you're thirty-five you're a little better than if you're forty-five. But the problem is that you get all these artists that are right at the beginning of their development. What they end up doing five years later is really different, because they're going through styles. They're developing. Generally you find that the best work is done twenty years later; the most authentic, original work. Because it takes a long time.

Q: Is there one piece of advice you would give beginners in your field about developing their artistic process?

A: Don't limit yourself too much too early. Curators and critics and collectors love signature styles. They love something recognizable, that they can hold on to and they can write about. "I'm a minimalist." "I'm a conceptual artist." "I'm a landscape painter." It makes everybody happy and safe. But it makes for crappy artists. Because you have to be willing to follow a whim. If you have a moment of lucidity about something you've seen or something you've always wanted to try, *do it*. It might be the thing that really opens up your artistic process *and* your career. Follow your nose and don't limit yourself. I see a lot of young artists come out of art school. They've got this slick, wrapped package all set to show to galleries: twenty paintings all in the same style so everybody gets it. But it won't facilitate your career as an artist, because you'll get bored, and people will get bored. One of the tricks to being an artist for a long time is staying interested. And one of the ways you stay interested is to be willing to follow your whims, popular or not.

2

Stoking the Coals
Idea Profusion

> New and stirring ideas are belittled because if they are not belittled the humiliating question arises, "Why then are you not taking part in them?"
>
> —H. G. WELLS

In my classes, I hear the same five words, "I've got so many ideas," invoked again and again the way a little boy might tell his confessor, "Father I have sinned so many times." When I play my part and respond, "And what are your ideas, my child?" my students—like the miserable but essentially innocent boy—usually can't come up with a very long list. Instead they offer a few ingenious but unformed plans and then trail off: "It seems like there are more, but I just can't think of them right now."

At first I puzzled over this. Were they having delusions of creative grandeur? Were they too shy to be explicit? Were they afraid I was going to steal their ideas and make a million dollars? Soon I realized it was none of these things. Like the boy stuttering in the confessional, they actually felt *guilty* about their ideas. They felt hounded by their brain children as if they were past sins lurking subconsciously day and night, just waiting for the perfect moment to rise up and drive them mad. So they did the most sensible thing: turned their minds to more practical matters and tried their best to forget.

If we want to forge a life from our creativity we must get over this guilt and embarrassment about idea proliferation. For most of us, too many ideas isn't the problem. The problem is our puritan view that we should confine our ideas to those we can realize; that anything else is just distraction and should be excised from our life like a bit of *E. coli* from a slab of meat. The real problem is that we don't lean into our ideas, we shy away from them, fearing that they will betray our true selves and show us up for what we secretly fear we are: losers.

But just because we can't act on all of them, ideas don't make us losers. Even the most impossible ideas—the ones you have absolutely no intention or interest or ability to carry out—foster other kinds of creative action. Why? Because they create a continuous creative high; they are a happy drug, an inner lover, a form of worship, and pure psychic nourishment. Though they spring from the same fertile ground as Martha Graham's "blessed unrest," ideas differ from amorphous hunger or vague inclinations. Ideas are hard chunks of reality waiting to be born. They have ingredients, names, purposes, and attendant tasks. They are the things we want to cultivate in the place of all those feelings that fill up our heads with abstract longing and dissatisfaction.

In order to disentangle feelings from ideas, I want you to buy two notebooks. One will be your Feelings Journal, the other your Adventure Book. Your Feelings Journal can function in much the same way most journals do: a place to vent angst, joy, sorrow, frustration, and the vaguest of longings (being a movie star, winning the lottery, feeling like a brilliant creative genius). These feelings all have their place in our lives, but this process is about pulling the vivid crystalline idea from the sludge of generic desire. It is only through this metamorphosis of desire into task that we ignite our commitment and go beyond the easy.

Your Adventure Book will be the place where you chronicle your weirdest creative ideas, your madcap moneymaking schemes, your annoying tasks and routine actions. Don't worry: Writing them in the book doesn't mean you are committing to them. Indeed, if you really use this book, you'll probably have enough ideas in the first two weeks to last you for two years. I'm afraid most of us *do* have too many ideas to actualize all but a tiny percentage of them. But the Adventure Book—unlike the Feelings Journal—engenders proactive dreaming rather than passive peeving. And if you're anything like me, you'll realize how uneven the ratio is between the two forms of thinking. I can fill up a Feelings Journal in a month, but one Adventure Book can last me a couple of years.

Not only does the Adventure Book allow you to keep a record of your creative spurts and slumps, it will serve as a catalyst to act on them. Rather than being forgotten, some ideas will cry out from the page, demanding to be born, and insisting that you be the mother. As you move through the exercises in this book, transfer your favorite ideas, tasks, and plans into your Adventure Book. As you act on these ideas, don't cross them off like a regular list of things to do, put a star next to them. After a year of keeping an Adventure Book, you'll have a record of your many creative achievements and you'll know how you've directed your energies. Plus there will remain an enormous well of ideas that you can draw on for inspiration, amusement, and action.

The Dangers of Abstraction

Like art, life doesn't exist in the world of general rules and abstract philosophy. Life is pink, smooth, liquid, loud, pigtails, guns, and crowds with faces, smiling or frowning. No matter how eloquent or insightful your ideas are about "life," these abstract notions never can fully embrace the rich smorgasbord of lived experience. Of course, our dulled sensitivity keeps us sane. We cannot feel the full impact of life at every splintered visceral second and still function. George Eliot in *Middlemarch* comments on this necessary softening of focus: "If we had a keen vision of all that is ordinary in human life, it would be like hearing the grass grow or the squirrel's heart beat, and we should die of that roar which is the other side of silence."

Yet if you have been studying writing or acting or dance or any art form, you understand the exquisite, if difficult, power of being specific. Concrete sensual details are the only way to breathe life into a vision.

Though we understand this as artists, as showering, burping, ordinary human beings we can continue to harbor very vague notions about what living actually entails. For example, I grew up believing that there were essentially two modes of living in the world: social and antisocial. The social person was kind, fun, and hopelessly unproductive. The antisocial person was obsessive, selfish, and creative. By maintaining this idea about the antisocial habits of self-directed people, I created a situation where I couldn't be both nice *and* creative. These cardboard ideas prevented me from observing actual people juggling lives that were both social and creative—despite the fact that they were all around me. I didn't have access to my observations because I was always categorizing them into the hermit slot or the socialite slot.

Abstractions about life may grow out of personal experience or they may be inherited from your family or community. In any case, it's good to simply look at your lived experience and separate it from your concepts about "life." If you can free yourself to focus on the actuality of the wrought-iron fence you have to buy for the theater set you're designing, your stomach grumbling for a decent meal, the exact word you

KEITH JOHNSTONE, TEACHER

Keith Johnstone, author of *Impro* and founder of Theatresports, took his knowledge of theater and psychology to create a synthesis of playful, insightful improvisation. Like all gifted teachers, he is constantly challenging himself to create new methods and ideas.

His interest in teaching art and theater grew out of his own terrible experiences in state schools in England. When he began studying theater and art in high school, he noticed that he became hopelessly blocked: "Mainly as a result of trying harder, which they always teach you to do. It was obvious to me that school was terribly wrong. I taught myself to read by reading comics at a very early age and then I'd get to school and children were punished for reading comics. Even at a young age, it was obvious that you were in the hands of very stupid people."

His teaching approach turned the authoritarian relationship on its head. He adopted a low status in relation to his students, sitting on the floor below them and telling them that if they failed it would be *his* fault, not theirs. He posited the then-radical notion that creativity is an essential part of human potential not limited to the work of specialized geniuses. "Everybody gets ideas," he says, "but they don't really listen to them. When you meditate you're swamped with ideas that you never knew you had. It's like diving in the ocean, it's always there. Most people are taught to discriminate, which ends up killing a lot of good ideas. Most people are in flight from them or their ego is tied up in it. If you remove the fear, you've still got the ego to contend with."

In teaching his classes in theater improvisation he talks a lot about the relationship between inhibition, creativity, and self-criticism. He likes to tell a story about the time the German playwright and poet Schiller received a letter from a critic who declared, "You're no smarter than I am, how is it you've been able to create so much more than I have?" Schiller responded that the critic only entertained good ideas but that Schiller let in *all* ideas. In this way, Johnstone has made the theme of his own childhood struggle with creativity the very basis of his lifelong work.

must choose to end your poem, then you can work with solving these problems. If not, gaping abstractions will consume your brain space, often substituting for more specific, immediate knowledge.

Let me be specific. If you believe that all things worth doing in life entail struggle, then when you receive a gift from the universe—like a job handed to you on a silver platter—you may be likely to miss the opportunity. If, on the other hand, you believe that all good things should come easily, when you hit a particularly sticky obstacle, you may see it as a sign that "you aren't meant to have it."

To disentangle your experience of living from the octopus of preconceived life, try out these definitions that distinguish "life" from living. "Life" describes that world of clear parameters, rules, and principles we were taught to accept as children. "Life" means that place of stasis that parents, teachers, and other culture keepers taught us to recognize as a shorthand for reality. "Life" is a coded language that we know so well, we are no longer aware of its encoding. We learn that if we break life's rules we invite danger, punishment, and generally bad things. When we talk about "life," we are talking about surviving—not thriving.

EXERCISE IN CONFRONTING ABSTRACTION

What does "life" mean to you? When you hear voices in your past or present whispering "That's life," what are they referring to? Write a list. Here are a few common examples.

That's life: When you shoot too high, you're sure to fall hard.
That's life: Not everyone can be successful.
That's life: There's no real justice.
That's life: If I try hard enough, I will succeed. If I don't, it's my fault.
That's life: You gotta pay the bills.
That's life: I can do whatever I want.
That's life: Suffer to gain.
That's life: If I only understood my emotional problems then I would be successful and happy.

Now write some of your own:

That's life:
That's life:
That's life:
That's life:
That's life:
That's life:

Many of your "life" definitions may ring true even when you reexamine them. That doesn't mean they're either true or false, but that they are now essential to your daily habits. Upon deeper inspection, some will reveal themselves to be impostors, false ideas that you believe emotionally but not intellectually. The important thing is to get them all out on the page so that you can see what seems useful and what may be getting in your way.

AN EXPERIMENT IN DIVINE DISSATISFACTION

Before we delve into the nuances of your past and the many possible shapes of your future, I want to take you through a step-by-step process moving from your vaguest longings to a concrete plan. In my classes this exercise takes between thirty and forty minutes and initially elicits a lot of grumbling and sighing. I tell my students again and again: It's only an exercise, you don't need to be brilliant or inspired, just answer the questions. They shrug and write down the first thing that comes into their mind and then stare at me with stone-faced displeasure. I have to resist the urge to stop class and deal with each of their complaints because, of course, complaining is what we do well. We do it artfully and with gusto, and although I personally consider it a pleasurable hobby, sometimes you just have to gag your inner whiner to let other voices (like your imagination) get a word in edgewise.

Theater director R. J. Cutler once told me a story about his early career. He was in a mentoring program at the La Jolla Playhouse and he was struggling with the play he was appointed to direct. He called up his mentor and began venting his angst that nothing he tried was working. The prominent theater director interrupted him, "Think, don't worry."

"That was very important," Cutler explained. "You spend the same amount of energy and time, but if you're worrying you don't get anything accomplished, and if you're thinking you get something accomplished and there's less to worry about, so I have learned to think more and worry less. And that's a good thing."

Exercises in Generating Ideas

1. To transform a worry into a thought, try the following exercise. It won't take longer than forty minutes. Answer each of the following questions in a fairly brief form: with a single phrase, a few sentences, or a short list.

- What is the one essence that you seek to bring out in your life and in your work? I'm asking for vague statements like "personal creative expression," "risk and peace," "beauty," "weaving together diverse threads into a whole," "humor and political purpose." Your answer doesn't need to be eloquent, it just needs to express your largest yearning.

- Looking at your essence statement, make a list of the arenas of work that you might be interested in working in and that reflect this essence. For instance, Katherine's essence statement was "creative expression" and the arenas she listed were painting, writing, and therapy.

- Based on your arenas and your essence, *invent* one small, specific project (such as a performance, painting, business, or event) which is in one of your arenas of interest *and* fulfills your essence statement. If you cannot choose between your arenas of interest, then invent a project that combines all of them. For example, Katherine conceived of a workshop in which she led people through a therapeutic process by having them write and illustrate a homemade book about their life. The most important thing is that it is *one* specific project and that you write it down.

- What's in a name? Names have power. They capture your idea and keep it alive, like a creature in a cage. Classes have names, rock bands have names, community centers have names, novels have names. It doesn't have to be a good name, just create the best name you can come up with now for your project.

- Who are the people involved in this project? You don't need to know them personally, just make a list of their general titles.

- Who is the intended audience for this project? Who are you making it for?

- What need does it fill in the world? What is its purpose?

- What are the existing opportunities in your life right now that would help you realize this project?

- What are the main ingredients you need to make this project happen? Specifically list your material needs: financial, spatial, legal status, time, equipment.

- How would you need to live your life differently in order to allow this project to grow?

- If you were to commit to this project tomorrow, what would be the first tiny step you would need to take?

The second step?

The third step?

Out of this simple series of questions, you can see how quickly a vague longing can transform into a concrete goal with a specific list of tasks. While you may now decide you have no interest in actualizing this project, you have at least practiced some proactive dreaming. But don't be surprised if you fall in love with this idea. Many of my students end up getting so excited about their project that they decide to make it happen.

2. Get a large piece of paper and a bunch of oil pastels, colored felt-tip pens, or crayons and make a big colorful drawing of your coming year as you envision it now. Depict both the positive aspects of the year and the obstacles you imagine encountering and their solutions. It might be entirely abstract—an image of color and line and shape—or it might be symbolic, or it might be quite literal, portraying yourself acting something out. It might combine all these styles. There is no wrong way to do it. Just do it and don't think too hard. It is weird for most of us to problem-solve by drawing with crayons, but that's exactly why it's useful. You are quite literally drawing into the unknown. Spend no more than twenty minutes on your picture.

Now you have an image of your finished year in front of you. Look at it while you answer the following questions:

What do like about your picture?

What do you not understand about it?

What do you dislike about it?

Analyze this picture on a deeper level, as if you were a psychologist or a tea leaf reader. What colors did you use? How hard did you press against the page? Did you cover the whole sheet? What part of the picture did you concentrate on most? Which parts are the most detailed, which the most general? What's the overall feeling you get from the picture? Restrained? Scattered? Exuberant? Passive? Flowing? Nervous? Melodramatic? Based on your observations, what do you think the artist of this picture needs to do? Does this person need to:

Scream?
Get out of town?

Focus on one thing?
Dive in?
Think logically?
Lighten up?
Enjoy their obstacles?

Write down your own prescription:

3. In the next exercise you will generate new work ideas by creating three interlocking realms: ideal tasks, ideal environment, and ideal content. This is a practical exercise for people who have trouble visualizing the ideal long-term work they want. My experience is that blurry vision in relation to even one of these three realms can be paralyzing. Fortunately, even the most confused person usually has at least one realm completely nailed down. Environment junkies know the kind of plants and people they want in their office, but they have no idea what field they are working in, or what it is they are doing. Task masters know exactly how they would sing blues ballads or facilitate meetings or call strangers in foreign countries to discuss travel plans, but they don't know the purpose of their work or where they want to be working. Cause devotees are certain that their work should promote safe drinking water for the spotted owl, but they don't know if they want to design T-shirts, clean rivers, or lobby in Washington and they don't know what setting will make them happy.

- List the actual tasks you most enjoy doing. Be specific (writing, talking on the phone, interviewing people, drawing, mixing sounds, conceiving of new business ideas, debating the interpretation of a piece of art . . .):

- What environment would you like to work in? (Describe the physical, organizational, and emotional environment. Example: in a sun-lit studio in the city with three partners, alone in an office in the country, or in a small start-up company with a boss who respects my expertise.) Don't clarify the kind of work you're doing, just focus on the context in which the work takes place.

- What fields are you interested in? This includes both professional fields like fine art or business or journalism and the work's purpose, like "creating beauty," "destroying hunger," or "saving the rain forest."

Using the three interlocking circles, imagine jobs in which all three of your circles intersect one another.

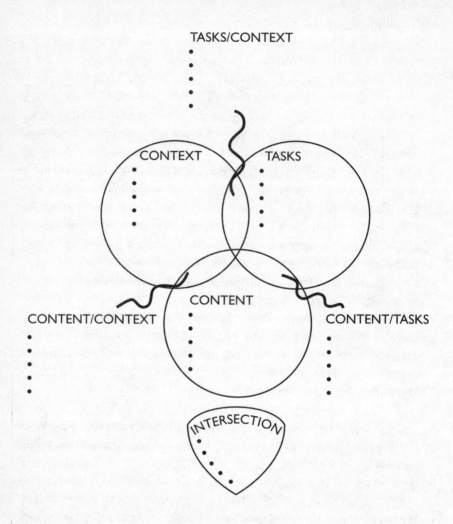

4. Personal Homework (I'll give you some to start you off):

- Buy two notebooks: your Feelings Journal and your Adventure Book.
- Transfer your ideas into your Adventure Book.
- If you feel so inclined, do the first tiny step of your invented project.

THE MONK BROTHERS, PUBLISHERS, VAGABONDS, WRITERS

Through audacity, ingenuity, and persistence, Michael Lang and Jim Crotty, founders of *Monk* magazine, carved a life for themselves out of a popular American pipe dream. Shucking their yuppie life in San Francisco's Castro district, they sold their possessions, bought an old U-Haul, and hit the road in the spring of 1986. They didn't know exactly where they were going, but they were determined to live a troubadour existence. They wanted to travel the country in search of interesting encounters and characters; they wanted to live freed from mundane obligations of rent, material possessions, and jobs. Both had been aspiring writers and entrepreneurs at various times in their lives, but neither had ever committed to either of these paths for long. It was through the pursuit of this nomadic adventure that they finally found the vehicle for combining all their talents and interests: a mobile magazine, which chronicled their travels and their underground investigations into the various places they visited. In the process, both found their voices as writers, learned about their particular skills in the realm of business, and achieved financial success from a wacky creative scheme.

I interviewed the Monk Brothers, as they are sometimes called, in their pink RV parked at Broadway and Houston Street in New York City. They had been on the road for over ten years. Michael Lang, the older of the two, is a soft-spoken yet tireless storyteller. His mystic/interpreter* personality has helped *Monk* expand from a newsletter to friends into a national magazine while staying close to its original spiritual and political values. His monocled monk[†] approach to life has kept their collaboration on track. Jim Crotty is brasher, more concise and explosive in his expression. As an interdisciplinarian,[‡] he has created more opportunities for *Monk;* as a realizer[§] he has helped to communicate *Monk*'s message to a broader public, raise funds, and think big. This interview reflects not only the remarkable complementary qualities of these two men, but the tension inherent in even the most ideal of collaborative partnerships.

(Michael and I begin the interview alone.)

---

*For definitions of the mystic and the interpreter, see pages 80 and 72.
[†]For a definition of the monocled monk, see page 178.
[‡]For a definition of the interdisciplinarian, see page 178.
[§]For a definition of the realizer, see page 70.

Q: How did you start Monk *magazine?*

Michael: *Monk* began in 1986 when Jim and I left San Francisco. I had met Jim a year earlier, on April Fools' Day in 1985. We'd lived together that year. I was totally stressed out working two jobs. I got to the point where I just wanted to leave the city. Jim and I came up with a plan to travel and look for a more rural place to live. I lived in an eight-room house in the Castro—it was the envy of everybody I knew, but I was never really into the yuppie lifestyle. So we dragged everything down to the street, sold it off in a big old garage sale. I loaded the left-over in the van along with my two cats, Nurse and Nurse's Aide. We just hit the road going north. The plan was just to get out of town, go out and stay with my friend up in Paradise, California. It was really silly because it was so unplanned for a major life change. Also I had a Mac-intosh computer and someone had just given me PageMaker and I thought, This is cute, we could make a little newsletter. I had so many friends who wondered what I was doing. So we wrote and printed out this little four-page newsletter and called it "Greetings from the Monks." A lot of our friends called us the Monks because we had no furniture and I was a total nonconformist Zen Buddhist. A month later we bought a van, a twelve-foot Conroy. We traveled up Northern California and Oregon. We said, Let's make a really fun newsletter. We spent the whole summer driving around, writing in our diaries, taking photos. By the end of the summer we had enough for twenty-four pages, so we sent a postcard to our two hundred and fifty friends and family saying, "We're going to travel for a year. Send us money if you want to get our newsletter." We came up with this subscription struc-ture: twenty-five dollars was the Feed the Monks Fund; fifty dollars was the Wool Sweater Fund to keep our cats supplied with wool sweaters because they loved to nurse on them; for a hundred dollars you would be a lifetime member of our newsletter. So we went to a printer in Ore-gon, had a thousand copies printed on newsprint, like a weekly.

We had fifty people who had sent us money up, so we raised close to seven hundred dollars, which was remarkable because if you've ever been on the road, if you can make even the tiniest amount of money, it's a revelation. I've traveled for decades and it's always been a rhythm of travel stop work, travel stop work. This really fueled our imaginations. We thought, Oh my God, you can write and get people to pay to read what you write when you travel? But the whole first newsletter was very personal, it was about what we ate, what we argued about. Later that year we went to L.A. and the money had run dry and we started gardening for money. We got to San Diego to visit my parents, and my mother, who is a dyed-in-the-wool entrepreneur, said, "Maybe you should sell advertising for this." We took her advice. We drove around San Diego County and we would literally go to a store and we would stay there for three or four hours and we would try to sell them an ad. We would try to get to know them, have lunch with them. Our first ad we sold was for the Bate Control Eye Method—a system of eye exercises for people who want to improve their eyesight. We spent six hours with this woman, heard her whole life story, had lunch with her, and finally we said, "Well, how would you like to advertise?" We hashed it over and she paid us a hundred dollars and that was our first ad. We were really excited. We spent the next two months writing a forty-eight-page issue on Southern California. We had a few little ads here and there—not much—and we were still gardening.

In the third issue, we got serious about advertising and we printed sixty-four pages and we made it look like a magazine and put a glossy cover on it. We printed up twenty thousand of them after we had sold a bunch of ads because we were going to distribute twenty thousand of them. Then we figured out how to get rid of them. It was like, first you sell the ads, then you print them and then figure out how you're going to get them to people. We hired these Tibetan monks to go up and down California, dropping off our magazines in bundles to give away for free at health food stores. That was the first days of it becoming a business. We had advertising, we had distribution, we had editorial. We didn't have a clue what we were doing. We were living in a van with two cats. From there we decide to take off for Sedona, Arizona, for the Harmonic Convergence. We got out there and it happened to be one of the vortexes of the whole scene. The New Age was crescendoing and everyone was there. Every channeler, psychic, you name it, they were all converging in Sedona. We became journalists for the first time. We started reporting on what we saw all around us instead of being idiosyncratic travelers. We printed a sixty-four-page magazine, still on newsprint but with a glossy cover, and we gave it to the Tibetan monks to distribute up and down California. Then a reporter from the *Los Angeles Times* called us up and said she wanted to talk to us. By then we were in Colorado, and she flew out and interviewed us, and it was the first time that anyone had really talked to us about what we had done. We didn't really think there was anything that unusual about what we were doing. We loved what we were doing. We thought, This is really cool, but we didn't think that it was mind blowing. She went back and wrote this two-page spread with photos in the Sunday *Los Angeles Times,* February 17, 1987. She gave our address at the bottom of it: "If you want to order their newsletter, write this address, send ten dollars." We got twenty thousand dollars over the next three weeks. It couldn't have come at a better time because we were so broke and we had no idea how we were going to print the fifth issue on Colorado. It was winter; it was cold; we were hungry. It was like the ultimate miracle. Sitting in this cold little van with the cats and suddenly we had all of this money!

So we went to the printer and we blew more than fourteen thousand dollars on printing this glossy full-color magazine. We didn't have a clue about color—we just said, "Oh, put color here, let's put some red here." Previously we had spent four thousand dollars on a print run. Consequently, it sort of put us into the realm of official publishers because the very next month we started selling national advertising. And from that point we got very, very serious about publishing. We expanded the editorial and we got more focused on travel writing. We went to Texas with a new vision and a new plan. The *L.A. Times* piece got syndicated, it was all over the country, and the next thing you know Paramount is knocking on the door and telling us it would make a great film and we got seduced into that bullshit for a while—just a total distraction. We got through that to just do the magazine. We had lost both Nurse and Nurse's Aide, but we found a new cat, Dalai Lama, who hopped on board.

For the next two years we published very funky magazines that were so undefinable no one knew what we were. We were very obsessed with health food—well, Jim was, I wasn't—he was obsessed with health food and I was focused on mystics and people who followed spiritual paths and so we wrote about our travels, about the weird people we met, and we had nothing but health food ads. In November 1989, we came on out to New York and that was a slap in the face. We woke up to the fact that we were publishers and this is an industry and we were fools! We were just clueless. That was part of our success, we were so clueless. We didn't have a single idea about anything like the ratio of ads to editorial or how to design it or package it or how to distribute it and we just totally made up our own rules. New York changed everything. The first change was advertising. Within the next six months we'd switched from natural foods to alcohol as an ad base and we'd gone from kooky mystical ads to publishing ads. Jim single-handedly attacked the New York advertising scene. That was the beginning of the third phase of *Monk,* and slowly we became known as an alternative travel magazine.

Q: You both write all the material in the magazine?

Michael: We have contributors, but we still write ninety percent of all the editorial. We take half if not more of the photos, though we have started to incorporate other people.

Q: Were you interested in writing or editing before you started this, or was it just something that happened as a result of traveling?

Michael: I'd always written journals, and in my twenties I was a very serious but unpublished poet. When I was in college I was writing short stories and sending them to *Harper's* and wherever I thought I could publish but I never did. I was attempting to write but was discouraged in my twenties and so I totally gave up the idea that anything could ever come of it. What fueled it for me was the chance to write from personal experience and send it out to people. Jim had also been an unpublished writer and so in a way it brought to the foreground what already existed, but I don't think that either one of us could have predicted that we would become travel writers. I like writing now because it allows me in full detail to tell the stories of the people that we meet. Oftentimes you meet so many people who are living these very intense lives and yet no one notices. That really was our forte early on, we took the ordinary and made it extraordinary. People who are very committed to their lives or their lifestyle are the hallmark of *Monk.* Whether it's Annie Sprinkle, postporn modernist, or the guy who's the head of the Oregon Christian Alliance. Two extremely different people, but they're extremely passionate about what they're doing and so we like to give them a voice.

Q: What is your typical day?

Michael: Nine times out of ten, we're parked in an RV park or on the street or in someone's driveway. Selling advertisements and taking care of business takes up a third or half of every day and then the rest is planning, researching, or out traveling around. Then at night, at least in the past few months, I've been writing every night.

[*Jim enters. He seems to be in a bad mood about the fact that he looked too conservative in a recent photo shoot. He announces that he wants to shave his head and Michael says he'll get out his clippers just as soon as the interview is over.*]

Q: What's your creative process as a team?

Jim: Complaining [*laughs*]. We started out as cookie makers and bakers of bread and pies in San Francisco—

Michael: Jim, Jim, I skipped that part.

Jim: We met—

Michael: Because I don't like that part.

Jim: April Fools'—

Michael: I told her that part.

Jim: When I moved in, we started various projects. First of all we were bakers. We wanted to make the world's most perfect portable treat—the healthiest cookie you could buy which had everything in it so you didn't need to eat a meal. We spent more time prototyping than we did manufacturing. Then we did pies. Then we did meals out of the home. And then we didn't have enough money to pay the rent and we left.

Here's the deal. Really quickly, we discovered that Michael is timely, he's a good planner, he's a good accountant, he keeps track of bills like you wouldn't believe and he's very, very meticulous about that stuff. Michael's in the southern tradition of storytelling. He just does it naturally. People just want to listen to him tell a story. He just keeps me entertained because when he meets somebody, he builds a whole story about it. Michael attracts the weirdest, wackiest characters on the planet. I meet these people too, but something about Michael's energy brings these people into his orbit and they begin to either reveal their deepest secrets or they have some sort of intense encounter with him that ends up as this amazing story. So Michael has great stories.

Q: What do you do?

Jim: My job is mouthpiece for the magazine. Michael might dispute this. I'm sure Michael could be superfamous on his own, but because I come from a more conventional midwestern doctor's-family upbringing, I think I have more of an ingrained understanding of how to take a really wild idea and market it to the masses. And so early on I had an ability to get publicity, to articulate the vision of *Monk* to someone who might be hostile to it if they just looked at the pictures. I made *Monk* more palatable. In some ways Michael's the conscience of *Monk*. I'm a little more skittish around sexuality issues because that's the hugest issue with my mother. Where I come from sexuality is definitely the taboo subject. You can be a drug addict, a drug dealer, or a murderer, but if you're a homosexual, that's a problem. I'm also a good marketer, publicist, and salesperson. I've sold almost all the ads.

Q: Obviously you're both creative, but how are you different in your creative inclinations? Some people have tons of ideas, some people are good at manifesting an idea.

Jim: We're both good at both. The unique thing about *Monk* is that we've taken an idea that everybody has at some point: to quit their job and hit the road.

Michael: There's big differences but we have a common thread. The differences are that Jim has the shotgun approach—like he'll have twelve ideas all at once—he has a whole bag of plans and projects and—

Jim: I'm the Prozac candidate.

Michael: My creative process is one thing at a time and that's really what kept *Monk* alive. One thing at a time. Only do *Monk,* only do *Monk,* only do *Monk,* the magazine.

Jim is way over on that end as far as spinning new ideas all the time. And I'm way over here, I just want to do *Monk* magazine. But we're both very good at manifesting. We both get the job done.

I had seven businesses before *Monk.* I've been driven. Everything I've done has been charged with the creative process, but this is the first time that it took off. I've always needed a partner to make a connection into the mainstream.

Jim: A partner or this particular partner, Mike?

Michael: I needed a partner and you came into my life. It takes a certain caliber of person—

Jim: Thanks, Mike—these ten years—that's real sweet.

Michael: Jim, I realize you want your hair cut but you don't have to be so—

Jim: I can't imagine that it's interchangeable, that there's nothing magical about the two of us, that you could have just gotten another partner.

Michael: If you would just let me finish my sentence—

Jim: Okay, I want to see you bail out now—

Michael: Before you launch a reactionary campaign.

Jim: Okay, bail out.

Michael: It's not a bailout, it's simply that I needed a partner, I prayed for a partner and you appeared.

Jim: I want to tell you more about the creative process.

Q: Speak.

Jim: Michael tends to not write everything down every day. He tends to let things sift through and then he comes up with a story. His natural talent is to take in the world and people deeply. And then tell a story. I tend to write in the moment because my memory isn't that deep. I write every day. I have a huge diary.

Michael: My creative process is taking the journey into someone. Really being a hundred percent present as often as I can. If it makes a deep enough imprint then a month later it will still be there.

Q: For someone who wanted to do something like you—not necessarily a mobile magazine but a troubadourlike, totally invented life—what advice would you give them?

Michael: My first advice is pick one thing and stick with it. No matter what. Every day, every hour, stick with it. Your focus is on that thing. Don't become afraid of the roller coaster.

Jim: Goethe said, "Commitment has power in it." It does. Michael's so right. He said early on, "You have to put all your eggs in one basket." The common wisdom, "Don't put all your eggs in one basket," is completely wrong when it comes to the entrepreneurial thing. Everybody says it different ways but it's always the same thing, you come up with your purpose, your shtick, your whatever it is that you're giving to the world and you just do that. "Just do it" is a Korean Zen mantra. Nike now says it, but it's a Zen idea. You just do it, whatever it is.

Michael: Within that thing you're going to find all of your life's lessons.

Jim: And you're going to get handed a lot of different things. All the things you thought you were missing out on, you'll find through that one doorway. Just through doing a magazine I learned all about business, publicity, marketing, writing, speaking. I've done talk shows, I've been in national magazines, I'm doing a movie. I'm making CD-ROMs, I'm on the Internet, I learn about cars, I learn about food, we learn about mobility, we learn about spirituality—everything—through that one doorway.

Lately I've been thinking about the reasons I'm always thinking about all these other things I could be doing. I think it's all because I'm in denial about death. If you're really in touch with your mortality, you know you only have eighty to a hundred years of your life (maybe a hundred and twenty if you're one of the few, but most people aren't that creative between a hundred and a hundred and twenty). So you have this limited time and as you get older you say, I'm going to do this one thing really, really well and yeah, I'm not going to be the actor; I'm going to be the magazine publisher. I'm not going to be the filmmaker; I'm going to be the writer. Those are hard decisions and that's a big lesson. You just have to say, Mind, shut off. I'm going to do this now as if it's the only thing I'm going to do for a hundred years.

Michael: That's the key. Do it, do it now, and if you want to change, you can change it. I've gone through seven career changes and I've never regretted any of them. It doesn't look like a mistake, even after I left them.

Jim: And you feel happy and complete with them because you did them a hundred percent, right?

Michael: Yeah.

Jim: That's important. Because they ended in their natural way. You know it's like a relationship. If you do a relationship with a lover one hundred percent, instead of tripping: Oh, this isn't the one. Instead, you really love this person and you do it one hundred percent, as if it were forever. If it's not meant to be, inevitably it will end, and it will happen in an organic process, because it's supposed to end.

PART 2

The Dig

You for whom I have looked so hard without ever finding. You whom I have longed for, called after, without ever seeing you come, you who are always present without ever existing—I am writing to you now. You who are basically only myself, but a much bigger and more noble self, an ingenious self, a self far from me, as real as the whole distance between the dream and the reality . . . You are my thought, I am your realization. An image carries you and your large open wings.

—MARIANNE WEREFKIN

In the next four chapters you will explore all the hidden crevices of your inclinations, needs, and desires, to uncover a holistic vision of your creative potential.

Excavating the Future

Searching Memory for Inspiration and Information

... I was *not* embarrassed at circuses. Some people are. Circuses are loud, vulgar, and smell in the sun. By the time many people are fourteen or fifteen, they have been divested of their loves, their ancient and intuitive tastes, one by one, until when they reach maturity there is no fun left, no zest, no gusto, no flavor. Others have criticized, and they have criticized themselves, into embarrassment. When the circus pulls in at five of a dark cold summer morn, and the calliope sounds, they do not rise and run, they turn in their sleep, and life passes by.

—Ray Bradbury

I stole this chapter's title from Mike Davis's wonderful book *City of Quartz: Excavating the Future of Los Angeles.* Even before I fell in love with the book, the phrase arrested my attention because it offered such a vivid description of the active, generative value of looking at the past and trying to understand it.

Archeologists dig up material that is already there—sometimes buried, broken, no longer functioning, eroded by time, entombed in some hidden vault. Then they lay it all out and look at it. They don't try to create anything. They are only exploring, attempting to understand the center of the culture's values and aspirations. They interpret the meaning of work, life, and creativity; they attempt to understand the invisible burning core that made the civilization live.

In the same way we may look at our own life—not as a doctor probing painful symptoms to see what diseases they reveal (as is sometimes the therapeutic model), but as an archeologist who has fallen in love with a mysterious civilization and in it seeks a new understanding of the present and the future.

This chapter will lead you through an exploration of yourself by examining memories that involve beauty, strength, and inspiration. If you understand the precise circumstances that once allowed you to be successful, confident, and creative, then you will be able to recreate those circumstances in your life now. The exercises will ask you to focus on the specifics of your experience and avoid generalizations. In this way, you will gather information about the kinds of people, environments, timetables, and tasks that bring out the best in you.

Through my workshops, I often watched how these memories of wonderful moments provided students with surprising insights that transformed into fresh new approaches to solving creative problems.

Sandy, a filmmaker and choreographer, lived in a big city because she wanted the community and the opportunities that a big city could offer. But when she began mapping out her memories from the exercises in this chapter, every positive memory involved being outdoors in a rural setting. Although she had not lost her drive to become a serious filmmaker, she had recently begun to feel burnt out. This made her listless about new projects, which in turn compelled her to question her talents. After recalling her childhood experiences with mud and trees and sun, she realized that the idea of being a filmmaker had been conflated with the idea of living a purely urban life. With her decision to make films, she automatically and unconsciously severed one of the main sources of her inspiration. She decided to start a film project that *required* her to be outside—at least some of the time. Making a film project while being in nature immediately refueled her creative energy.

The memory exercises in this chapter are designed not only to give you more clarity about the kind of life you want to live, but to reveal the conflicts between our career ambitions and our ideal lifestyle. By analyzing the memories of your peak experiences, you can see the ways in which your professional ambitions clash or cohere with your other, more private longings.

Though this chapter is all about looking back, it will prepare your mind for action. Before you begin a reorganization of your life, you must first feel that you're coming from a place of uncensored knowledge. I cannot emphasize enough how crucial it is to go ahead and dig up *all* evidence of buried desire—from every tattered, half-baked art project to every whispered daydream. Lay all the evidence out and look at it on the table. If you don't allow yourself to go through this process, you may find that you have once again led yourself down a dead-end trail.

Tricia, an aspiring opera singer and entrepreneur, waited until our last meeting to tell us that what she *really* wanted to do was graphic arts.

"It seemed so impossible," she shrugged when the rest of us expressed surprise at her not having told us before. How she had convinced herself that professional opera was somehow less competitive than commercial art, I don't know, but because the idea of being a visual artist was so precious, she rejected the notion a priori. She had spent several weeks of class focusing on her "second choices." Don't make the same mistake. Allow yourself to consider all your ideas seriously. There will be time later to make commitments to specific goals and eliminate certain options. If you eliminate your ace of spades now, you're going to be playing with a short deck.

If your memories point you in many directions, so be it. One of my students, Michael, a solo performance artist, said that his memories led him to believe he wanted to be "a farmer, a priest, or a porn star." Don't try to be coherent; open your mind to the great contradictions of human desire. When the time comes to make serious plans, the unearthed treasures of your psyche will already be handy.

When my student Meredith did her excavation, she remembered a series of peak experiences that all entailed working with people. She had been slaving rather unhappily under the dream of being a big-name conceptual artist. Now she no longer felt inspired to do her sculpture—she couldn't force herself to do it and she didn't know why. Through these exercises she remembered that some of her happiest projects were collaborative and that she had the most fun when she wasn't responsible for the actual physical production. She also noticed that the projects didn't need to be visual in order to fulfill her creatively. In the ensuing year, she explored a wide array of projects and roles within creative groups. She produced a radio drama based on the work of a local novelist, she created several CD-ROM titles in collaboration with other people, and she made a documentary film about her new favorite sport: surfing. She found that her new role as a producer allowed her to work alone on creating concepts and then collaborate in the actual production of a project. Invigorated by these positive experiences, Meredith approached galleries with new sculpture ideas. Within the year she was showing her art in two local galleries as well as continuing her other collaborative projects.

SARAH SHELTON MANN, CHOREOGRAPHER

Throughout our interview, choreographer Sarah Shelton Mann refers again and again to a tool she developed as a child growing up in a dysfunctional southern family. Finding herself neglected and often alone, she poured her energies into a process called "tracking" that she still uses to this day. "It's like an animal tracks prey," she explains. "You study the territory. You study the seasons, when it's time to hibernate and when it's time to come out. You know what the animal eats, if it's after you or you're after it." For Mann, tracking describes the continual activity of observation and questioning essential to staying creatively alive: "Because I had no discipline as a child and no one cared what I thought or did, I would give myself exercises and tests. Whether it would be in the sandbox, making cities, and having to develop neater holes, larger rooms, deeper tunnels; or climbing a tree and getting one branch higher. I made up structures all the time. And I had no one to play with so I had to figure out how to keep learning. I'm still studying tracking."

Through staying in touch with her childhood process, Mann has carved out a remarkable career for herself. She is the grand dame of a fertile dance theater scene in San Francisco, and the founder and choreographer of Contraband, a cutting-edge collaborative dance company that fuses live music, acrobatic movement, and larger-than-life visuals into impassioned kinetic spectacles. In addition to her art-making, she has studied a multitude of bodywork techniques and spiritual disciplines. Her punk-spiritual approach combines an unusual mix of daily actions: writing, coffee, and cigarettes followed by an hour of meditation and then yoga.

Mann believes that everyone is an artist but that most people don't have the chance to develop what they love: "I once heard about an ashram in southern India where the meditation was the opportunity to learn anything. You could just choose to train as anything you wanted. So someone who came there as a carpenter would end up in Ayurvedic medicine. They actually had the opportunity to find what they truly loved. We have to continually answer the question, What do you want to be when you grow up? You look at Daddy and it's 'I want to be a fireman' and you look at Mommy and it's 'I want to be a cook.' Or it's 'I hate Daddy, so I'll never be a fireman.' And a lot of people who are stuck creatively become supporters of artists when they're actually extremely talented themselves."

In the same egalitarian spirit, she understands that despite her past successes she can't remain creative while resting on her laurels. She must continue to reinvent her creative process. "As a child I had no life, so I had to create one in order to actually hold one together," she says. "Everything was falling apart. So in my creativity I have this cycle of destruction and putting things together and then destroying them again. I hesitate to say this but I'm beginning to think all of my work has been channeled. I don't think I've ever done anything. If that's the case I need to have a lot more respect and discipline, to honor what is being given to me."

Mann's humility toward her own creations reflects an overriding philosophy that being an artist is not the goal itself but a means to a more transcendent end: a spiritual life path. In offering advice to aspiring choreographers and artists, she echoes this belief in a higher purpose while encouraging the artist to follow his or her interests: "What I would say is, your job in life is to find out who you are, and that's the only thing you need to do. Do what you actually enjoy."

Moving into Memory

The acting technique called "sense memory" is designed to bring back vivid memories of physical and emotional sensations when they are needed to help create a reality for the actor on stage. The actor recalls drinking hot coffee until the constellation of sensations is instantly accessible: the warm ceramic against the hand, the scorched-earth smell, the steam, the wetness, the quickening of the pulse. When the actor finds herself on stage, the cool empty plastic mug can evoke the essence of real java.

Now, as you begin to look closely at some moments in your life, use "sense memory" to bring back the original details. You'll need time and a quiet place to focus, relax, and write. When you think of a memory, close your eyes and use your imagination to recreate the environment. When the memory is full and rich, pick up the pen and begin writing freehand—working through the following exercises. As soon as you lose touch with the vividness of the memory, stop.

EXERCISES IN EXCAVATING THE FUTURE

1. Think about your earliest memories when you did just what you wanted to do. They don't need to be productive activities. No matter how seemingly unimportant, let your mind revisit your original inclinations and desires: for example, "I loved to play with small things, like tiny stamp envelopes—the tiny world made me see things in a new way. I loved to touch them, feel their tininess and think about how perfect they were. . . . "

    Now jot down images from these memories.

2. Using the same attention to sensory detail, list some things you loved doing; for example, "sloshing in the swamp behind our house, reading philosophy, inventing cities out of trash" . . .

    • as a toddler:

    • as a child:

    • as a teenager:

    • as a young adult:

3. Pick out the five most powerful memories from the above lists.

    1.
    2.
    3.
    4.
    5.

Apply the following questions to each of your five memories:

What part of this experience gave you pleasure?

What circumstances allowed you to concentrate?

Was there anything in the environment or the social setting that contributed to the joy or the heightened clarity? The time of day? The weather? The color of the room?

Was the action meant to benefit anyone else, like a gift? Was it a collaboration? Was it highly private?

Was it intended to impress, rile, or protect someone?

Was your mind completely involved in the action or were you spurred on by the idea of what the finished product could do? Did this project have a purpose outside the action itself?

What belief did this action express?

4. List your five most essential beliefs. Here are some typical ones:

    *   Loving people is more important than art or money.
    *   We have a responsibility to be politically active.
    *   Human beings are more savage than animals.

    1.
    2.
    3.
    4.
    5.

Now look for times or events in your life when you were best able to put these beliefs into action. These memories may differ markedly from the previous exercise in that they do not necessarily represent the environments or challenges that brought out the best in you. They may, however, represent the work to which you aspire in the world.

Memory connected to belief 1

Memory connected to belief 2

Memory connected to belief 3

Memory connected to belief 4

Memory connected to belief 5

5. Compare the memories in exercise one with these memories. Are there any overlapping memories? Do you see any contradictions between your beliefs and what ignites you to inspired and joyful action? Can you spot any false beliefs that you feel you have difficulty living up to or that you cling to for some reason?

ERIC MC DOUGALL, ENTREPRENEUR AND CREATIVE PRODUCER

Eric Mc Dougall always knew he wanted to work in a creative field, but given his many interests, he had a difficult time devoting himself to a single discipline. Like many interdisciplinarians,* he thrived in working environments that included both solitary pursuits and collaborative projects, physical action and intellectual work. While studying architecture at UC Berkeley, he played drums for the college jazz band and became involved in organizing a jazz festival of college bands. This experience led him to producing the Berkeley Jazz Festival, which in turn landed him a job with a large production company. Later, as a designer and producer at FM Productions, he applied his knowledge of space and music to create sets for large rock tours. Eventually, he decided to start his own production company, McDougall Creative. Since then he has produced a wide variety of large-scale events, from an Apple computer conference to the gala event for the fiftieth anniversary of the United Nations, attended by Bill Clinton and Boutros Boutros-Ghali.

In his current work he can make the most of his generator/maker[†] nature. Drawing on a fabulous inventory of skills and interests, he gets to compose music, design sets, work with writers, direct videos, and work with actors, as well as oversee the conceptual aspects of his business.

Q: How do you describe your work to people who have had no exposure to it?

A: Corporate opera. I call myself a producer or creative director of live events. We also produce film and video. Conceptually, we help a company shape its messages. I think my background in design and architecture has really helped me. In architecture you solve problems by looking at things schematically. You're designing a building and you create a program for the building. For instance, certain things need to be next to each other—the bathrooms are near the elevators because of the flow of the piping through the building. These are schematic, abstract arrangements that dictate the final form. I bring that kind of design process to corporate communications.

---

*For a definition of the interdisciplinarian, see page 178.
[†]For definitions of the generator and the maker, see pages 75 and 65.

Q: Within your job, do you do mostly conceptualizing, or concrete creation—i.e., film, music, visuals . . . ?

A: I am lucky to have a healthy mix of creative direction and hands-on creation. I find myself working as a set designer, a graphic designer, a video director/producer, a music director sometimes, and music producer often, going into the sound studio and choosing a mix or choosing sounds. I also enjoy designing lighting.

Q: What does your workday look like?

A: It's pretty varied. A lot of it is working with people. I spend a lot of time on the phone. This friend of mine and I decided there are different levels: When you're at level five you're one week before an event and you're deadline-oriented, and your efficiency is at its best. You're able to talk to fifty people a day, write fifty E-mails, finish a script, and go to three meetings. And then there are other times, like now for example, when things are kind of slow and mellow, and you're thinking about long-term stuff.

Q: What do you see as the different elements of your creative process?

A: You ask a lot of questions in the beginning. First you try to understand what the goal is. You can go in twenty million different directions, but you have to hone in on where in general you want to go. The next part involves collaborative problem solving. It's that "one plus one equals three" phase. You can have a good idea—you think it's the best idea in the world—but then you put it next to other people's ideas and you become very humble very quickly! Then we use a big white board or chalkboard or big pieces of paper and have a brainstorming session.

Then there are moments when you need solitude. Just to sit down and center yourself, and look through your notes. That's when you get "quantum leap" moments of brilliance that happen after you've asked all the questions and assimilated all the possible ideas.

The most important thing for a creative person is not to become too attached to your own identity. It's the worst thing in the world. Because you completely lose your objectivity. If you think you've got the best idea in the world, you're totally blind. When you're the kind of creative person who makes a product with your hands, it's really hard to take criticism without taking it personally. But I think in a lot of ways I've been able to divorce myself from criticism of the object equaling criticism of me. I feel that my ideas are just a malleable plastic ooze that can be molded into one form or another. If the idea doesn't work, I extend my creative process by reworking the ooze.

Q: How have you learned this?

A: It takes time. In the beginning you're really married to every concept you have. You acquire the ability to incorporate others' ideas and change your own without compromising the value you bring to the endeavor. It also has to do with ego. Ironically, I think you end up with greater ego satisfaction by being above your ideas and being able to manipulate them as if they were somebody else's, than by being holed up in your own creative cave. So you're either looking at the forest from above, or you're in the trees.

Q: Do you have any daily practice that helps your creativity?

A: Yeah, you've got to do *other* things. Explore in totally diverse realms that are completely outside what you're doing. I get no ideas by looking at corporate communication magazines. If I want a creative infusion, I'll go to a film archive and see some films, or I'll exercise, or I'll go to a bar and have a conversation with somebody who I've never met, or I'll read a book about ants. I have a lot of friends in the art world. People who help me see things in a different way.

Q: After studying architecture, how did you know this was what you wanted to do? Did you fall into it or say to yourself, "I know I don't want to be an architect"?

A: Berkeley's design school focuses heavily on environmental design, with emphasis on process and theory. But I'm not really doing now what I have set as my ultimate goal. I fell into this. Because of my background in music, business, and design, I became a set designer. That led to creative direction and so on. I don't feel alive unless I'm learning, moving, changing, growing.

Q: You're a generalist.

A: Yeah, I'm the ultimate generalist. Being a producer like this is perfect for me because I can keep my fingers in a million little pots, and hire the best people possible to manage those pots, then I glue it all together. I find that there are not a lot of people who can do that, can manage a lot of things simultaneously but pull them all together and make a really strong product. Movie directors do that; it's a bit of a dictatorship but a collaborative dictatorship. And the dictatorship part comes from just having a strong sense, an unwavering sense, about what an end result should be.

Q: It takes a lot of chutzpah to start your own company. Where did you learn this self-directedness?

A: I've always been an independent, self-starting, self-motivated person. Having a lot of confidence helps too. A sense that you can do anything, even when you don't know how. I had never produced a video before, and a client said, "We need these videos done, these interviews, and we need graphics, and you guys do that, right?" I'd never done it before but I said, "Yes." When we got back, we laughed. Then I got serious and called in the most experienced video producer I knew and I stuck to her like glue. Now I can budget a video or film, I can edit in off-line digital, I know what it takes to get titles to happen—you just learn by doing it. *Just say yes.*

Q: Did you have any role models or mentors for what you do? Or for a vision of a creative life that inspired you?

A: I had an opportunity to work with fashion designer Karl Lagerfeld once. Looking at a guy like him, I realized that you can draw the line wherever you want to, arbitrarily. You can draw it really high, or you can draw it really close to the chest. At that time he was designing three collections for spring and fall for Chanel, for Chloe, for Lagerfeld, writing children's books, and doing photomontage spreads for his own books. I also love looking at certain eras when a critical mass of creative people came together— like Paris in the twenties with Hemingway, Coco Chanel, and others. I look at these periods of creative ferment, wanting to create that. I'm still trying to create that or be a part of that. I think that would be wonderful.

Q: Have you had an emotional support system through all this?

A: I think ultimately when I've been smartest, when I've found myself making the occasional brilliant move, it's been because I've been with a girlfriend who has been smarter than me and was able to really clarify issues and guide me in the right direction. When I look at my turning points, like when I decided to start a business, it's because someone was supporting me. Someone I could bounce my ideas off, someone who gave my ideas a really sane look. I can imagine that you could have the same kind of relationship with a really good shrink or psychologist. In fact, there are people who specialize in working with entrepreneurs, who charge a lot of money, but they're that kind of person. You go in and bounce your ideas off them, and they steer you and guide you.

Q: Do you have any tricks that you play on yourself when you don't feel like working? Or do you always feel like working?

A: No, I don't always feel like working. There are things you do. I'm very environmentally sensitive. So sometimes I'll change my space, I'll rearrange my space to make it feel more conducive to what I'm trying to do.

Q: Like furniture?

A: Furniture, yeah, rearrange things, go to a different place. For example, when you're at college, and you're sitting in your hovel, in your studio apartment hovel, and you're not inspired to read about Mesopotamia, what do you do? Well, I would go to the reading room in the library, a giant oak hall, a great piece of architecture. Suddenly I would feel academically inclined with the critical mass of other people burning the oil there. Things like that really make a difference.

Q: Talk about some of your failures, where you hit an obstacle you felt like you couldn't get past.

A: I had a partnership with another guy, and it felt like it wasn't going in the right direction. It's the biggest agony: You're a year into a partnership, you're making money, people like you, and you're doing interesting projects, but you know there's something fundamentally wrong. It was the hardest decision to decide to end the partnership and start over. You have to incorporate a new company, come up with a new name, try to find an office. . . . You have to act on those difficult feelings, and do something about them, and try to make that into something positive. How do you take a problem and make it into an opportunity? If you have a problem and it stays a problem, you haven't really done anything. But if you can take a problem and turn it into something positive, that's clearly a good thing.

Q: Has your idea about what motivates you, or what success is, changed since you started?

A: Yeah. You know, when you're younger you think success is money. Success isn't money. You may go through phases where you think success is power. Success is just, to me, recognition for doing the best that you can do in a given realm. That's it. There's nothing more.

My goal is to make enough money doing something really fulfilling that is valuable and smart. To me it's about education, and planet preservation, and quality of life for human beings. And what else is there to live for? Otherwise you're just using resources and taking up space. I'd like to get to the point where I have enough resources to do something that makes up for my taking up the resources on the planet.

Q: If there's one piece of advice you'd give to a person like you what would it be?

A: Ask yourself what environments have you been around in the past that give you a lead on other things. You've got to synthesize all the things that are around you in your life, and take advantage of all these things that can help you. You can't just go off on your own. It's weird because we grew up in the Me Generation, and the focus was on the individual. What about where you've been, what your family lineage is, what your training is, what you were curious about when you were a kid, what toys you played with? Your history, your connections, your original impulses—all those things are vital to understanding your future. Like I played with Legos. Legos were this undifferentiated form and I could make it into anything I wanted. I think that says something really essential about the way I think.

Q: It's a perfect clue to your work now.

A: Yeah, if I had been deeply into a *20,000 Leagues Under the Sea* submarine kit, then I would have been focused on a very literal, equipment-based, technological reality—but I had Legos. One block could equal the size of a supertanker or the size of one block. The imagination determined the scale.

When you're considering which direction you want your life to go, it's important to strip down all the artifice that you've created around you, your work, your life, and look at the essentials. If you had a fire in your house, what four things would you want to keep? If you were to save one photograph, one book, one object, and one idea, what would it be? What four things are at the core of your being?

Then you need to go through some different exercises: self-searching. When you think of your strengths and the things you've done in the past, what gives you the biggest feeling of accomplishment? That feeling of pride, pride of accomplishment—that's the biggest motivator there is.

Kaleidoscope of Creativity

Understanding Your Artistic Profile

I live my life in growing orbits
which move out over the things of the world.
Perhaps I can never achieve the last
but that will be my attempt.
I am circling around God, around the ancient tower,
and I have been circling for a thousand years,
and I still don't know if I am a falcon, or a storm,
or a great song.

—RAINER MARIA RILKE

Color-wheeling our parachutes, diapering our inner children, stalking down our totemic animals, we engage again and again in the great search for the elusive self. We study (and invent) the systems of self-hood—from the science of psychology to the cosmic numbers of the Enneagram—all to uncover our individual place in the galaxy of "personality." Self-knowledge is important for all of humanity, but it is especially crucial for people who want creative lives. In many of these self-knowledge systems, however, the "artist" category only occupies a single lonely spot. All artists are lumped together—marked by generic descriptive adjectives such as "unconventional," "imaginative," "independent," and "intuitive." In my experience, however, there are a wide variety of creative temperaments—each with their own habits of mind, body, and spirit.

The creative profiles in this chapter are derived neither from ancient mysticism nor modern psychology. I just made them up. They are tools for probing and exploring. Batter them, hybridize them, take issue with them. Use them as a miner's pick to dig into the uncharted territory of your creative self.

The types I've listed can help clarify your career path by uncovering how your lifestyle or livelihood runs at crosscurrents with your natural creative tides. For example, many people think that because two people share the same artistic aspirations, they should also be happy working in the same day job.

Consider the following scenario. You are a novice actress. You look up to your friend Bernadette, who works as a cocktail waitress while pursuing her acting career. You have a full-time day job at an insurance company that prevents you from fully pursuing your dream. Bernadette, on the other hand, never misses an audition and she's always practicing her witty repartee with customers. You decide to take the leap: quit your job and make a commitment to acting. You jump at the opportunity when Bernadette offers to get you a job at her restaurant.

After a week of spilled drinks, awkward interchanges, and sore feet, you receive a letter informing you that the one agent who had expressed an initial interest in you "is no longer accepting new clients." That night, as the last swerving suit disappears behind the red vinyl door, you slump into a booth and announce your plans to return to school to study environmental science.

"Why are you giving up?" Bernadette asks, snapping her Juicy Fruit.

"Because I can't take this," you answer. "I don't like working at night or chatting up strangers. And I hate being told what to do. I'm just not cut out for the life of the struggling artist."

"Suit yourself," says Bernadette.

"If you can't stand the limelight," sneers the cook.

But no one asks you, What does waitressing have to do with acting? Just because it works for Bernadette doesn't mean it has to work for you. Maybe Bernadette is an "interpreter," and is happy refining her people skills within the larger business of a restaurant. But maybe you are a "generator," full of private brainstorms and ideas with little urge to nurture customers' desires or socialize throughout an evening. So what can you do? This fictional "you" must find work which both creates happiness and supports an acting schedule.

The types I have observed fall into two basic modes: collaborative types and individualistic types.

COLLABORATIVE CREATIVITY
Leader
Teacher
Realizer
Healer
Interpreter

INDIVIDUAL CREATIVITY
Generator
Inventor
Maker
Mystic
Thinker

Though all have the capability to work through every stage of creation, each type prefers a certain moment in the creative process. The generator, for instance, loves the moment of conception—where there are tons of ideas and no limits. The interpreter thrives on the final stage of creativity, when the work becomes polished, clear, and strong.

Allow the following profiles to help you explore your artistic essence and give you a sense of the sorts of work relationships that support your blend of creative colors. Each person probably draws from a combination of types, so don't feel compelled to fit yourself into a single profile.

Maker

Alan is an abstract painter. He does not translate concepts into things, like conceptual artists do. He does not tell stories with his paintings. He makes things. Visually arresting things. Things that are wonderful to look at. When he talks about his work, he talks about the kinesthetic action, the colors, the making of a mess. He is the very embodiment of a maker.

For most makers, their greatest joy springs from creating things with their hands. They value craftsmanship and material creation over abstract conceptualization. They want to be close to the means of production. They are not satisfied with daydreaming; they doodle. They would rather dance their idea than chat about it.

Makers often lean toward the creation of physical objects, whether they are painters, sculptors, furniture builders, computer artists, or cooks. Although there are a lot of makers in the visual arts, you need not be involved in making a material object in order to be a maker. You might also be a drummer or a dancer. For makers, the central act is the complex moment of touching, moving, working, and thinking. Makers tend to be physically vigorous and emotional rather than intellectual or conceptual. They often enjoy working alone because solitude allows them to go deep into their action and work without interruption. While they are interested in the process of making for its own sake, they also derive great joy from observing the work evolve before their eyes.

Practically every artist has something of the maker in her. The urge to bring something tangible into being lies at the very core of creativity. If you yearn to garden, braid hair, fix toilets, paint canvases, or beat bongo drums, you may be working with the spirit of a maker.

Makers face special obstacles in adjusting to traditional employment. While they might have the skills for producing a feature film or running a large company, the pain of working in an abstracted work environment—where the most sensual material is white bond paper—is unbearable for them. In David Hare's play *Plenty,* Susan, a secretary, articulates the maker's dismay at a life of shuffling papers: "They get heavier and heavier as the day goes on, I can barely stagger across the room for the weight of a single piece of paper, by the end of the day, if you dropped one on the floor you would smash your foot."

Since our culture doesn't tend to value those jobs that touch or make the object itself, many maker jobs don't necessarily conjure images of privilege. Aside from a few cherished jobs like the fine artist and surgeon, our society reserves the highest prestige for jobs that are removed from the action. For makers the very prospect of a traditional career can be disheartening.

If you are a maker seeking a way to have your workday enrich your artistic life, then consider the following array of options: gardening or any outdoor work; plumbing; teaching children (always visceral and active); working in film; installing art; working in museum shows; construction; working in a restaurant; or working in a "craft" form (pottery, glass blowing, tile painting, furniture making, fashion, graphic arts, house painting, or massage).

Maybe you are not 100 percent maker, but you have been working in an environment that neglects that side of your artistic urges. Our relationship to our hands is an often overlooked element in beckoning the muse—even for artists who are not involved in hands-on object creation. At one of her lectures, in response to someone's question about her daily process, novelist Doris Lessing claimed that before she writes, she cleans house, washes dishes, and putters around until she feels inspired. She suspects that she is preparing her mind for creativity by stimulating and working with her hands in simple, repetitive tasks.

Maker Exercise

If you are a maker, try building the elements of your perfect working environment and look for clues within that. Physically assemble every necessary piece—if only in miniature—of the ideal setting for your work. Now look at your collage or installation or furniture rearrangement or shoebox stage set, and ask yourself the following questions:

Are you attracted to working outdoors? Do you need to produce a number of things each day, or would you be happier working on a long-term project? Do you need to work alone? Do you want to use your whole body the way builders do? Or do you want to use your hands and eyes the way jewelry makers do? Must the product be useful? Must it be beautiful? Is it three-dimensional or two? Is it a time-based art like film or performance?

Take a pen and scribble down some jobs that possess these elements. Use this piece of paper as a bookmark in the exercises of chapter 6, where you will find use for these ideas again!

Teacher

Teachers enjoy giving people information, ability, and knowledge. Preferring informal, intimate groups over large, formal gatherings, they are less interested in possessing power than they are in transmitting it. Some teachers who haven't found a healthy outlet for their teaching energies can become obsessive helpers, nags, and know-it-alls (I can vouch for this, personally.) However, if they can create a situation in which their impulse to teach is put to good use, they can flourish both psychologically and creatively. With the proper outlet for their pedagogical genius, they will focus on their own dreams more effectively. The personality of the teacher tends toward the jovial yet emotionally detached—exhibiting a strong pragmatic drive to solve problems (often other people's) through a mix of logic and imagination.

Though teachers usually feel comfortable speaking in front of small groups, they may shy away from large public-speaking forums or performances. They yearn for interactive learning and dislike unnecessary personal attention, in spite of the pleasure they glean from being in charge. They work well under short deadlines within a structured framework, especially if the framework is of their own design. They may have more difficulty working toward long-term, unstructured goals. Articulate and communicative, teachers often have the best access to their own creative energy through the process of working collaboratively.

The teacher's creativity has often been belittled in our society with such ridiculous maxims as "Those who can't do, teach." But the creativity of natural teachers is as versatile and vibrant as that of any other creative type, it's just that they get excited by the immediacy of learning, communication, and interaction.

Sometimes teachers use their teaching skills to develop themselves within their art form. Natalie Goldberg, author of *Writing Down the Bones,* began teaching writing before she herself was widely published. She first became renowned for her intuitive, spontaneous teaching techniques, which in turn led her to write two books about the craft of writing, then an autobiography, and finally a novel. In this way, natural teachers can put their teaching talents in the service of their artistic aspirations.

If you find yourself volunteering to teach nieces how to drive, friends how to do the macarena, bosses how to use their still-untouched computer, you may have a talent and affinity for teaching. If you can find a job that uses this talent, you may have found work that can breed richer creativity in all aspects of your life. Here is a list of unorthodox teaching situations you might not have considered: English as a second language; coaching a sport; inventing and starting your own classes; working as an artist-in-residence in a school, community center, or institution; working as a "specialty arts" teacher in an after-school program; teaching special classes within corporations in writing, public speaking, or acting; starting a school of your own; starting a summer camp for children; working as a private tutor.

Teacher Exercise

Draw up a lesson plan for one hour of the most wonderful class in the world. It doesn't have to be a class that exists, you can invent it.

What are you going to be teaching? How will you begin the class? How will you structure it? What will the students be doing? What will your role be? Once you have a clear picture of this class through a complete lesson plan, then determine the size, setting, and audience for the class. Make a list of three possible places you could teach this class—if only on a voluntary basis.

Now put this exercise as a bookmark in the exercises of chapter 6, where you will be able to use the information again.

Thinker

The thinker simply enjoys thinking. Mind-boggling, eh? Doesn't every-body like to think? Well, yes and no. Many people like to think in rela-tion to someone else or something else. For instance, some people think as they talk; the talking catalyzes the thought. Other people think as they read; the activity of reading makes their neurons fire. For thinkers, however, thinking is its own reward and needs no external impetus. They consistently prefer introverted activities over interaction. They value the idea as much as, if not more than, the communication or realization of that idea.

Thinkers enjoy measuring, interpreting, analyzing, and theorizing. Their art is the art of allowing an observation to bear fruit in the mind. They feel at home in abstractions and take pleasure in seeing and inventing patterns in the world. If you find that you are satisfied with contemplating an idea and then become bored with the mundane details of communicating or manufacturing your ecstatic vision, then you may be working with a thinker's mind. Because thinkers feel so comfortable and connected to the ideas themselves, they don't always see the point in spending so much time on the crafting of the form.

Some examples of famous artist-thinkers are writer/librarian Jorge Luis Borges, postmodern choreographer Yvonne Rainer, and concep-tual artist John Baldessari. Borges explored arcane philosophical conundrums in his short stories. When he was asked why he didn't write novels, he answered that it was because he didn't read novels— he got bored after ten pages or so. He was interested in the kernel of the thoughts themselves, not in long, elaborate narratives. Rainer, dis-carding the old concept of dance as beautiful artifice, made thought-provoking rather than aesthetically pleasing dances out of everyday tasks, game structures, and theories. She pared the craft of dance down to its skeleton in order to physicalize her intellectual ideas. In

Baldessari's early groundbreaking work, he neither painted nor photographed, but acted as part archivist, part theoretician—creating provocative visual statements through the juxtaposition of still images spliced from old movies. None of these artists were interested in the flourish of emotion or the flaunting of virtuosity, or even getting messy with voluminous production. Their art was the art of seeing things in a sharp, strange, new way.

For career and creative ebullience, thinkers need to put themselves in situations that at once boggle the mind and require them to practice consistent action. Their creativity thrives in the half darkness of confusion, when the unsolved problem grows beautiful as it is turned over and over, the way a coarse rock is made smooth in a rock tumbler. In the work world, this means working in a job that requires continuous learning such as scholarship, museum work, journalism, or research. Thinkers often feel most comfortable surrounded by the physical artifacts of thought: They work in libraries or on archeological digs, in churches and archives. Examples of thinker-friendly day jobs range from used-book seller to mathematician, political analyst to computer programmer or business consultant.

Thinker Exercise

If you are a thinker in search of the right working situation, then let your mental habits lead you to some new ideas. Go to a library and look through biographies of people you admire. Look at the course of their careers and how they found jobs that served their creative ambitions. Make a list of your favorite creative thinkers and their jobs. Now sit and write a list of the jobs you think will keep you in a constant state of curiosity and intellectual challenge.

Put the list in the exercises of chapter 6 for future use.

Realizer

Realizers are the people everyone else depends on to get things done. They relish the process of problem solving with lots of elements, people, and materials. Limelight and fanfare may result, but ultimately these things don't really make the realizer happy. Instead, realizers often prefer to stay behind the scenes, providing the driving energy for pulling together an entire project.

Versatility and excellent communication skills allow realizers to create multifaceted projects, events, and organizations. Using networking and brainstorming as tools for building momentum and community, they tend to work well with groups. They understand how to get the most out of their time. Once they have fastened onto a project, they are extremely motivated, especially if they are working in an environment that gives them the freedom to work in their own rhythm. When I interviewed Chris Wink of Blue Man Group, he talked about one of the other Blue Men as a classic realizer: "Phil knows how to get things done, he realizes things in the world. Where my job might be to go away and read a book, his role will be about getting our work out in the world."

While realizers are often encouraged to pursue business, administration, and publicity, they can unleash their creative and logistical skills on almost any endeavor, especially in the collaborative arts of film, theater, multimedia, and music. In terms of transitional work or day jobs, certain kinds of work lend themselves to the realizer's well-spring of know-how: events planning, producing, publishing, marketing, catering, managing, styling, volunteer coordinating, fund-raising, or union organizing.

It is precisely the realizer's attractiveness as a collaborator that puts his or her fantastic organizational skills in constant danger of being kidnapped. For this reason, realizers must guard themselves against saboteurs of their dreams.

Do you find yourself reorganizing your desk—or (heaven forbid) someone else's? Do you find yourself taking on the responsibilities of planning your sister's wedding? Remember: Your talent for making things happen is as rare and precious as pure gold and should be treated as such.

Realizer Exercise

Plan a one-time event which will bring you closer to the people, situations, or activities that you want more of in your life. For instance, if you are an aspiring actress, organize a play reading with a director you would like to work with. If you are a painter, create an open studio for a small number of invited curators, artists, and collectors. If you are a dancer, sponsor an event that supports your dance form. Write a list of things to do, as if you were really going to plan this event—complete with lists of phone numbers, tasks, and ideas. Then choose one of the following options: Either carry out the plan or invite a small group of friends to your house to brainstorm on your job situation and the viability of this idea.

Put the plan in the exercise section of chapter 6 for future use.

Interpreter

Interpreters play with stuff that is already there—bringing it to life in new and fresh ways. Their creativity is built upon understanding how things can be made better. Through elaborating, improving, and evolving raw material, the interpreter manifests and perfects the work in a new form. For instance, all performing artists—dancers, musicians, and actors—must have the gift of the interpreter. Performers are the mediums through which creative work meets the world. They work with the last stage of creativity—not the initial concept or the hammering together of a temporary shack or blueprint—but the phase which sees a work to its completion or improves upon its original plan. Great editors exhibit the interpreter's ability in bringing a book to fruition, just as a cinematographer interprets a script to transform a film into a visual experience.

An asset to any large-scale creative work, interpreters often make good consultants, cinematographers, lighting designers, editors, academics, actors, musicians, dancers, and directors. In many ways, interpreters are among the luckiest of the artistic types in that they enjoy and are good at creative, reasonably well-paying jobs like editing, producing, consulting, and music production.

The essence of interpretive work combines intellectual acuity, steadfastness, and flashes of visionary genius. Interpreters possess two distinct talents: First, they can envision a finished work where only a model or a partially created piece exists. Second, they possess the patience and specificity of mind to work toward a finished piece detail by detail.

Interpreters sometimes choose to work on other people's projects over their own, finding themselves drawn to a project's potential for "really happening." Their diplomatic and efficient style allows them to work both with others and alone. Not overly proprietary, they tend to be driven by the purposefulness and quality of the work itself rather than their role in the process.

When interpreters lack the time or interest to clarify their own creative path, they may find themselves caught in the role of midwifing for other people's creative work. The interpreter's rush to perfection, so valuable in the later stages of creativity, runs at crosscurrents with the tumult of confusion that surrounds the early stages of creativity. If you are an interpreter who is having a difficult time giving full attention to one of your own as-yet-undeveloped ideas, you must let yourself wade through the darkness of the early creative process.

It is also crucial that interpreters tap into work that they feel utterly passionate about. Without that sense of passion and importance, interpreters will be tempted to shift their focus to a project at a more developed stage.

Interpreter Exercises

1. For individual projects: Take a piece of paper and make a mess of it. The next day come back to it and play with it some more—painting over what you did the previous day, cutting out patterns, gluing stuff onto it. The only rule is that by the end of the day, it must still be a mess. Work on the piece every day for six days (perhaps instead of your daily action). On the seventh day, do whatever you can to finish the piece to your liking.

2. For collaborative projects: Make a list of the people or organizations you know who are working on projects that you like. Do you have ideas on how you could improve these endeavors? Call and tell them you might be able to contribute to the project. Maybe your brainstorm will unearth some new ideas that will lead you to a fantastic freelance situation.

Put this list in the exercises of chapter 6 as a bookmark for future use.

ADAM BECKMAN, CINEMATOGRAPHER

Cinematographer Adam Beckman grew up fascinated by cameras, composition, and the language of visual imagery. While his classmates at NYU film school aspired to the highly touted title of director, Beckman chose to focus on camera work and cinematography. He saw that the job of the director, despite its creativity and centrality, was somewhat removed from the actual *filmmaking*. He knew that *he* wanted to be the person looking through the viewfinder and creating the imagery. He also had little interest in working with actors except as material for lighting and composition. Once out of school, he worked for little or nothing to gain experience in the field. Before long he met a veteran cinematographer who took him under his wing. "This business works through mentoring and personal relationships," he says. "On the one hand, there's this vicious hierarchy. On the other, people are always looking for someone to help them and someone they can help."

After ten years working first as a camera assistant and then as a cinematographer, shooting everything from commercials and MTV music videos to independent features and documentaries, Beckman is still trying to find a balance between lucrative, less-fulfilling work and more creative, low-budget projects.

He recommends that would-be film workers choose the process that gives them the most pleasure: "If they pick editing, they'd better like the sound the computer makes. If they choose lighting, they should enjoy looking at gels and climbing ladders. A lot of people look at the film industry as something that's hip, cool. To me, hip and cool connotes some kind of fun, relaxed environment, and a film set can be anything but fun and relaxed. Unless you're working in an area whose everyday process you simply enjoy, the stress can be overwhelming."

He also advises that beginners dive in and work at all levels.

Be a production assistant on a decent-sized shoot. Really overstep your bounds on shoots where you have nothing to lose and really understep your bounds on shoots where you do. Volunteer. Even if you want to be a director, shoot medical videos; even if you want to be an editor, work with sound on the set. It's all interdisciplinary and you have to know everyone else's job. And at the same time, go back to your school and shoot as many of your own projects as you can. Don't delay your creative work.

Though in the past Beckman has been cynical about the value of film school, after being in the industry for ten years, he now appreciates the fact that it allowed him the opportunity to explore the medium without being distracted by the politics and hierarchy of the film world. "The best thing about film school," he says, "was meeting other people who are all on the same level in terms of real knowledge. You're all learning together and your goals have nothing to do with commercialism."

In recent years Beckman has been approached by a number of people asking how they can get into film. While eager to help them, he has begun to question why so many people are attracted to filmmaking: "A lot of people associate filmmaking with film watching, when they are completely different experiences. Watching a film is essentially solitary, passive, and very sensual. Filmmaking is technical, proactive, and strenuous. You certainly have to love film to be a filmmaker, but you need to have other qualities as well. Sometimes when people enter into filmmaking and discover it's not what they expected, they're very disappointed."

He also wants to warn people about the stresses of the film lifestyle: "In freelancing there's a lot of unseen work because you have to take care of yourself financially and there's no guarantee that you'll ever have work again. If you need regularity in your life, the film industry is not going to provide it. But if you love what you're doing, there's just nothing better. Throw yourself in one hundred percent."

Beckman's quiet, self-reflective personality clashes with the stereotype of the brash, fast-talking schmoozer who makes it in the world of film. While he acknowledges that it helps to have a certain amount of charisma, he dimisses the notion that getting ahead in film hinges on a person's ability to brazenly sell oneself and climb social ladders: "My success is in being really quiet. If you present yourself as something you're not, the people who have a lot more experience are going to see through it. Everyone values honesty, integrity, and passion. Don't impress them with your knowledge, impress them with your interest in the medium."

Generator

Generators manufacture ideas and schemes. They have enormous enthusiasm and a surplus of initiative. For the generator the best moment in the creative process is the first stage of conceptual ecstasy. In ideal circumstances they are high risk-takers, boldly leaping into their idea like a cliff diver plummets into the blue sky. Generators adore brainstorming and despise repetition. They have more ideas in one week than they can carry out in a whole lifetime. They live in a state of creative rush. Ron, one of the most classic generators I have ever met, was a visual artist working as a freelance advertiser. His conversations were spotted with, "Oh, I've got a great idea," "Wait, that reminds me, we really should—," and "Oh, no, I've got it—" His friends call him Idea Man. Thrilled with the search and unattached to the outcome, generators are focused on the sheer production of ideas themselves.

This exaltation of the idea can create a postpartum depression when the difficulties and complications of carrying a project through to completion arise. The surfeit of ideas also makes it possible for generators to begin many projects without finishing any of them.

Young generators often get stuck in "no-brainer" jobs like restaurant work, where they have ample time to flex their dream muscle between slinging cappuccinos. Ironically, these jobs usually entail an enormous amount of repetition, which ultimately drives them nuts. They have little patience for fulfilling people's needs, because their minds are involved in creating their latest scheme. If you consider yourself something of a generator, and you are toiling in a monotonous job and you want out, consider the following option: Invent your own job (or three if you can't stand the idea of doing one thing). It could be a service, a business, a job you create within an organization. Or enter a field that demands a high output of new ideas. Marketing, advertising, journalism, graphic design, consulting, and curriculum design all require a generator's aptitude for spinning new theories and ideas.

If you are a generator stuck in a job that bores you but you don't feel you can quit just yet, try using your generative power to destroy the drudgery. Many years ago, when I was a waitress, I noticed that the restaurant where I was working had no desserts. I offered to bake pastries and cakes for their lunch shift at the same hourly wage. They bought it. Even though I was only fifteen and had no formal culinary training, I created a project that made the work less boring and gave me pride. I learned that I could put my generator self into action in all sorts of unlikely places. The next summer I didn't even bother to look for a job; I started my own catering company with a couple of friends.

If being a generator is an essential part of you, you must find a situation where you can put your conceptualizing power to work. Generators must remember that now is the best time to start one of their ideas and carry it through. The ideas will build on each other and lead to new projects, but remember: The trap of being a generator is developing a big fat dream muscle surrounded by flaccid action flesh.

Generator Exercise

Make a list of all the projects you'd like to do. Pick one of your smallest, simplest ideas and execute it from start to finish.

As you increase your belief in the power of your own action, you will be able to juggle more projects and finish them. As you work through this singular project, write all your competing ideas down on a single list.

Put the list as a bookmark in the exercises in chapter 6 for future use.

Healer

Healers access creativity through the part of them that wants to console, nurture, and cure. Morally inclined and very intuitive, their art springs from their sensitivity to emotional states. Many healers have been through tumultuous experiences that give them special insight into life's frailty and complexity.

Healing provides fertile ground for the energies of socially conscious, creative souls. Anna Halprin, choreographer and founder of the Tamalpa Institute, has been working for thirty years exploring the expressive and curative powers of dance. In addition to her classes on body-based healing arts at her school, she creates giant participatory movement rituals for people with HIV and other life-threatening illnesses. Many of the people in my workshops chose to support their art with a day job that was more directly connected to physical or psychological healing. One dancer worked as a massage therapist and bodyworker; a painter taught painting at a convalescent home; a young writer led workshops in journal writing. Other possibilities include community art projects, tutoring, career counseling, therapy, yoga, alternative medicine, and the whole array of services created to help people physically, spiritually, and emotionally.

Healer Exercise

If you are a healer and you want to refocus your creativity toward an individual, self-generated project, then try making the outcome of the project be a gift for a friend or family. This deadline and clarity of motivation can give you the impetus to create. If you have a lonely grandmother or a tortured teenage grandson and you are a poet, write poetry just for them. If you are a budding entrepreneur, write a business plan for a company that will help a specific person in your community. Write a list of the creative projects you can do that would support your creative aspirations through your impulse toward service and giving.

Put that list as a bookmark in the exercises at the end of chapter 6 for future use.

Leader

Leaders have a talent for moving people toward a common goal. They can perceive a dream in vivid detail. Their words make a distant blur seem real and immediate. Along with this skill for persuasion comes responsibility and power.

The leader's ingenuity comes from the ability to work with people, just as the potter works with clay. Most leaders are good public speakers with infectious wills. Once they set their minds to realizing a vision, they are utterly unstoppable.

If you are a creative leader, you may have trouble finding situations that fully utilize your special talents. Most job descriptions are looking for "team players," "assistants," and "responsible employees," not "wacky inspired leaders." Few ordinary jobs require individuals to exercise the talents of creative leadership. Creative leaders tend to rankle under the restrictions of most traditional employment hierarchies. The frustration festers like a blister and even going to work becomes impossibly painful.

An exemplary creative leader is choreographer Margaret Jenkins. Though she began as a dancer and traditional choreographer, she eventually became the artistic director of a large dance theater company. Not only does she collaborate with writers, musicians, set designers, and costume designers, she collaborates with her dancers in creating their own movement. In changing from a crafter of movements to a conceptual director, she had to develop the leadership skills that would allow her to communicate her vision without squelching her collaborators' creativity.

Do you find yourself creating things that involve the contributions of other people? Do you have an easy time delegating? As a child, were you the one who decided where home base was in the game of tag? Did your friends accept this role from you? Must your role be central in a project in order for it to excite your interest?

The pitfall of being a leader is that if you can't exercise your visionary, trailblazing instinct, you can become disconsolate and lethargic. For creative leaders, the best day jobs are those that can either provide you with a lot of autonomy (independent contractor, consultant, freelance anything, taxi driver) or give you the opportunity to work with your raw material: other people (project director, film director, volunteer coordinator). The most important thing for the leader to do is to *begin leading now*. It doesn't matter what your interests are or whether or not you are paid for it. Just start it: punk band, CD-ROM project, invention group, art salon. Put your creative energies to work in a way that will widen the area of your life that you want to expand. Whether it is in art, business, or politics . . . you can begin some part of the creation process now without a *license,* a *job,* or *money.*

Leader Exercise

Develop a formal plan and description for a project in which you will be the leader. Include a mission statement, a budget, and a ten-step plan for executing the idea. Gather a few friends together, present the idea, and solicit feedback.

Now put this plan in the exercise section of chapter 6 as a bookmark for later use.

Inventor

Inventors create new forms, objects, and ideas. Their talent lies in dreaming up new thingamajigs and then trying to create them. Like generators, they are harebrained, madcap brainstormers, but the inventor's product is not the idea, but the project itself. Their creative process is not complete until they have tested their theory, painted their vision, blown up their basement. The madness of the inventor arises from both their weird ideas and their willingness to act on them even when other people are calling them crazy.

The danger lies in the fact that inventors can lose track of "reality," or worse, lose their ability to communicate the usefulness of their creations to others. While the strength in their ideas springs from their bizarreness, the inventor's work is not finished until they see it manifested in the world. Inevitably, inventors need to believe in themselves because, initially, no one else will.

Do you invent new gadgets, services, words, animals, scientific advances, political systems, dance forms, musical instruments? Do you enjoy both the process of imagining and the hands-on making of your creations? Is originality of great importance to you? Do people often tell you you're a lunatic?

If the answers are predominantly "yes," then stop masquerading as a normal person and give in. You are an inventor! If you feel that your job doesn't facilitate the wild inner terrain of your mind, then think about making a partnership with an interpreter, a realizer, or a leader and collaborating to get your work into the world.

I have witnessed several such partnerships in my workshops. One woman who was a wildly inventive and eclectic craftsperson formed a business with a woman who wanted to start a creative company but wasn't interested in the physical production of the things themselves. A young man who invented small scientific toys joined with a graphic designer (who was a classic interpreter) and a writer/architect (who was a classic generator) to begin a new toy company.

Though you may not consider yourself a joiner, you should at least know a little about the organizations that represent your field. There may be an inventors' group, an artists' salon, a radical collective, or a product design group that perfectly satisfies your needs for role models and collaborative peer support.

If you are an inventor looking for a good day job, look for jobs that link you to other artistic types in your field or support your eccentricities. I have seen inventors working in offbeat restaurants, copy stores, companies, and corporations. I have also seen inventors flourish as directors of tiny, one-person operations: from sign painting to grant writing, pie baking to hair styling. Because inventors like to be involved at every stage of creation, one-person businesses are ideal for their renaissance spirit. Of all the artistic types, inventors have the the most difficult time "passing'" in the workaday world. You need to be able to be yourself and not waste any extra energy masquerading as a team player.

Inventor Exercise

Invent a job description of your ideal work. Then spend a free day pretending you have that job. Simulate the experience from the environment to the task to your interaction with other people. Spend the entire day in this self-invented life. At the end of the day, write down all the ideas for working situations that you thought of over the course of the day. Pick the best of them and begin it.

Now put the list of ideas in the exercise section of chapter 6 as a bookmark.

Mystic

Mystics tend to be less product-oriented than many other artistic types. The ideas and objects that spring from their labors are side effects rather than the culmination of their creative process. Mystics understand the ineffable relationship between our hearts and the giant river of creativity. Like healers, mystics tap into energy through engaging their ethics and their spiritual beliefs. First and foremost, they live creative lives—moment by moment.

Mystics create moments, moods, ambience. Sometimes these things come out as art, sometimes as cherry pie or a whispered bedtime story.

What we call great art may arise from their actions, but mystics won't really be interested in that label. They will remember small, detailed, sensual observations and feelings rather than the grand facade of product. Since their art is ephemeral, they make wonderful performers, musicians, and interdisciplinary artists.

Choreographer Sarah Shelton Mann expresses many of the traits typical of a creative mystic. Everything seems to flow together in her conversation. One moment she is talking about an epiphany on a mountain in Hawaii, the next moment about her latest dance project, the next about the kind of artistic community she wants to create or the internal workings of her process. This lack of regard for conventional categories reflects the fact that she is constantly processing all experience—artistic or otherwise—through the lens of her spiritual eye. Her creation of art is just one manifestation of a much quieter, subtler process of living. Mann combines this mystical inclination with a leader's ability to gather and direct people's creative energy and the maker's purity of pursuit in making her choreography. Her creativity combines equal attention to the most ethereal and the most brass-tacks aspects of the work. When I asked her how she moves from idea to production, the mystic, the leader and the maker all have their turn: "The first thing that happens is that I dream things. The next process is trying to bring that vision into time and space, dealing with the restrictions of what I have chosen as a business venue, which is the stage and presenters and the dance world. So the first element is a dream, the second is a group of people and movement, and the third is—What does it have to do with reality? And what is the larger focus of it in the world? What is the relationship between the personal and the universal?"

With their purity of vision and strength of convictions, mystics can have a tough time in our materialistic, logic-based culture. As children, they often encounter abuse, ridicule, and a general lack of understanding. As adults, they are often adored because of their ability to connect with others in intimate and creative ways, but in the professional world, they are still expected to be hard-nosed and clearheaded. But if mystics don't get all the respect they deserve in our product-oriented society, that doesn't keep them from valuing their own elusive talents. Driven by a burning core and nothing else, they are fiercely independent thinkers.

Do you stare out windows absorbed in the details of the senses? Are you comfortable with silence? Does your hunger for a better world color your everyday actions? Are your feelings and the feelings of others among your highest values?

Mystics tend to make good poets, choreographers, visual artists, and composers. They are less likely to to be interested in business or large-scale organizations. Prone toward monkish lifestyles, they do best living lives of simplicity. Since mystics tend to be unwilling to work the system, networking their way through a hierarchy or schmoozing their way into a job can be an onerous and unnatural chore. Mystic-friendly day jobs include freelance work that is single-focused and doesn't require a lot of marketing, like technical editing, teaching yoga, graphic design, and running small workshops or therapy groups.

If you think you are a mystic and are seeking employment, look for gentle work environments or jobs with a lot of privacy so that you can work in your own style.

Mystic Exercise

Make a list of the essences you want to bring into your life. Create a ritual (or perhaps an invented beverage) that symbolically incorporates all these essences. Perform this ritual with the intention of imbibing your new life into your body. Okay, now that you feel truly transported, meditate on the perfect situation for your career and creative woes. At the end of the meditation, write down your ideas and put the list in the exercises section of chapter 6 as a bookmark.

Using These Types to Understand Your Creative Colors

Again, these artistic profiles are tools to be used to understand your own kaleidoscope of creativity. For example, I recognize myself as both a teacher and a generator. While the generator in me likes to come up with a lot of wacky schemes; the teacher in me creates forums for manifesting these schemes. For instance, I wanted to create a day job for myself that would nourish my desire to write. As a fairly social, pragmatic person, the concept of sitting in my room writing all alone without a greater community seemed abysmal. So I created a small school called The Writing Parlor that offers fiction and nonfiction writing classes. This ideal day job provided me with a context for teaching as well as the opportunity to study with other writers whose work I admired. It gave me time to write in the morning and time to fraternize at night. The job also required that I generate lots of new ideas—classes, poster designs, literary readings. The outcome was a day job that indulged my innate impulse to scatter my energies, brainstorm, and teach while allowing me to become more committed to my writing.

Margaret, an aspiring designer, recognized herself as a mixture of realizer, maker, and interpreter. She was stuck in a job in a large company in the special events department. Although she had a flare for the aesthetics and planning aspects of the job, she yearned to practice her art in a more hands-on context. She was also tired of being a cog in a large system that didn't have the same aesthetic sensibility as her own. Since her job as an events planner was her most obvious marketable skill, she decided to create a part-time business of planning small alternative parties and weddings. In the long run she wanted to phase out of events planning, so she designed the business not as a full-blown career, but as a part-time job she could maintain while she returned to design school. Six months after starting the business, she quit her full-time job and survived on planning one or two events a month. In this way her interpreter and realizer selves earned her a living and gave more time for her maker self to play in her studio.

As you begin working on the following exercises, consider these questions. Which one of your types can help you earn money? Which of your types expresses the very kernel of your creative aspirations? Do your various creative styles compete with each other, each with their own art form? How do your more introverted aspects interact with the more collaborative parts of your creative process? By analyzing how these facets of your creative kaleidoscope work together, you may be able to generate a more complete picture of your current career problems.

EXERCISES IN STRETCHING THE DREAM MUSCLE

1. Draw a pie chart of yourself and the artistic types you think you encompass.
   Example:

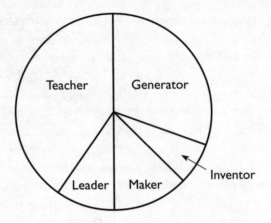

   Which of the archetypes motivate you to action?

2. Create a pie chart that reflects the archetype or combination of archetypes you wish to become.

Creative Pie Charts

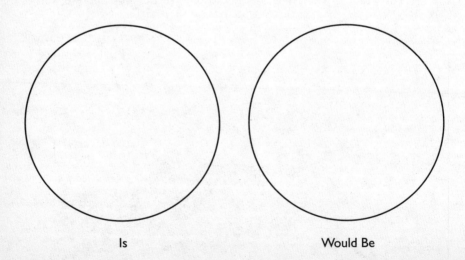

Is   Would Be

3. Write down a list of three specific ideas for expressing these archetypes within yourself.

1.
2.
3.

4. Shazam, you are a human cat. If you had nine lives to devote to nine different careers, what would they be?

1.
2.
3.
4.
5.
6.
7.
8.
9.

   Look at the careers you have chosen. Do they reflect your artistic archetypes? Go through and mark next to each one of them which archetypes that career brings to mind.

5. Describe your ideal role model or mentor for the artistic type you wish to cultivate in yourself. Create a vivid picture of him or her, how he lives his life, and how she helps you with yours.

6. Personal Homework: Transfer your ideas into your Adventure Book.

7. Ecstatic Task. It's been two weeks. Are you still doing your daily action every day? If not, why not? Do you need to change the time, the activity, the attitude? Write down your daily action and the time when you will do it here:
   How many days will you do it?
   (Seven, yes?)

8. What did you learn from this chapter? Are there any related issues you still want to explore?

MARY GAITSKILL, NOVELIST AND SHORT-STORY WRITER

When asked about where she learned to write, Mary Gaitskill doesn't list her university courses in creative writing and journalism. Instead, she talks about a single teacher from a small community college who pored over her papers, set up an accelerated schedule for her, and read her short stories. After college she moved to New York, where she learned that a bachelor's degree in journalism did not amount to the practical, marketable skill she had believed she was developing. For the next ten years, while she read and wrote fiction, she worked her way through a panoply of starving artist jobs—from working in a bookstore to prostitution. Aside from two essays in the *Village Voice,* Gaitskill had no success in publishing her writing until Poseidon Press made the unusual decision to publish a book of short stories by a completely unknown author. Since *Bad Behavior,* she has written an acclaimed novel, *Two Girls, Fat and Thin,* and another widely acclaimed collection of short stories, *Because They Wanted To.*

Gaitskill now lives a quiet life of tumultuous passions. She writes fiction and the occasional essay and often teaches creative writing at a university. Unlike many of the artists I spoke with, her art is governed by neither a strict schedule nor a puritanical work ethic. Though she does have certain routines, she displays the mystic's classic lack of aptitude for dogged action. Ranging from meditative to obsessive, Gaitskill's art springs from a mind that cannot help but bring everyday life under the microscope of her fiercely perceptive and emotionally uncompromising vision.

Q: What is your workday like?

A: I don't know if I have a workday most of the time. It's horrible how disorganized I am. I get up and—I don't know if I want to talk about this but [*whispers*] I meditate. Then I spend a huge amount of time staring into space and getting oriented toward the day. Then there's eating and talking on the phone and all these time-consuming activities. Invariably there's something I have to do, like get my hair cut or do the laundry or buy something or go for a long walk, because exercise is important. Then there's dinner. Then, after dinner there's a long working-up period when I realize I've put it off all day and I have to get serious and do something. That's when I sit down and write, usually.

Q: You write in the evenings?

A: Unfortunately, yes. A lot of the procrastination is sheer neurotic anxiety. But also there may be another, more dignified reason, which is if I'm really uncertain about the direction of a story, my intuition has to come into it strongly. For that to happen I do have to go through the day with the story in the back of my mind, and then zero in on it.

Q: Can I ask you about meditation?

A: Well, I've never studied, I don't know the various kinds of meditation. I do it standing up, I breathe deeply and relax and quiet my body. The reason I like to do it is that if left to my own devices, my mind jumps around way too much. It's not intelligent or productive, it's just like a radio bouncing from one station to the next really fast. I can get wound up and then I can't concentrate at all. So for me meditating is good because it just slows it down right at the start of the day and gets me more—I'm trying to articulate this without using cliches—

Q: Centered?

A: I was going to say "in tune with myself," which is worse! Underneath all the mental hopping around, there's usually a quieter, stronger, organizing pulse of thought. If I can get past the chatter and sink into that deeper thing, it's much better for me.

Q: Do you do it for a certain amount of time?

A: It varies. Sometimes I do it for maybe five minutes, and other times I do it as long as twenty minutes. It's very productive, 'cause a lot of imagery comes to mind and I just sort of follow it. It's almost like dreaming, only you're conscious. You can also guide the dream if you want to open it up. It's not only calming, it reminds me of the part of myself that's always creating stories and images.

Q: Like focused daydreaming.

A: Yeah. I once heard someone describe it as picturing your thought passing through your mind without focusing on the thoughts at all, just focusing on your mind as a container. And then you do the same thing with your heart; you let whatever feelings are happening exist and you focus on your heart as a container for them. It sounds weird, but the thing that got my imagination was when he said, "Then you feel your infinity." And you do. You're like a plant—an organic thing that's just a vessel for all this stuff.

Q: What are the other elements of your creative process? Are there any other things that you use?

A: I've always had this ability: Even when I'm really emotionally upset about something I can detach from it. I go up in the corner and look at it from a distance. I first noticed it when I was about twenty-three, and I was in this terrible, heartbreaking situation with this turd I was involved with, and I was going over to his house to yell at him. I'd called him up and said, "Can I come over and talk to you?" He was such an asshole, he knew I was coming over so he took a bath, so I had to wait for him to come out. And while I was waiting—one of his roommates was having a loud argument with another girl in his room, and then in the other room, another roommate was fucking some girl, so all around me there was moaning and yelling and huffing and puffing. And then—this was before answering machines—there was a notepad by the phone listing phone messages, and one of them was, "Lisa says to tell Bill to fuck off." And part of me was like, "How hilarious," even though the other part was totally embroiled in the pain of it. So there's always a part of me that's saying, "Gee, this could be a really fun story."

Q: Sort of a narrative eye.

A: Yeah. Some people could see it as a problem because it is emotionally detached, but it can also work for me.

Q: Did you have any role models or mentors when you were younger?

A: When I was a teenager, my mother would paint and draw. And it was always good for me to watch her. I always felt it was very important to her even though she didn't do it professionally. I began to paint with her. We created a very nonjudgmental environment where we would do this stuff and mutually support each other. Also, she had a friend who was a working artist and she would come over and rant about the horrible Detroit art community and her problems at various venues, and other bitchy artists, and sexism in the art world. And this was really electrifying to me, to see an older woman—she was only thirty, but to me that seemed really old—who dressed more like me than like my mother, and was engaging with the world in this way. My sisters and I would always kind of hang around when she was there.

Q: What kind of support system do you have now?

A: I've always been resistant to the idea of a support system for some reason. When I was younger I never had it. In my twenties I hardly knew any writers. But when my first book came out I did slowly become acquainted with some more writers and editors—and I do show my work to them and ask them what they think. I like to think of myself as incredibly independent, but I think the truth is I'm horribly susceptible to what people say to me. Especially at the larval stage of a piece. Once, I was really upset about something another writer had said to me about a story and this older writer friend of mine said, "Why do you show your stuff to people anyway? You're acting like an amateur. You shouldn't ask people what they think, especially if they're other writers. Of course they're gonna say something jealous at some point, of course they're gonna want to take you down." I could understand her point and I was kind of embarrassed, actually. But on the other hand I thought, even if someone says something you don't like and it upsets you, it still could be helpful in the long run.

Q: What were some of your early day jobs?

A: I worked at a bookstore for a while. I was a receptionist at a medical office for a while; that was horrible. I was a freelance proofreader, legal proofreader; that was good because it paid a lot of money and I could determine my own hours. That was the best job I ever had, being a writer. I was a naked art model. I was a prostitute.

Q: That's quite a variety. When did you start writing and earning a living as a writer?

A: I always wrote, even when I was a kid. I drew pictures and told stories, like cartoons. I did that all through my kidhood. When I was a teenager I wrote these interminable journals where I agonized about how awful the world was, and how terrible my boyfriend was, and how everybody was having fun but me. But then I got serious again about doing stories when I was in my late teens, and when I was about twenty-one I decided I really wanted to write, and that's when I sat down and I wrote my first serious story, in the sense that I intended it to be artistically created for other people to read. So I guess I started when I was twenty-one, and started making a living from it when I was thirty-two.

Q: Do you have any tricks that you play on yourself when you don't feel like working?

A: Well, in the beginning I would just say, "Nobody's gonna see it, nobody ever has to see it. It doesn't have to be any good at all. In fact it can be shit!" And that would work for some reason. If you become really self-conscious, you just freeze. So I often have to go through this process of making myself not self-conscious by reminding myself it doesn't have to be good. Other than that I don't really have a trick, it's more that there's a certain point of resistance that if I can get past, it will be okay. I don't even know what the resistance is. It could just be massive laziness, or fear that what I do won't be good. But I know that if I can get past it and kind of sink down into it, then I'll be okay.

Q: *Do you still do that with yourself?*

A: Occasionally. Not so much, because now I feel like it *does* have to be good [*laughter*]. But I still remind myself that just because you write one thing that's good . . . you can still write things that are bad, and they can even be published and people can laugh at you, and you can write something good again.

Q: *How many projects do you work on at once? Do you just work on one until it's finished?*

A: I'm really monomaniacal. I have to work on one thing usually. Sometimes I put something aside and pick up something else and then return to the first thing. I like the idea of being able to do a lot of things at once but I find it very hard to switch my attention from one thing to another.

Q: *What was the most frustrating period of your development, in relation to becoming a full-time artist?*

A: Probably my late twenties. I kept trying to sell my stuff and people didn't like it. I was thinking, "This is a waste of time, you're never gonna get anywhere."

I was feeling like I was never gonna get published, and perhaps I just wasn't any good and maybe I should just stop. And in New York especially, you just feel like a fool saying you're a writer because everybody is acting like they're a writer or an artist or an actress. You say "I'm a writer," and people smirk at you. It was a horrible time of my life. Nothing was working in any area. Nothing.

Q: *Do you remember any time when you were tempted to quit?*

A: Oh yeah. In fact I think I did quit for about six months. I just thought, I don't want to do this, this is too painful. But it was quite hard to quit, because it was kind of like the backbone of my life. Part of my ambitious nature was saying, Well, if I'm not successful by the time I'm thirty I'm gonna kill myself [*laughter*]. I actually had that thought. And then I thought, How ridiculous. Why would I have to kill myself? If I don't succeed as a writer, I can still do other things. And if I just forget about being a writer, perhaps I can even enjoy myself more, I can just travel around and be a bum and do whatever. It wouldn't be so horrible. And I actually think there was some connection in that change of attitude, and the fact that I did get published. It didn't happen like that [*snaps fingers*], but I think it happened a couple of years afterward. But my attitude really relaxed and I thought, Yes, I would like to be published, but it should not be the driving force behind my self-esteem. I think somehow in some weird cosmic way that helped make it happen.

Q: Have your thoughts about what success means changed since you started writing?

A: I became more successful much more quickly than I imagined. Even though it took a long time, if you consider eleven years a long time. I pictured it happening more slowly. I thought I would get things published in quarterlies or magazines here and there. I wasn't expecting a book to come out and to be able to make a living from it all at once. So I was very startled by it. It exceeded my ideas of success. At that time my idea of success would have been to have a story in a good quarterly, and to be known on that circuit. And to have a story in a big magazine like the *New Yorker* would have been the ultimate. So I wasn't expecting a whole book. I wasn't expecting the glamour part either, like to have my picture in magazines and stuff. Which I liked [*laughter*]. That's very seductive, the glamour thing.

Q: Do you ever feel like it affects your creative mind?

A: Probably a little, and I think it really could have if I'd been younger. I'm actually glad I didn't get published when I was in my twenties, because the hype stuff would have overwhelmed me. I would have taken it much more seriously than I did when I was older. I would've believed it had something to do with who I am, which it does, but only tangentially.

Q: But you don't find it affecting your actual writing?

A: When my first book came out and I got some pictures in magazines and so forth, it probably made it harder for me to write. In terms of publicity in America it was nothing, it was just a little blip. But to me it felt like a lot, and it just makes you really self-conscious about the image other people hold of you, and part of you wants to live up to the image because you know it's there. And another part of you is embarrassed by the image, or frozen by it, or disconcerted in some way. So it fucks with you.

Q: What would you say motivates your writing? Do you write for certain people?

A: I think ambition was much more important to me when I was a lot younger, in its base form—i.e., I just wanted attention. I wanted people to listen to me and to think I was important. And that's become less important to me, which is good because I think that attitude is very insecure. When you're driven by that you're really looking for something to fill you up and make you feel good. I've become somewhat more secure as I've gotten older. Not that I'm completely secure; I don't think anybody who has a brain ever is.

Q: What drives you now?

A: There's still the ambition thing. But there's something deeper that I think everybody has, anybody who wants to do anything that's creative in any way, whether they intend to do it professionally or not. It's a desire to take your way of looking at the world and bring it out in a way that people can understand. To communicate that in an artful form is deeper and potentially more potent than regular talking. It creates a profoundly satisfying exchange, because to read—to really receive it—is dynamic too.

I'm really embarrassed to admit this because this is so small and personal, but oftentimes what motivates me to write a story is something I'm really emotionally upset about. Sometimes I'll have these situations that cause me so much anguish because I feel like I haven't been able to communicate with the person involved. That's very painful to me. Especially if it's compounded by being an erotic situation. So sometimes I've written stories wanting that person to read it even though I know they won't. That's basically who and what I'm writing it for. It's small and personal but it does give it a lot of power because you're really putting yourself in it, it makes it very intense. Later the other person fades away; years go by and the other person is forgotten, but it still comes out a very strong statement because that very personal force is behind it.

Q: Some writers say, "I can't talk about it, because if I talk about it then I'll have already communicated it."

A: Yeah, and if you can't talk to the person, you *can't* communicate it, you have to write it [*laughter*]. Also—this sounds like phony altruism—but I also sometimes write because I want to affect the world. I want to bring out something I feel people are overlooking. I write essays for that. A lot of times people deny the raw, painful emotions. They don't mind looking at them in a big, gaudy form, like a talk show, but when it comes to sitting there and feeling the weak, ugly stuff, they want to pretend that belongs to somebody else. I know; I've done it. But your weakness is a hair's breadth away from your strength. If you can't feel the weak, ugly stuff, you'll never know the strong part either. But people hate the ugly thing, and they never see how beautiful it can be. We want fake, easy beauty. I'm the same as most people that way, which is why I have to deal with it in my writing.

Q: If there was one piece of advice you would give a beginner, what would it be?

A: Basically not to listen too much to what other people say about your work, or make yourself too open to what other people's ideas are. There's a certain kind of purity of perception that everybody has, but I think it gets occluded in many people's lives very early, because we get so many ideas about what things are supposed to be like, what we're supposed to think or feel, or what things are. We often don't see things just through our own eyes. And I think that's the most important thing, to be able to see things through your own eyes and be able to say what you see without worrying about what other people have to say about it. I think first you have to have that base of knowing what you think and feel. Later you can learn from taking in other people's ideas. But first the base has to be there. That sounds less complicated than it is, though, because it's very hard to do that, more so than you'd think.

Neglected Needs
Time, Money, and Desire

> Keep the faculty of effort alive in you by a little gratuitous exercise every day. That is, be systematically ascetic or heroic in little unnecessary points, do every day or two something for no other reason than that you would rather not do it, so that when the hour of dire need draws nigh, it may find you not unnerved and untrained to stand the test.
>
> —WILLIAM JAMES

In the first two chapters, you launched the process of refocusing your daily life through instituting the ritual of the daily action and priming the mind for new ideas. In chapters 3 and 4 you explored facets of your own creativity through your memories and artistic inclinations. This chapter explores the parameters of your worldly needs: money, time, and other basic conditions of your everyday well-being. Without understanding your immediate needs, any grand plans you make for your ideal creative life will almost surely fail. Once you accept the fact that you have needs outside your art, you can begin to craft a life that will survive the hardships of a creative career.

People often don't see that a lack of progress in their creative life comes from an unwillingness to acknowledge their daily concerns. They think: I have low self-esteem; I'm lazy; these obstacles are too huge; but in reality, they just haven't realized that the hungry, naked animal living inside us doesn't trust the artist to feed, clothe, and care for it. The animal of necessity creates such a ruckus of fear and consternation that the artist cannot begin to plan for the future, much less take action in the present. This chapter will help you reveal the needs lurking behind your creative obstacles.

Analyzing Artistic Angst

Katrina is an impish thirty-seven-year-old inventor, painter, and videographer. She has started two small businesses and has held a panoply of unsatisfying day jobs, from office drudge to ditch digger. She started my class with a power plant's worth of energy, proclaiming that she wanted to find a new focus and make a commitment to her creative work. At the fourth meeting, however, she came in looking like a failing forty-watt bulb.

"What happened to you?" another student asked.

"I just keep hearing this voice inside my head, saying, 'If you haven't figured it out by now, you just don't have what it takes. You must not want it badly enough. What's the point? You're almost forty.'"

Perhaps you have similarly discouraging voices sounding off inside your head. Maybe they're the voices of real people echoing from your past, or maybe they've just oozed up like flotsam from the cultural sea that values child protégés and enfants terribles over the rest of us.

Sure, there are young people and even children who have been blessed with the innate talent or circumstances to excel in a given arena. But the existence of a few especially gifted individuals should not prevent the rest of us from diving in and falling in love with creating those things we would be most proud to give the world. Creativity is not a limited resource, like gold or oil; it is not a zero-sum game. There is no physical law out there limiting the number of people that can be creatively fulfilled. These angst-ridden feelings are often disguised fears about time, money, space, and people. But the fears don't declare themselves openly. Instead they seep into our most vivid desires and make everything murky and dull. The following process will compel you to peel back the layers of desire and fear and reveal the essence of your basic needs.

When that voice whispers, "Maybe you don't want it badly enough . . . maybe you're too old to do it . . . maybe you haven't got what it takes," toss away your pessimism the way an astronomer discards the assumptions of an outdated cosmology (if only reluctantly). Instead, demand from yourself that you be specific. What is this "it" you are always yearning for?

What does creativity and success actually mean for you? Is "it" a lifestyle; a measure of skill, fame, respect; or simply an inner sense of confidence and fulfillment? Let's begin by defining what you seek to gain in working through this process. Write your objectives in the space below.

Did you use any of the following generalities?

> remake my life
> find the perfect job
> get it together
> be more creative
> get focused on . . .

These and other stock phrases frequently hide very specific needs or desires. We often express ourselves in euphemistic terms so that we can pretend to communicate to our friends or family without revealing much about the actual substance of our ambitions. Sometimes it's shyness, or modesty, or hard-earned protectiveness. Kindly friends and family nod and say, "Yeah, I know exactly what you mean," thereby allowing the conversation to move on to dishing out gossip or peach cobbler. Our loved ones can't know exactly what we're going through because we haven't told them. Sometimes we're not exactly sure ourselves.

Write down *exactly* what you want to gain from this process. Replace abstract phrases with specific ideas. For instance, "I want to become more focused on my design ideas" might become "I want to choose and complete one prototype from my pile of sketches." Or, "I need a job I don't hate" might become "I need a part-time job paying at least eighteen dollars an hour working with a mentor figure in the field of environmental education or the arts."

Don't feel like it has to be either high-flown or humble, just *concrete*.

This exercise is the first of many that will push you to articulate the concrete details of your creative desires.

Now make a list of the things you perceive as the main obstacles to achieving the above goals. Include internal issues, such as, "Whenever I try to make a specific decision, I get disoriented," as well as nuts-and-bolts problems: "Alaska doesn't have a very well-developed film industry."

Post this list of obstacles somewhere in your home or workspace. Look over your list. Do your concerns touch on money, stability, or time? Do you have any judgments about whether or not you should even have these concerns?

I have noticed that many of the artists I worked with had concerns that they didn't feel they should have. For instance, Maria, a young choreographer, didn't think she should really need that much time to become a great dancer. She rationed her time in dance classes, then felt bad about her slow progress. After Jessica graduated from conservatory, she decided she was self-indulgent for using a rehearsal space to practice her flute; as a result (surprise, surprise) she never practiced because she didn't want to bother her roommate.

I used to think that my daily concerns about money and an enjoyable day job indicated that I was hopelessly normal and essentially uncommitted to a creative life. I thought that if I wasn't willing to undergo intense hardship and risk, I just wasn't cracked up to be an artist. Not all of us are willing to embrace the life of the starving artist. Nor do I think we need to. But the more material needs we have, the more initiative we must take to establish a life that meets both our creative *and* our worldly needs. That means we need a stratagem.

Uh-oh. Here comes the business-speak with the eight-point plan to "micromanage your emotional state and impact your dreams into spiritual profit." While the word "strategy" does suggest corporate boardrooms, stockbroker trading rooms, and Pentagon war offices, "stratagem" has quite another feel. Stratagem means "a clever, often underhanded scheme for achieving an objective." The sneaky connotations of this word give a fairer representation of how the process of building a creative life really works. You are not out to dictate to yourself, but to coddle, coax, and seduce yourself into tasting a sweet, spicy new life.

Here is the basic stratagem I've come up with for aspiring artists to reinvent their lives:

1. Know your needs. (This includes distinguishing between false and true needs and accepting your true needs.)
2. Know your creative desires and inclinations.
3. Create a vivid vision of your ideal life.
4. Devise a plan that provides both for your true needs *and* your creative plan.
5. Begin implementing the plan now, attending to both your creative desires *and* worldly needs simultaneously.
6. Create daily habits that support these goals.

A stratagem is the necessary difference between people who successfully build creativity into sane, healthy lives and those who create dichotomies between creativity and money, art and sanity. Granted, "sane and healthy" is a pretty subjective description, but everyone has certain needs outside their creative urges that are essential to a good life. When artists neglect these needs, they begin to equate their creativity with that gnawing feeling of deprivation. Just as insomniacs who force themselves to lie in bed wide awake teach their bodies that "bed" means "restlessness," so too do artists who sacrifice their daily needs on the altar of creativity teach themselves that "art" means "pain."

Here are some of the questions you might ask yourself when you think about your worldly needs.

1. *Exactly* how much money per year do I *need* to make?
2. What kind of housing situation do I require?
3. What form of transportation do I need to use?
4. How much time do I need to develop and maintain my art?
5. What kinds of recreation and companionship do I need?
6. What kind of respect, love, and sense of purpose must I have to fulfill my ethical, political, and spiritual life?

Your answers describe the ingredients you need for happiness. Kwame, a young playwright, discovered he had few material needs, but a lot of educational and emotional requirements.

KWAME'S COLLECTION OF NEEDS

I need time for writing in the morning. I need $1,300 a month after taxes. I need a space to do my work where I have privacy. I need friends to read my writing and support my weird ideas. I need a forum for sharing my expertise with other people: a day job with a lot of autonomy. I need hobbies where I am a rank beginner to keep me honest. I need good food, exercise, and a stable emotional life.

Elaborate on your basic needs, adding any other conditions that allow you to do your creative work consistently.

Whether your needs are ridiculously luxurious or nearer to the monkish ideal of bread, water, and a horsehair shirt, it doesn't matter. You must take them seriously, because until you face these needs, they will float about like orphan ghosts, crying in your dreams, muddying your thoughts, and eventually getting in the way of your ambitions.

Strangely, when people are finally on the road to being creatively fulfilled in their work, their most pressing needs vanish into the ether.
The joys of money, praise, and fancy consumer goods pale in compari-
son to the pleasure of doing work we feel passionately about—just as a
child forgets she is hungry when she is totally absorbed in a task. At
the beginning of the journey, however, when the night is dark and the
road filled with potholes, you must keep yourself strong, healthy, and
clearheaded. You are like a mother with a carriage full of hungry
babies and a long journey ahead; you have to feed those screaming
mouths if you want to make the trip.

Once you understand the needs, how do you proceed with determination and faith that there is a situation out there that will meet both your
personal *and* creative requirements? The reinvention of a life is a big project, and though it doesn't happen overnight, it does happen in the present. We're talking about attending to your creative urges now, letting
them dominate your long-term plans but not sacrificing your life today.
So instead of thinking in all-or-nothing terms ("I'll either quit my job and
move to Paris to become a painter, or stay here at my present job, pay off
my debt, and kiss my art goodbye"), realize that there are many paths
that connect the place where you are now to the place where you want to
go. Your present task is to know the terrain and your daily limitations,
draw up a map, and begin bushwhacking a path of your own.

Practically all innovators throughout history have had to discover or
create a life to match their creative form. Neither life nor art springs
from thin air; people make concessions, devise stratagems, take risks,
and even learn other skills in order to maintain a life that focuses on
their highest goals.

Here are some ways creative people remade their lives to give their
art more time and space to grow. Some attended to internal issues, others to external issues, but the important thing is that they figured out
what they were lacking and set about getting it.

- Jackson, a screenwriter, stayed in school as long as he could to fend
  off his school loans. When that money ran out, he lived in his
  mother's garage and worked eight hours a day finishing his screen-
  play.
- Ruby, an actress who was ready to give up on theater, figured out a
  way to become a copy editor at home so she could make her own
  schedule and be available for auditions. Through editing, she got to
  engage in intellectual work that not only supported her financially

but counterbalanced her highly social, group-focused life as an actress.

- Sarah, a modern dancer, learned to be a sign language interpreter. Not only was the work high-paying and flexible, she got to travel around the country attending conferences and concerts. The work also had a subtler benefit: She became fluent in yet another language of movement. Her day job shared an essential element with her creative work; her body became a medium for expressing feelings and ideas.

- Faith, a conceptual artist, found herself disillusioned with the current politics of the art world. Instead of quitting to study law or accounting, she got a job as an art director in a multimedia software company. She made money, fell in love with the new technology, and found new confidence in her visual talents. Oddly enough, after she got the full-time job, she became much more productive and creative in many areas of her life—including her fine art.

- Kenneth house-sits in a beautiful home in Oakland, California, and sells his paintings in a gallery in New York. He makes a modest living on his art, surfs, and goes to a lot of raves. His decision to live a simple, unmaterialistic life gives him the luxuries only time can afford: friends, art, and recreation.

Musings on Dead Presidents

Of the many needs that confound the aspiring artist, the two most common are money and time. When I work with students who feel their main obstacle is a lack of money, I try to get them to open their minds and see the wealth of possibilities that can provide them with money or save them enough money to do what they want to do. During brainstorms, I toss off every idea I have—especially the taboo and unsavory. "Can you borrow money from your father, your great-aunt, your brother? Is there any way you can get everything you need for the project for free? Maybe you could barter your services? Sell your firstborn? Ever tried phone sex? Is there anywhere in the world where the things you need (film stock, canvases, computers, vacant space) are being thrown away?"

While my attitude is that there is always a creative solution to money problems, I do realize that many artists face a singularly difficult plight in trying to earn a living "doing what they love." One young performance artist had read numerous books about money and was livid. "They say all I have to do is pursue what I love and the money will follow. Like I'm really going to get rich by sabotaging Barbie dolls and replacing their voice boxes with phrases like, 'I'm hungry. Dexatrims make my tummy hurt'?"

She could have moved to Amsterdam or France (where performance art is more generously funded). She could have allowed Mattel to sue her and then tried to get publicity from giving prison interviews. But she didn't want to do these things. Nor did she want to "sully herself with the marketplace." While I sympathized with her position, I also began to see that her very attitude toward money was getting in her way. She seemed to have such a complicated set of standards about how she should make money that she had difficulty earning any money at all. When she couldn't make money off her experimental performance art, she would find herself in low-skill, low-wage jobs that she loathed but which protected her from the feeling that she was selling out.

Before reading any further, let's explore some of your ideas about money.

- How little money would you be happy to earn if you were doing work that you absolutely loved?
- How much money would you want to earn if you had a full-time job that you didn't find creative?
- Is there any amount of money that could buy your creative time away from you?
- If you had "enough" money coming in would you be tempted to live above your means?
- Do you use extra money to put aside time for your creative work, or does money end up taking away your time (in the form of shopping, bar-hopping, and so on)?
- If you had five million dollars, what would that mean for your creative work?
- How do you feel about asking to be paid for your creative work? Does it feel different from getting a paycheck from a job you don't like?

SALLIE TISDALE, WRITER

At twenty-one, essayist Sallie Tisdale was a single mother on food stamps. Aside from her writing, she had few marketable skills. After a short stint reporting for a local weekly, she realized she wasn't interested in becoming a journalist. Although on her own she would have been happy enough scraping by with a low-paying day job and living the life of a starving writer, as a mother she felt she had to make a decent living. After amassing an impressive pile of rejection letters for her personal essays and giving up on the idea of getting a job related to writing, she decided to become a nurse: "So I went to nursing school and didn't write for two years. I was very depressed and very poor."

Ironically, it was this concession to the real world that eventually allowed her creative work to blossom. "I went through a very powerful maturation process during nursing school. Just before graduating, all these words started to bubble out. It was like my writing had grown up too in that quiescent time."

She began working as a nurse, but in the final analysis she knew that her real path was writing. "I wasn't a very good nurse," she says. "I wasn't willing to give it the time and attention it needed. I'd rather be writing. I think nursing is a lot like writing. It's very creative, if you do it well."

Based on her own realization that finding her voice was intimately linked with growing up and learning something about the world, she recommends that aspiring writers chart a similar course: "Write a lot, read a lot, and take jobs that have nothing to do with writing. Write what you really need to write. Don't get caught up in the neuroses: 'I am a writer, I am an artiste, my life is tragic.'"

Despite the obvious difficulties in combining a creative career with being a single mother, Tisdale credits her motherhood with shielding her from many writers' worst nightmare. "I've been a mother as long as I've been a writer," she says. "So I've never understood writer's block. The hours and minutes were so few, there was never time to let that develop. When the kids were little, days would go by when I wouldn't be able to get to my study or even my notebook. The desire to write would just build up like sexual anticipation. So maybe I *have* had writer's block and I have been able to be changing diapers at that time."

Now her day resembles a full-time freelance writer's. After her children and husband have left the house, she makes her way to her study, where she writes most of the day. She also meditates every day as a part of her Zen Buddhist practice, which she began thirteen years ago: "I used to fantasize about being a nun, and during my midtwenties I went on a religious search and found Zen Buddhism. It seems like a contradiction, but a lot of people in Zen are ambitious, externalized, nervous creative people."

Many artists have conflicted relationships with money. They want a luxurious life but no signs of filthy lucre passing through their hands. They want stability without savings. They want to be poor and righteous and generous of spirit on the one hand and they want to be rich and fabulous on the other. They want to do wonderfully healthy things for the world for free and, at the same time, work in high-powered, prestigious fields and get paid by the truckload.

If you have this internal battle with greed and guilt, hedonism and morality, you may be suffering from the effects of extreme thinking. From this black-and-white perspective, the middle ground of getting paid for good, hard work reverberates with negative connotations: boring, staid, conventional, capitalist, careerist. Some creative people I have worked with have had so many jobs they dislike that they have begun to equate earning money with discomfort and humiliation.

In the days of patronage or a hefty NEA budget, artists could harbor the idea that their pristine artistic sensibilities were above the stench of fresh cash. Today, however, artists must develop healthy, pragmatic relationships to money. Not only must they be voraciously resourceful and optimistic to propel their careers forward, they need to remember that money itself is not the thing that corrupts us. Rather, it is the things we exchange for it (respect, happiness, our ethics, and our very life) that finally distort our sense of dignity.

Consider for a moment the positive aspects of doing work you love and value in return for fair compensation. Money, when coupled with genuine interest, can give you permission to do something well. In fact, it often *demands* that you do. Employers know this—that is why they don't run companies on volunteer labor and summer interns. Granted, making a living wage for what you love may not fit your image of the long-suffering mendicant or the glamorous superstar. But it may be a necessary step in learning how to give the very best of your being.

The transition from being a wage slave (making money from things you don't like to do) to a self-employed creative person (making money from things you love to do) is the most difficult transition for many people to make. Exiled from the small, protected space of a conventional job, it's often hard to comprehend the expansiveness of the new terrain. Just as chemicals in the brain block perception to prevent sensory overload, you may unknowingly avoid the idea of earning a living from your creative work as a way of defending yourself against the vertigo of possibilities.

Once you have established a rigorous practice for your creative work—art, invention, ideas, whatever—you will learn to value your work enough to demand proper compensation. If asking for money persists in being a problem for you, then you might begin by asking for pittances and then work slowly toward your ideal wage.

In the beginning, I gave Life Worth Living sessions for free; next I traded them for lunches and favors, then low fees, then, finally, professional rates. Although I always enjoyed the work, being paid definitely changed my attitude for the better. I became more focused, more demanding of myself and, in turn, more effective. Had I never been paid, the work would have become a time-consuming, draining hobby that I squeezed between a day job, writing, and my personal life.

Time, the Ever-Hungry Beast

If frustrated creatives often overestimate the need for money, they tend to undervalue the need for time. Time is an insatiable beast, eating away at your life, consuming your energy and your ideas. The beast of time can never be fully tamed, but it can be disciplined, nourished, and cared for. If you wrestle with the beast of time by trying to accomplish more in an afternoon than you can get done in a week, you are probably losing the fight. If you wish to live a self-directed life, you have to change your relationship to time. It must become less embattled and more cooperative. You must feed the hungry beast and thereby win it over to your plan.

What Does All This Mean?

Your life is time. How you spend your time is how you spend your life. In Keith Curran's play *Walking the Dead,* Bobby quips, "Be careful of how you live your life, you may end up having to live your life that way."

Creativity takes time: time for doing the work, time to rest and replenish your imagination, time to study your craft, time to dream. With the knowledge that creativity is a time-consuming process, you might approach the other activities in your life with an eye to having them work double duty. For instance, if you have a day job that not only earns you a living but helps you study your craft, then you'll have fewer activities to juggle during your free time. Similarly, if you need daily physical exertion and swimming has always driven you into a dreaming, creative trance, then by all means quit your aerobics class and find a place to swim.

Use these questions to explore some of your attitudes and ideas about time.

- How much time do you need for creative work?
- How much time do you need for resting and replenishing your imagination?
- How much time do you need for your basic human needs: sleep, food, cleaning, and exercise?
- How much time do you need for socializing? Family time? Alone time?
- How do you spend your most creative hours of the day?
- Is there anything that you "don't have enough time for" only because you misconstrue how much time it actually requires?
- What activities in your life do you consistently overestimate in terms of their need for time?
- What activities do you consistently underestimate in terms of their need for time?
- Are you often late? Are you late for certain kinds of activities and not for others?
- Do you make deadlines? Are you more likely to make a deadline for a job than a creative project?
- What do you wish you could change about your relationship to time?

I hope this chapter has given you clarity regarding those unspoken needs that prevent you from moving forward. Some of these needs you may want to satisfy; others, like the constant need for money, you may learn to work with in a new way. In any case, understanding how these needs dovetail or clash with your ambitions will serve you well as we look at day jobs and how they relate to your creative work.

EXERCISES IN FINDING AND FEEDING NEEDS

1. Narrate your perfect day from the moment you wake up to the moment you close your eyes. Write in the present tense, allowing yourself to experience the moments as they unfold. This is a *working* day—not a holiday that finds you lounging on a tropical island sucking on a giant alcoholic slushy. This is a day where you are doing all the stuff of your dreams. If you need to change your place of residence, your job or your financial or living situation, go ahead! This is not a pretty-good-if-I'm-realistic day, it's your ideal day.

2. Based on your new understanding of your daily needs, think about what kinds of help you might like from other people. Make a list of those people who could help you on your journey. They might be close friends, distant acquaintances, people you don't know, or people who are dead!

3. Personal Homework: Transfer your ideas into your Adventure Book.

4. What did you get out of this chapter? Any realizations? Undiscovered needs? What do you still want to explore?

MICHAEL LEHMANN, FILMMAKER

Filmmaker Michael Lehmann is known for his quirky, satirical movies about American life like *Heathers, The Applegates, Hudson Hawk, Air Heads,* and *The Truth About Cats and Dogs.* In an industry that hailed him as both a "young and hot will-be" and a "not-so-hot has-been," he weathered the storm of public opinion by cleaving to his original intention: to make interesting movies. With the innocent but restless energy of a realizer, Lehmann thrives on the multilayered demands of filmmaking: pragmatic problem solving, interpersonal communication, creative inspiration, and intellectual analysis.

His life exemplifies that of a typical interdisciplinarian.* His days include attending business meetings, creating budgets, doing research, writing or reading scripts, holding conceptual meetings with collaborators, working with actors, shooting films, and doing postproduction work. Lehmann possesses the qualities necessary for filmmaking: a highly social personality, an ability to synthesize information, and a compulsive work habit.

Many of his earliest experiences paved the way for his life as a filmmaker. He studied painting and philosophy in college and later worked in technical and administrative jobs at a large film studio. Although in each situation he realized that he "did not have the temperament" to be a painter, a philosophy professor, or a technical or administrative genius, each endeavor developed certain skills he would later use as a filmmaker.

Q: How did you become involved in filmmaking?

A: I moved to New York to go to art school because I was committed to being a painter. Then I decided art school training was too limited, so I left the School of Visual Arts to study philosophy at Columbia University. I stopped looking to school for anything directly related to my creative interests and I looked to school for an intellectual education. I do think studying philosophy helped me. It's given me a great basis for approaching anything. When I went to Germany to study for a semester, I took a film class from a depressed Czechoslovakian woman who had us watch a Wim Wenders movie over and over. Even though it was incredibly boring, I fell in love. I fooled around with half-inch black-and-white video and I just thought: This is crazy. This is what I should be doing.

*For a definition of the interdisciplinarian, see page 178.

I realized that my early interests in photography, stories, and painting had come together in film and it was really a matter of whether I had the confidence to pursue it.

The first thing I did was apply to film schools at UCLA and the University of Southern California. While I was waiting to find out if I got in, I tried to get a job in any capacity at a film company in San Francisco. I had no money. I spent the year house-sitting. I didn't want to take any money from my parents. I figured I had gone to college; I was a grown-up; it was time to take care of myself. For about three months I mooched off people and lived off my savings and spent every day calling everybody I knew who was remotely connected to filmmaking in the Bay Area. I didn't really know too many people, but a friend of mine had been an assistant sound editor on *Apocalypse Now,* and he put me in touch with the guy who was in charge of hiring people at Zoetrope, Francis Ford Coppola's company. It took a couple of months and I tried all sorts of other ways to get jobs that didn't work, and finally I got a call from Zoetrope. They said, "Our receptionist is quitting. Do you want to answer the phones?" I said, "You bet."

Q: Was it exciting?

A: Yeah. Not only did this job get my foot in the door, it was a good position to learn about how the company worked. And I don't think I've ever done a job better in my life. I was a great receptionist. I had no attitude about it. It kept me busy all day and I got to know every single person in the company because I gave messages to them. And it was fun. Sitting in the entrance to the company so that anybody that came through the door had to talk to me first. I got to look at a lot of famous, cool people even though all I was saying was, "Go up to the third floor." And everybody at the company got to know me.

I got word back from UCLA that they accepted me and I deferred acceptance because I thought: I'm working for a movie company, why go to film school? USC never sent me an answer. But I didn't care because I was working at a film company. I had begun working in the postproduction facilities and from there I got involved with the electronic and video equipment.

Q: Eventually you ended up going to USC for film school. How did you finally decide to get an M.F.A.?

A: It was a really difficult decision. Two and a half years later USC found my application and they sent a letter saying I was accepted and I thought, What harm can it do? It was going to cost me money, but I was convinced that if I didn't leave my job at Zoetrope I would never do anything creative in film because I'd be doing things that were technical and administrative and I have no genuine aptitude for anything technical or administrative.

By that point I was acquainted with a lot of people who worked in film, and I asked everybody for their opinion. You have to ask everybody everything. If you're interested in pursuing something, ask everybody's opinion about it who works in that area, because nobody minds being asked a question. The worst they're going to say is "I don't have an answer for you," which you get a lot in film: "There's no standard way to do it, so I can't really help you." But the fact is that if you ask enough people you get some insight as to how it works. So I asked everybody, "Should I go to film school?" I remember asking a young guy only five years older than me who had already directed four huge movies and he said, "Don't go to film school, you're crazy. I never went to film school. It's a waste of time, it's a waste of money." Coppola said, "Well, film school is a good place to meet other people who want to do the same thing you do, but do you really need to learn what they teach there?" Another friend with an undergraduate degree from film school told me, "Film school doesn't really help that much. Here I am, out of film school and I'm just trying to raise money to make a movie." So a lot of people gave me reasons not to do it. But I looked at all the filmmakers who were working in the American film industry that I admired—not just in Hollywood—and almost all of them had gone to film school. And if you look at the people who are making movies now, it's even more true.

Q: How did you earn a living during these years?

A: I took out student loans and was a teaching assistant. I also got hired again by Zoetrope to supervise the installation of a sound mixing studio. They paid me well enough, and after that I supported myself completely on student loans. I cowrote a script with a friend that we optioned for ten thousand dollars, I wrote a treatment that I got a thousand dollars for, and I ate a lot of peanut butter and jelly sandwiches. My girlfriend, who's now my wife, had a job and sometimes she paid the rent. I barely squeaked by. I was determined to make money on my creative work if I could. Ultimately, I got a job as an extra on a beer commercial and I got upgraded to a principal because they used a shot of me holding a beer bottle, and so I made twelve thousand dollars for four days' work and had health insurance for two years and it was the luckiest thing that ever happened to me. And without that I don't think I could have held out to make my first movie.

Q: Is there anything you look back on now that you wished people had told you?

A: Nobody told me how miserable film school would be. Nobody told me how competitive and how emotionally damaging that experience could be. People said don't go to film school because you know this stuff already or because it's a waste of time, but nobody said don't go because you'll be in a situation like a marine boot camp, which is designed to turn you to jelly or make you stronger. I don't believe in that. In fact, I survived it really well, but I watched a lot of my friends who I thought were really, really talented get destroyed by film school. If somebody had laid out to me how slim a chance there is of following that route and doing what you want to do, I might have thought differently about it.

Q: You mentioned before that when you decided to make films the decision was all about confidence.

A: That was one of those basic motivational things where you ask yourself what you really want to do with your life and if you don't pursue it, then what are you doing? You can pursue it and fail and then say, "That's what I wanted to do, but it didn't work so I'm doing something else now," but what conceivable excuse could you have for not pursuing it?

People say to me all the time, "I want to be a director, what do I do?" Well, I don't know—you can do a million different things to get there but if you don't do anything, you won't do it at all. When people say to me, "I know I could do it really well, I just haven't done it yet," I always just say, "You should start doing it now, because it doesn't get any easier."

Q: Have your ideas about success changed since you began?

A: First of all, because I'm Jewish, I don't feel like I've achieved success. Over the years I've realized that success isn't a thing. It's not an object. You can't quantify it, you can't hold it in your hand. People say "You made *Heathers;* that's a cult classic," and I say, "I also made *Hudson Hawk,* which is a famous disaster."

My idea of success has changed in that I've realized that it's a relative thing. I have friends who are really talented and yet they haven't been able to do what I do. That I've found a way to do the work I want to do for me is success. And I certainly think that it was as much fun to struggle and to look up and say, "Gosh, I wish I could be doing that," than it is to have done some of these things and look back at them and go, "How will I ever find another script that good?"

Q: What personality traits or habits do you think you have that have allowed you to achieve what most people have such a hard time achieving?

A: Luck. In the arts, you can't get away from it, luck is key. Because there are too many weird factors that you just can't control.

But aside from luck, there are two things. One, it helps to be articulate. It helps to be clear about what it is you want. And it helps to understand the conventions of how people work in your field: the history and the current conditions that factor into people making decisions to support you or not. Let's say you're a painter and you want to get your work out. It helps for you to know what the gallery system is, what painters have done in the past, it helps for you to know what the people who control the power—the economic power—what they're looking for and what language they speak. It doesn't mean you have to be like them. In fact, you don't want to be them, and that's not why they respect you. This is an ability I developed. Anybody can develop it. Before you go in and get somebody to support you in what you're doing, don't just think, This is what *I* want to do, this is how passionate *I* am, think about it from their side: What are they looking for? How are they seeing me? It's not about tailoring what you do to be what they want, it's about recognizing the factors that influence their decision. If you're able to do that then it helps you find a clearer way to convince people that what you're doing is also good for them. And that also holds for collaborations between artists. Be cognizant of why it's good for them and make sure that *they* know that so that the collaboration is real.

The ugly word for it is being political but the nicer side of it is being aware of other people's needs in any situation where you're trying to get their help, and acknowledging their needs without changing your vision and without pandering to them.

Q: What do you do when you experience creative blocks?

A: Get really weird, ugly, and unpleasant. I don't know what you do about that. Sometimes the ideas don't flow. I remember I was talking to a friend who was a really great comedy writer and he told me, "I smoked pot every day for fifteen years," and I said, "And you did all those great creative things? I can't work if I have a drink." And he said, "Well, I'm having a really hard time working without being stoned." And at that point I was working on a script and I was totally blocked and I said, all right, I'm gonna smoke some pot and see if that helps me. And so I did and it completely panicked me. I couldn't do a thing. So that didn't work.

Q: Did you have any role models or mentors? People that you knew or didn't know?

A: There were filmmakers whose work I really loved: Luis Buñuel, Stanley Kubrick, Francis Coppola, Wim Wenders, Roman Polanski— and I looked at how they pursued their lives. I read a lot about these people and thought, I'd love to be doing what they do, but what I realized is that everybody did it differently, so it's hard to model your life after them. Still, it's important to ask yourself the question, when you make a choice, Would so-and-so who I admire have made that choice?

Q: Was there anybody you could talk to about your creative issues?

A: In terms of mentors? No. I was too scared to do that. But other than that, I would discuss anything with anybody. All my friends. Film school was just like Coppola said it would be—I met all these people who wanted to do what I was doing and we could help each other do what we wanted to do.

Q: There was a community of artists all working at the same level.

A: Exactly, and I still have that. I'm talking to other directors all the time and we'll talk through ideas and frustrations. We talk out creative problems: How can I get this performance out of an actor? Or, how can I find this kind of music?

Q: Can you talk about some of your failures?

A: You don't want to think of your failures as failures with a capital F. I think it's really healthy to have things not turn out. It's really important to get better for trying hard and failing and then looking at it and saying, "Okay, why did I fail? What could I have done to avoid that, how can I avoid that in the future? Will I not avoid that in the future because that's just part of me?" I don't think of anything I've done as a failure. I think of them as disappointments. Failure seems too defeatist.

Q: Do you have one of those personalities that's never defeatist?

A: I have a personality that is entirely defeatist and it's so much so that it doesn't matter if I'm really defeated. I noticed this early on. I made my student film, *Beaver Gets a Boner,* and it isn't very good but it was a student film. It wasn't supposed to be good, it was supposed to be a learning experience. I was very disappointed in how it turned out, but I didn't care because I was really happy that I got to make it. When we started to screen it at school, all the students (politely and nicely, because they were my friends) said, "Well, it's too bad you fucked up. The script was really good"—it was written by somebody else—"and you guys had the best crew in school and worked really hard, but the movie isn't any good." I thought that my filmmaking career was over and my attitude was, Hey, it's great, I made a film, I went to film school. So then the movie screened six or eight months later and suddenly my phone machine is filled with calls from producers and agents who want to meet me or represent me and I thought, This is a fluke, 'cause I still thought I had a failure on my hands. When *Heathers* came out and was a big hit, I can quote you every bad review, but I have no idea what the good reviews said because I read them and thought, These people don't know what they're talking about. So then when a movie comes out like *Hudson Hawk* where they said, "one of the worst movies ever made"—when you read something like that in the *New York Times,* you can't look at it as anything but failure. But then I said, "I don't know, I tried as hard as I could under very difficult circumstances to make an unusual movie, and it was an unusual movie, evident from the degree of hatred that people expressed toward it." So I looked at this and said, "Well, this may be a failure on everybody's terms and I acknowledge that and I'm not going to live in denial of it." But I was also proud of the fact that I got under so many people's skins, because I was just trying to do something different. I can look at it and say, "I know why they hate it, I probably would hate it too if I were them," but I wasn't so cynical going into it. I was just trying to make an interesting movie.

In other words, failure happens, don't make excuses for it, but don't be paralyzed by it. I'm more paralyzed by success than by failure. Failure basically says great, you have a clean slate, go out and make it better.

Q: Have you ever been tempted to quit?

A: I remember right before I got a film made in film school I was ready to quit. I couldn't get the faculty to approve my projects. I had left a good job and put myself deeply into debt. I thought, Maybe I should just leave school. But I only had one more semester left and I thought, I might as well just get my degree. I was very discouraged. Then I thought, Wait a minute, maybe they're not approving my projects not because they're assholes (which is easy to say because it's true, but trivial), but because I'm not submitting stuff that they perceive as being the best thing I can do. So what is the best thing that I can do? I went back to the things that were really true to me. It's tempting to do things that are cool to other people or trendy. You do yourself a big favor by going back to what's right for you. What are you about? What sort of emotions are you going to be conveying? What sensibility do you have? When I was about to quit, that's when I got in touch with what I wanted to do and that's when I got ahold of the *Beaver Gets a Boner* script—it was kind of a John Waters–style, nasty, satirical, stupid movie that had a lot of attitude.

Q: What do you think is the most common problem for people who want to get into film but aren't doing it?

A: Focus. People ask me all the time for advice about "How do I get to be a director?" or "How do I work in the movies?" and I say, "Well, figure out exactly what you want to do." And they say, "Well, I'm not really sure, there are a lot of things I *would* do," and I say, "Well, fine. As long as you feel that way, you're subject to the winds of fate." And as soon as you say, "I want to do *this*," you have a clean line of sight.

Q: Do you do anything like meditate?

A: I talk on the phone a lot. I'm basically gregarious and I like collaboration. Even when I write I have a better time when I'm collaborating with a partner. That's why I want to be a director and not a writer. A lot of screenwriters say, "I want to direct because I don't want people ruining my work." Try being a director. Everyone ruins your work! You have studios, producers, investors, test audiences. It's not about that. Most writers who get to direct figure that out. The question is, Do you want to be the person that everybody asks questions of all day long? Do you want to be the person who figures solutions out to all these problems?

Q: How does self-discipline function in your life?

A: You need ways to motivate yourself. You don't have a timetable, a boss; nobody's going to chastise you at the end of the day if you don't get something done. I'm actually not as disciplined as I'd like to be. What I've found after doing this for a long time is that the only time I want to be disciplined is when I have a project that's really getting made, then everything is organized, everything is disciplined. But between projects, when I'm trying to be looser and more creative, I don't exercise that much discipline.

Q: What does your workday look like now?

A: If I'm not in production, I'm on the phone by nine or nine-thirty. In the morning I read screenplays and get phone calls. I work on maybe three or four projects at a time. Right now I have a movie that I've been working on every day for the last three months. I still don't know if it will ever go into production. I'm also trying to executive-produce a movie for a friend of mine who's a screenwriter who wants to direct. I'm also doing a project for HBO. Since I've moved out of Los Angeles, I needed to work as a director without being tied up forever on a feature, so I started to do commercials—which I have really mixed feelings about—but as work, it's great because the shoot usually only takes a few days, pays well, and you work with good people.

Q: Do you work seven days a week?

A: Sort of. I try not to work seven days a week because I have kids, so I like to spend the weekend doing less, but every day of my life I do some kind of work. It's just a general overriding sickness. It's a bad compulsion and I don't like it.

Q: Is there any advice that you would give a beginner in your field?

A: Think about *why* you want to do what you want to do and when you've figured that out, then think about how you want to focus your intentions, and set really specific goals. Not timetables and not ultimatums, but think about where you want to be headed and pursue it and always keep an open mind about unexpected things. Set goals and be disciplined and focused and then maintain a balance that allows you to be open to the things that come out of nowhere. That's the trick.

6

The Drudge We Do for Dollars
Day Jobs

To be ill-adjusted to a deranged world is not breakdown.
—JEANETTE WINTERSON

If most creative people are locked in a continual battle between their art and their daily needs, then the most dangerous front is that of the "day job"—a phrase that drips with torpor and dissatisfaction. We give up our "days" (usually an eight-hour slot of time) for a "job" (not a career) so that we can get "real work" (our creative projects) done at night and on weekends. (I'm using the term "day job" to include those bread-and-butter jobs that occur at night as well.) While many creative careers eventually become lucrative enough to make day jobs unnecessary, the day job syndrome afflicts all but the luckiest or the wealthiest of artists at some point in their careers.

The day job syndrome manifests itself in a variety of ways. Some individuals, seduced by the illusion of security and comfort, become slaves to their day jobs and lose track of their original creative intention. Others live with intolerable, low-wage day jobs—sacrificing so much for their art that they cease to have lives. Then they blame their art for their poverty, discomfort, and insecurity when really the fault lies with their annoying day jobs. If you are still struggling to earn a living with a day job and not yet getting money for your creative work, you are in the most difficult stage of the artistic life. While these early stages can be extremely frustrating, the lessons you learn during this period will serve you well when you start experiencing success. Many of the artists I interviewed maintained that it was during this period of struggle that they developed strong work habits, emotional maturity, and greater powers of concentration. This chapter examines this hectic period in a creative career and the ways your day job can support or undermine your creative pursuits.

I have identified four basic types of day job most artists must consider when planning their lives.

In the Big Tent

These jobs may not require the actual skills of your art, but they do put you in contact with the people, organizations, and publications that produce your art. When director Michael Lehmann worked as a receptionist at a film company, he took advantage of being in the Big Tent. He met people, learned new skills, cultivated friendships with directors, and got to see how the industry functioned.

The downside of Big Tent jobs is what I call the "midwife syndrome." The midwife syndrome puts you in the role of fostering and developing other artists (you're cleaning up after the lion when you want to *be* the lion), while neglecting yourself as an artist. Symptoms of midwife syndrome include feeling despair at the end of your workday that you'll never really be considered an artist or innovator in your own right; worrying constantly about what kind of impression you're making on your bosses (who, if they so desired, could further your career); and feeling cynical about the medium itself.

In considering a Big Tent job, ask yourself the following questions:

- Could you learn from being around professionals?
- Do you need an education in how the business functions?
- Will you be frustrated and impatient if you are called upon to attend to other artists?
- Will you embrace the opportunity to schmooze?

Big Tent jobs work best for highly ambitious artists in the earliest phases of their professional careers. Having already committed themselves but having not yet gotten their big break, they are focused and hungry to network. Many Big Tent jobs require a high tolerance for shoptalk, since they tend to deal with the business of marketing and selling art rather than the creation of the art itself.

No Contest

When it comes to decisions between No Contest day jobs and your art, there's no hesitation, you know where your priorities lie. Waiting tables is a classic example of a No Contest job. No Contest jobs never tempt you away from your dreams; you never worry about them when you are not punched in. Often they require little formal education and no long-term commitment. General office work, telemarketing, waiting tables, digging ditches, and taxi driving are all good examples of No Contest jobs. Sometimes these jobs expose you to an unfamiliar part of the world that provides fertile soil for your imagination; other times the work and environment embody your very idea of tedium.

Maggie, a successful rock singer, built her music career while working in a hip but down-and-dirty diner. The job was essentially a no-brainer and she was constantly getting in trouble for getting calls from her booking agent and recording label on the pay phone in the middle of the lunch hour. Because the job had such low stakes, she was able to focus on her real work. Furthermore, as a hangout for the young and artsy, the job gave her visibility in the rock 'n' roll community. Best of all, she could be her goofy, irreverent, eyebrow-pierced self at work.

The nasty side of No Contest jobs is that they usually require hard work, they may not pay extremely well, and they may lack creative challenge. They tend to be repetitive and can feel like drudgery if you don't enjoy the environment, the people, or the daily tasks. While younger artists are often drawn to No Contest jobs for their freedom and simplicity, many older artists are less enamored with the idea of working at a job with little creative or intellectual challenge.

Sometimes you can combine a No Contest job with the networking potential of a Big Tent job for pleasing results. When Julian Schnabel was a struggling painter in New York, he got a job as a fry cook at a local hangout for artists and gallery owners. At the end of the night he joined them and stayed into the wee hours of the morning, arguing about art and getting soused. In the beginning he had to suffer the slings and arrows of an art crowd that ranks you according to the status of your gallery. Since Schnabel had no gallery, he hardly registered on the scale of existence. But eventually the bar helped him build personal relationships with the people who could help his work find a home in the world.

DAN PERKINS, CARTOONIST

Before he began making a living from his political cartoon "This Modern World," Dan Perkins, aka Tom Tomorrow, did what millions of struggling artists do to stay alive and off the career track: temp work. Like most fellow artists, he disliked the work while he was there. Now, however, he sees that temping gave him many of the elements he needed to develop his art: "It's horrible, demeaning, mindless, difficult work, but that's how you purchase your autonomy. If you learn to play that game, you can have a pretty autonomous life, which is presumably the goal for someone who wants to be an artist."

Though he was usually working full time, he learned to steal time back for his creative projects. "I would do a lot of writing while on the job—what an employer might uncharitably consider daydreaming," he says. "It was actually really good because I had to sit in one place and I had to be doing something else and my mind could wander for hours."

While his No Contest day jobs allowed him to get bits of creative work done while paying his rent, they also steeled his commitment to change his situation. The more time he spent "in sterile offices" with "mindless Republicans," the clearer he became about his goal: to make a living off his creative work and never again have a day job.

His experiences in the corporate world also contributed to his dark satirical sensibility, the hallmark of his four-panel cartoons lampooning current events and politicians. His earliest pieces were published in the anarchist zine *Processed World,* then gradually he began to get picked up by alternative weeklies and, finally, national magazines. As his reputation and readership grew, Perkins made the unusual decision not to join a syndicate, which can take as much as a 50 percent cut. Instead, he continued to mail his cartoons out directly to his roster of newspapers and magazines. At the end of every week, he prints up his new cartoon and does a mass mailing, which he has gradually honed down to a deft three hours of work. This way he maintains control over his distribution and promotion and shares none of his income with a middleman.

In deciding whether or not you might want a No Contest job, consider the following questions.

- Do you want your art to be the sole focus of your life—unhampered by other responsibilities?

- Do you have a lot of physical energy?
- Do you want a job you don't have to think about?
- Are you willing to sacrifice work that's mentally challenging or socially relevant in order to maintain a clarity of commitment?

Counter Balance

The Counter Balance job demands that the artist do something very different from his or her art form. Gail, an aspiring graphic artist, found that having a job doing HIV street outreach balanced out the many hours she spent alone, bent over her desk, immersed in design, form, and color. Joseph, an actor who worked part-time as a freelance technical writer for geological surveys, enjoyed relief from the boisterous, emotional world of acting through the quiet, meticulous study of rocks. Eric, a science fiction writer, worked as a mathematician by day, crunching numbers at a federal lab. His math work allowed him a middle-class lifestyle and an access to concepts for his science fiction. The disadvantage was that he had to fit his writing around his full-time career. Yet because of the many perks and challenges of his math job, he decided to keep it until he could support himself exclusively with his writing. The Counter Balance job often exposes artists to a whole different walk of life that provides inpiration and important life experiences.

On the other hand, Counter Balance jobs often require a high degree of skill or commitment. They may distract you from your chosen path or demand long working hours. And there is the danger of actually caring about the job, which means you may have a hard time quitting when your creative work demands it.

Wellspring

The Wellspring job directly feeds the source of your craft or art. For instance, a novelist I know who works as a scriptwriter for educational CD-ROMs makes good money using his storytelling skills. The job allows him to make a living practicing his craft, if not his individual art. Teaching, art for commercial purposes (for example, dinner theater, industrial films, journalism, MTV choreography), and consulting within your field on other people's projects are common examples of good Wellspring jobs.

Rita, a costume and furniture designer, makes her living by sewing fabulously strange costumes for a local film production house. While her real love is designing costume for avant-garde theater, doing freelance work for film earns her excellent money as she practices her art.

While there are many desirable attributes to Wellspring jobs—good pay, access to resources, and fun creative work—they can take the same place in your life as your art. It inhabits your imagination, your artistic skills, and your prime hours of creativity. Moreover, the self-promotion needed to keep the work coming in demands a level of time and energy that you may not want to give.

Art Forms and Their Demands

In the upcoming pages, I will discuss the everyday needs of ten distinct arenas of creativity and a selection of day jobs often associated with them. I interviewed groups of innovators in each field, asking them about the jobs they had early in their careers. Take this section as an invitation to meditate on the actual demands of your art form and the types of day jobs that will most support your goals. Remember that the right job should not only pay the bills but pave the road to creative success. If you spend a good portion of your waking life working a job at odds with your creative ambitions, then now is the time to think about finding a new day job.

Acting and Performance

The life of the modern actor requires a combination of freedom and structure, social life and solitude. One of the most peculiar aspects of the acting/performance career is auditioning. All of us have at some time experienced the strange sensation of having our fates decided by strangers. In job interviews, contests, grades, we learn to accept others' judgment of our abilities as part of life. Yet only acting requires its professionals to participate in such a prolonged and continual process of binary judgment: Either you get the job or you don't. The omnipresence of auditioning in the actor's life creates very specific needs.

First of all, actors need a flexible daily schedule in order to attend auditions whenever they arise. Flexibility is also necessary for the on-again, off-again nature of the acting jobs themselves (theater work at night, commercial work during the day, and film work at the ungodliest hours). The solution may be doing freelance work or a mix of odd jobs, running a business, or working a flexible night job. Actors also need time to develop and maintain their craft. This may mean classes or coaching in acting, dance, music, voice, or meditation. Finally, actors need time to organize their self-promotion: sending out résumés and head shots as well as contacting and maintaining relationships with agents, casting people, and directors.

Though actors don't need a lot of start-up money to launch or maintain a career, they do need to make some initial investments in professional head shots, resumés, classes, and possibly voice-over tapes. They need money to maintain a selection of clothing and makeup for auditions as well as a little left over to attend plays, performances, and films.

Perhaps more important than any other element is the actor's emotional support system. Friends, mentors, and fellow actors can provide emotional support to soften the stresses of auditioning. They can also be a great source of artistic inspiration and practical exchange. With the right community, certain things that usually cost money will take care of themselves. For instance, an actor's "workout group" (scene study and improv groups organized by other actors) might take the place of an acting class for part of the year.

Generally, because of the heavy emotional strain of the entertainment industry, Big Tent jobs are especially difficult to make work. If a beginning actor is struggling to develop her confidence, she doesn't need a day job that constantly reconfirms her lowly status in the hierarchy. A good part of the business is maintaining an image of professionalism and confidence in the face of fear and self-doubt, so certain day jobs, though they may put the developing artist in contact with professional directors or casting directors, are only for real go-getters. One young woman who had auditioned unsuccessfully for a prestigious Shakespeare company accepted a job as a backstage dresser, hoping she could get to know the company. Because she was so self-assured, she made what could have been a really disheartening job safety-pinning bodices work to her advantage. Not only did the directors get to know her, but she made friends with actors who then cast her in their smaller production the following year.

The great majority of actors work in No Contest jobs like waiting tables or office work. Ironically, these jobs allow actors to keep their priorities straight only as long as they are *not* getting a lot of work. If Mark, who waits tables at night, gets a part in a play, he must quit his job because rehearsals are primarily scheduled at night. If Whitney, who works as a receptionist by day, gets a three-day film shoot and her boss won't let her take the days off, she will need to quit her office job or sacrifice her movie debut. Either way, actors need to beware of those day jobs that punish them for succeeding. That usually means finding bosses who understand your priorities.

Waiting Tables
Pros: No Contest, social, dramatic, low commitment
Cons: hard, physical, repetitive, public, stressful

Theater or Film Administration
Pros: Big Tent, stable, close to business, working with artists
Cons: little money, potentially tedious, midwife syndrome

Freelance Editing
Pros: Counter Balance, flexible, money, calm, challenging
Cons: unpredictable, demands skill, requires computer

Cleaning Houses
Pros: No Contest, own business, flexible, simplicity
Cons: physically draining, not entirely stable

Telemarketing in Arts
Pros: No Contest, other artists, easy to get, requires acting
Cons: repetitive, midwife syndrome, frustrating, little money

Tax Consulting for Actors
Pros: Counter Balance, good money, flexible, skilled
Cons: tedious, seasonal, requires skills

Teaching Acting to Chldren
Pros: Wellspring/Counter Balance, kids are wonderful, part-time
Cons: exhausting, emotionally taxing, inflexible

Teaching Acting to Adults
Pros: Wellspring, adults are wonderful, creative, part-time
Cons: midwife syndrome, requires experience

Teaching ESL
Pros: Counter Balance, stable work, creative, decent money
Cons: repetitive, not theater-oriented, inflexible

Dinner Theater
Pros: Wellspring, acting, good money, contacts
Cons: takes prime performance time, not always artistic

Music

Whether you are a rapper or a concert violinist, an avant-garde composer or a bongo drummer, you probably have a lot in common with your other musical cousins. For one thing, you need a place to make noise: a place to leave your instruments and equipment, and a place to rehearse with others. Despite the near universality of this need, many musicians deprive themselves of rehearsal space. They think it's a luxury that they only deserve if they are successful. It's not. It's a basic necessity, a prerequisite to success. Whether it's a closet, a nearby park, a studio, or a garage, you need to have a place where it's safe to sound good, to sound bad, to sound boring, and that is available when you are.

A great majority of musicians need their nights free for rehearsals and performances, so many normal nine-to-five jobs do not impinge on the typical musician's schedule. However, the high-powered full-time position may not work for the currently performing musician. The late nights of many music scenes (from punk rock to classical) make jobs that allow you to sleep in especially attractive.

Musicians need to make an investment in their instruments or equipment, ranging in price from a couple hundred dollars for a used guitar to several thousand for a new piano. Some musicians also need funds for ongoing lessons. While Big Tent jobs can muddy the musician's sense of identity within the industry (you can get known for being a great audio producer and everyone can forget that you're actually the next Jimi Hendrix or Yo Yo Ma), they can also help you navigate the twisted waterways of an industry that drowns many a talented soul. For the youth-oriented rock 'n' roll business, many musicians choose No Contest jobs to stay focused on their goals. Classical musicians, on the other hand, often find homes in Wellspring jobs such as teaching or composing for commercial venues.

RETAIL IN RECORD STORE
Pros: No Contest, music, fun, social, discounts
Cons: not challenging, dealing with public, inflexible schedule, little money

AUDIO PRODUCTION
Pros: Counter Balance, flexible, challenging
Cons: unpredictable, requires equipment and skill

TEACHING MUSIC TO INDIVIDUAL STUDENTS
    Pros: Wellspring, continued learning, social
    Cons: unpredictable, midwife syndrome

RECORDING STUDIO
    Pros: Big Tent, independence
    Cons: midwife syndrome, investment in equipment, highly skilled

PLAYING PARTIES
    Pros: Wellspring, celebration, good practice
    Cons: repetitive, unpredictable, artistic compromises

COMPUTER REPAIR
    Pros: Counter Balance, flexibility, independence
    Cons: career track, repetitive, possibly corporate

FILM, TV, RADIO COMPOSING
    Pros: Wellspring, lucrative
    Cons: danger of refocusing creativity on commercial work

MUSIC CRITIC
    Pros: Big Tent, interesting, intellectual, develops second art
    Cons: midwife syndrome, critical not creative, requires writing skills

Dance

Every dancer needs time and space to practice, no matter if the aspiration is balancing on a toe in a national ballet company, bumping and grinding in a sequined swimsuit on television, or doing a dance with a chair in a rehabilitated mayonnaise factory. Because dance requires such a large amount of space and time, most professional dancers continue to take classes throughout their careers. Where a pianist might meet with a teacher one hour a week, most serious dancers spend a couple of hours in classes every day. The enormous physical energy that dancers expend makes peak hours of the day one of the most precious commodities of the dancer's life.

Since most dance studios offer classes in either the late mornings or early evenings, and companies vary their rehearsal schedules from afternoons to nights, dancers must fit their work schedules around their classes, rehearsals, and performances.

Because of the physical demands of their art, dancers often seek out especially healthy work environments, such as spas, alternative medicine centers, and art centers. Later in life, when many dancers crave more intellectual challenges and fewer physical ones, some choose to slowly develop another career or art form as they continue to pursue their dancing. Then, if they ever want to move on, they have another career in the works. Of course, there are many older choreographer/dancers such as Merce Cunningham and Martha Graham who continued to perform into their golden years. There are also dance innovators like experimental choreographer Anna Halprin who change their approach to dance in later years into something less focused on formal performance and more on community organizing, running a dance school, or developing a movement-based healing practice.

As a result of their deep and abiding understanding of the body, many dancers choose physical fitness, rehabilitation, and medicine as their secondary jobs. One choreographer friend of mine runs a Pilates studio out of her home while studying acupuncture and running a small dance company. Others lean towards Counter Balance jobs that offer intellectual training and a quiet, peaceful workplace. Though Big Tent jobs are rather rare in the underfunded dance world, they provide wonderful opportunities for young dancers. Working a few hours a week in a dance studio provides many dancers with unlimited free classes. By doing administrative work for a small modern dance company, one young woman I knew eventually began dancing with the company after the choreographer invited her to join in rehearsals.

SIGN LANGUAGE INTERPRETATION
Pros: Counter Balance, language of movement, part-time
Cons: unpredictable income, requires special skills

TEACHING DANCE
Pros: Wellspring, community leader, part-time
Cons: midwife syndrome, limited pay

BODYWORK/ALTERNATIVE MEDICINE
Pros: Counter Balance, flexible, part-time
Cons: unpredictable, demands training, running business

AEROBICS/PERSONAL TRAINING
Pros: Wellspring, body consciousness, physical
Cons: repetitive, physically demanding

COMPUTER PROGRAMMING
Pros: Counter Balance, challenging, intellectual
Cons: career track, demands training

FILM SOUND "FOLIO" (SOUND EFFECTS)
Pros: Counter Balance, perennial
Cons: demands training, sporadic but intensive

MUSIC VIDEO CHOREOGRAPHER
Pros: Big Tent/Wellspring, fun
Cons: Corporate, demanding work schedules, difficult to get

Visual Arts

Whether splattering, framing, molding, or staining, all visual artists need the same basic ingredients for work: a place and time to make a mess. Without work space, there is always going to be a reason why the work can't get done. How big, how fancy, how equipped your studio needs to be depends upon you and your medium, but you should take your need for studio space seriously. I knew a painter who worked in tiny studio apartments—breathing fumes all night, tiptoeing naked among vermilion and sienna puddles on his way to the bathroom. Essentially, he was sleeping in his studio rather than painting in his bedroom. Since he made substantially sized work and dealt with toxic materials, this sleep/work space was not the happiest of arrangements. Eventually, even the most self-sacrificing artists realize that studio space is not an extravagance but a basic requirement of their work.

Although supplies are expensive and artists often feel the impulse to work long hours in order to buy them, time is still their most valuable creative resource. Styrofoam packing peanuts, dry leaves, and moldy old bread can be transmuted into evocative, thought-provoking art, but only in the alchemical laboratory of time and inspiration. While considering your monetary goals, remember not to shortchange yourself in terms of time.

Because visual artists most often work alone, they greatly benefit from having an emotional support system of friends and a professional community of other artists. Sometimes these support systems can be provided by a good day job. Certain Big Tent jobs can help fine artists, while others may impinge on their sense of creative identity. For instance, some young artists get jobs selling art in galleries only to get sucked into the administrative side of the art world. While they are getting to know curators and gallery owners, the curators and gallery owners are getting to know them as gallery attendants. Freelance hanging and repainting gallery walls, on the other hand, may not be glamorous, but these jobs allow you to meet the art crowd without developing an ongoing relationship with them as fellow administrators. Teaching children or adults can be a wonderful part-time job for fledgling as well as established artists. Whether the students are second-graders, retirees, or M.F.A. students, teaching can provide the solitary artist with an ongoing creative community.

GALLERY ATTENDANT
   Pros: Big Tent, stable
   Cons: selling, midwife syndrome, wrong side of the art world

FREELANCE COMMERCIAL ART
   Pros: Wellspring/Big Tent, lucrative
   Cons: difficulty getting work, self-promotion, drains creativity

SET PAINTING
   Pros: Big Tent, lucrative, social, using craft
   Cons: midwife syndrome, repetitious, long hours, unpredictable

TEACHING
   Pros: Wellspring, social, continued learning
   Cons: midwife syndrome, possibly unpredictable income

COMPUTER ART DIRECTION
   Pros: Wellspring, steady income
   Cons: long hours, corporate setting, technology, highly skilled

SIGN PAINTING
   Pros: No Contest, flexible, creative
   Cons: unpredictable income

FRY COOK
   Pros: No Contest, social
   Cons: hard, repetitious

Writing

Writers are lucky. All they need is a pen, a paper, and brains. They can write anywhere, with the most primitive tools, with little jots of time and inspiration, right? Well, yes and no. If it's so easy, then why are there all those books about how to "survive a writer's life," "break through writer's block," and "find time to write"? I think part of the difficulty in getting to the page has to do with its deceptively facile surface. "Just do it!" the whiteness seems to scream. "You don't need anything but talent." Your mind mirrors the page: blank, blank, blank. "Well," the page smirks, "I guess you should try again another day, or how 'bout another life . . . "

So you move out of your writing space, maybe carrying your journal with you, promising yourself to scribble down something when the muses arrive. They missed their appointment again. Those flaky muses. Oh well.

The absence of material demands makes it all the more necessary that writers create a clear physical space and specific times to write. Though this may take on a variety of forms, the most conventional home for writing is a quiet place in the morning. There are, of course, notable exceptions. Colette wrote in bed at night. Balzac wrote all night, charged up on espresso after a day job as a physician. Harriet Beecher Stowe wrote *Uncle Tom's Cabin* at the kitchen table amid the cries and dirty diapers of children.

Novelist Jonathan Lethem supported his early writing with a job in a used-book store. When asked about the advantages of this job, he mentioned several benefits: being surrounded by books, *not* writing on the job, and knowing other writers.

There are no rules except that you find the situation that works for you. Think about your writing patterns, your somatic logic, your environmental needs. "A good job" may mean having your mornings free, being worry-free about money, doing a job connected to words or literature, or finding a job that reminds you what it means to be human.

JOURNALISM
Pros: Wellspring, educational, interesting
Cons: midwife syndrome, career track, full-time plus, uses writing energy

WRITING CD-ROMS
Pros: Wellspring, lucrative
Cons: corporate world, career track, uses writing energy

RETAIL IN BOOKSTORE
Pros: No Contest, stable, near books
Cons: low-income, repetitious

ACADEMIA
   Pros: Counter Balance, intellectual
   Cons: career track, demanding, critical thinking, full-time plus

TEACHING ENGLISH/WRITING
   Pros: Wellspring, helping, steady income, social
   Cons: midwife syndrome

EDITING
   Pros: Big Tent, working with words, ongoing learning
   Cons: midwife syndrome, full-time, corporate

CONSTRUCTION WORK
   Pros: No Contest/Counter Balance, physical, culturally different
   Cons: hard work, long hours

PUBLICITY
   Pros: No Contest, working with words, possibly lucrative
   Cons: corporate, midwife syndrome, hype

ADVERTISING COPYWRITING
   Pros: lucrative, working with language and ideas, creative, social
   Cons: may drain creative energy, full-time career, corporate

Design

From floral fabrics to sculpted bushes, from camera angles to cars, from lighting to baby bottles to computer screens, almost everything we touch, see, and use has a designer's eye behind it. The influence of design upon our lives is everywhere, yet it can be a difficult field to participate in as an individual artist. The high price of equipment and the prevailing need for corporate designers has created an environment in which design schools and large organizations seem to have a monopoly on training designers. If your present situation doesn't allow you to practice your art because of a lack of facilities or equipment, consider looking into those day jobs that can give you access to the tools of your art. For instance, I knew a visual artist who wanted to learn to be a computer graphics expert but had no experience, no money, and no computer. She got a job as an administrative assistant at a computer magazine; in her spare time she taught herself to use all the graphics programs they had. After a year, she began to get freelance work creating posters and flyers for small businesses.

You also might consider starting a small side business that would allow you to acquire the proper equipment. Entrepreneurial ventures are a great way for young designers to learn about their trade in a short time and become experts without having to climb the design-firm ladder or attend an expensive graduate school program. In many cities there are apprenticeship programs in traditional crafts like carpentry and furniture building that can lead directly to paid work.

PRODUCT DESIGN
   Pros: Wellspring, creative, lucrative
   Cons: possibly corporate, high competition

RETAIL IN DESIGN STORE
   Pros: No Contest, living with design
   Cons: midwife syndrome, low income

FREELANCE DESKTOP PUBLISHING
   Pros: Wellspring, flexible, lucrative
   Cons: business of getting work, repetitious

DESIGN/PRODUCTION FIRM
   Pros: Wellspring, social, steady income
   Cons: midwife syndrome, competitive, corporate

CINEMATOGRAPHY/ART DIRECTION IN FILM
   Pros: Wellspring, lucrative, variable, travel
   Cons: long hours, exhausting, unpredictable

CONSTRUCTION ARTS
   Pros: Counter Balance, outside, learning crafts
   Cons: physically demanding, long hours

MUSEUM DESIGN
   Pros: Wellspring, educational, travel
   Cons: business of getting work, unpredictable

CRAFTS
   Pros: Wellspring, hands-on, flexible
   Cons: possibly repetitive, selling

TEACHING CHILDREN
Pros: Wellspring, part-time, playful
Cons: midwife syndrome, low income

Film, Video, and Theater Direction

Although film, video, and theater each have their own industry, the evolution of the director's career often intersects all three. There seem to be three different paths by which people become directors: They go to graduate school for directing, they just begin directing their own projects, or they work their way into the field by doing related jobs. For instance, if they want to direct film or video, they might start with some screenwriting, lighting design, producing, or cinematography. If they wish to direct theater, they can infiltrate the field as actors, stage managers, or casting directors.

What route you decide to take depends on a number of factors. If you have an idea and no patience, you might just dive in, buy a cheap Super 8 camera, or stage an outdoor performance. No matter what happens, you will learn something and you might make the next *Slacker* or discover you're the next Grotowski. If you want to learn about the craft first and watch the art form in process, you should consider a job in the industry. If you crave intensive learning and peer support, then consider entering a training program or graduate school. Most typically, successful directors have chosen all of these paths in their development. They work on larger productions in the summer while attending graduate school during the year, and every extra penny they get they put toward their own projects.

No matter how tiny the project, the director needs all of the following to create his or her art: skills, an idea, a script, funding, contacts, money, equipment, and a team of people. After deciding which of these elements seem like the greatest impediments to your goal, look at the jobs below and see which of them might furnish you with some of your missing pieces.

CAMERA/LIGHTING-RENTAL SHOP
Pros: No Contest, great connections, stable, good community
Cons: low pay, repetitious

PRODUCTION IN AD AGENCY
Pros: Big Tent, understanding business, lucrative
Cons: corporate, competitive, career track

PRODUCTION ASSISTANT
 Pros: Big Tent, education, flexible, accessible
 Cons: midwife syndrome, low pay, long hours

CAMERA ASSISTANT
 Pros: Big Tent, skilled, good income, flexible
 Cons: unpredictable, hard work, not creative

FILM/SOUND EDITING
 Pros: Big Tent, lucrative, variable
 Cons: far from action, midwife syndrome

TEACHING VIDEO
 Pros: Wellspring, creative, part-time
 Cons: far from professional peers, low income

TELEVISION STATION WORK
 Pros: Big Tent, stable income, educational
 Cons: corporate

THEATER ADMINISTRATION
 Pros: Big Tent, stable income, educational
 Cons: midwife syndrome, low income

CASTING DIRECTOR/LITERARY MANAGER FOR A THEATER
 Pros: Big Tent, intellectual, exposure
 Cons: hard work, low income, midwife syndrome

STAGE MANAGER
 Pros: Big Tent, good income, close to action
 Cons: midwife syndrome, boredom

GARDENING
 Pros: No Contest, Counter Balance, outdoors
 Cons: low income, hard work

Entrepreneurship

Few career paths encompass as many climatic zones as that of entrepreneur. Whether you sell mushrooms at a roadside stand or are the founder/CEO of a multimillion-dollar software manufacturer, your business began with two simple ingredients: an idea and a willingness to work. Your final recipe might call for much more: business partners, employees, business plans, capital, trademarks, publicity packages, equipment, products, services, and legal identities—but no entrepreneur can start cooking without the first two elements.

Like any business, the start-up usually needs a site (a desk in your living room or a rented work space) and communication (usually a phone). Nowadays most people would say that you also need a computer and a fax machine *before* you start a business, and in some cases that might be true. But if you're not starting your business because you can't afford a computer, you're probably dragging your feet, rather than thinking smart.

When Genny entered my class, she had never considered starting her own business because she assumed she needed "capital"—an awful, intimidating, abstract term for a stack of idle cash. (And let's face it, only the ultrarich can afford such an odd luxury.) She had no savings, no computer, and no place from which to conduct business. Yet once she refined her idea—personalized memory books for weddings—she slowly began gathering the necessary ingredients for *her specific* business. She cleaned out a place in her garage to create a work space; she found a secondhand computer; she began collaborating with a friend who made handmade books; she reorganized her hours at work; she designed a brochure, a business card, and a few prototypes. In other words, launching her business came before all the necessary ingredients. Getting them together was part of the process, not a prerequisite.

As with other creative work, starting a business requires consistent effort. The best day jobs for nascent entrepreneurs entail working in a related field or under the wings of another, preferably brilliant, businessperson. Producer Eric Mc Dougall worked for Bill Graham, the events producer. Interface designer Loretta Staples worked for Apple Computer before she launched her own design firm.

But most of the entrepreneurs I spoke to were more like artists than one might expect. They learned the most when they were "being foolish": doing things their own way, making their own mistakes, and taking lots of naive risks. Whatever day jobs didn't interfere with starting their businesses could work in the short term. Eventually, however, each described arriving at the moment when they had to turn away from a regular paycheck and delve into their own vision.

DAY JOB IN AREA OF INTEREST
Pros: Big Tent, educational
Cons: feeling stuck, less control

PUBLICITY, PROMOTION, MARKETING
Pros: Big Tent, high intensity, creative, stable income
Cons: midwife, stressful, less control

ORGANIZATIONAL CONSULTING
Pros: Big Tent, social, intellectually challenging, good income
Cons: lack of autonomy, teaching instead of enacting

TEMP WORK
Pros: No Contest, access to computers, low stress
Cons: tedious, unstable, low income

DIGGING DITCHES
Pros: No Contest, physical, outdoors, plenty of thinking time
Cons: hard work, full-time, not a learning environment

Nonprofit Innovation

Like entrepreneurs, nonprofit innovators usually develop an idea out of working in their field and wanting to change the status quo. Nonprofit innovators spring from many backgrounds, including law, social work, political activism, and education.

Most of the nonprofit innovators I have encountered worked extensively in the nonprofit sector or in a related for-profit field before they started their own organizations. Within that field they were more likely to be someone who actually was a "direct service provider" or shaped the vision (like a program coordinator, a volunteer coordinator, a grant writer, an executive director, or a teacher) than someone in a purely technical or clerical position.

There is one important element that young nonprofiteers often overlook. Because they are dependent on the good grace of the larger community for volunteers, funding, partnerships with businesses, and alliances with other nonprofits, nonprofit innovators must build strong working relationships with all levels of the community. You cannot say, "I'm not interested in dealing with rich people," because wealthy people might be willing to fund your project. You can't look at similar nonprofits and say, "Those are my competitors—I won't help them," because someday you may want to create a partnership with them. If you are creating a community-based organization, everyone is your potential partner. Your early day jobs should pave the way to building these strong community ties.

HOMELESS PROGRAM COORDINATOR
Pros: Wellspring, autonomy, creative, often part-time
Cons: working in a larger bureaucracy, low pay

VOLUNTEER COORDINATOR FOR A HOTLINE (AIDS, SUICIDE, BATTERY)
Pros: No Contest, learn how to organize people, part-time
Cons: low pay, repetitive after initial learning curve

TEACHER FOR LOW-INCOME AFTER-SCHOOL PROGRAM AT YMCA
Pros: Wellspring, demanding, creative, important, part-time
Cons: low income, limited autonomy

ASSISTANT GRANT WRITER
Pros: No Contest, creative, educational
Cons: stressful, bureaucratic, highly skilled

CANVASSER FOR WOMEN'S LOBBY
Pros: No Contest, discussion of issues, outside
Cons: low income, exhausting, asking people for money

Invention

Whether blowing up the tool shack in the backyard, bent over a bubbling pot in the kitchen, or isolating genes in a laboratory, the independent inventor usually needs a place to experiment with raw materials. But the most crucial element is developing the thinking habit. Successful inventors carry their problem solving with them wherever they go: in the shower, commuting to work in the morning, in bed watching television. While the initial investment of materials and equipment depends on the specific project, the inventor may also need money for patents and possibly the development of a prototype.

Because many independent inventors need access to certain kinds of industry or technology to test their invention, some choose day jobs within a larger company. For instance, I knew a young inventor who worked in the marketing wing of a biotech firm. While the *content* of her day job had no relationship to her invention, the setting allowed her access to equipment, scientists, and information. Although she had no science background, she did have plenty of science-related ideas, and she met an astrophysicist who wanted to be her partner and could provide the technical know-how.

The independent inventors I spoke with repeatedly expressed the intense frustration they experienced in bringing their projects to a mass audience. Most had the tools and resources to create a makeshift prototype in their studios, but the process of reproducing this thing in a cost-efficient, timely manner pushed them to learn the entrepreneurial process of making liaisons with manufacturers or—even more involved—to manufacture, market, and distribute their invention themselves. For this reason, many inventors choose day jobs that teach them aspects of this process. Others choose Counter Balance or No Contest jobs that take their mind off their project completely.

GARDENING
Pros: Counter Balance, outdoors, independent, conducive to thinking
Cons: physically exerting, sometimes tedious

MARKETING ASSISTANT IN RELATED FIELD
Pros: Big Tent (perhaps), access to resources, stable income
Cons: midwife syndrome, usually full-time

DEMONSTRATOR IN A SCIENCE MUSEUM
Pros: Big Tent, fun, working with other inventors
Cons: midwife syndrome, low income

TEACHING SEMINARS IN INVENTION PROCESS
Pros: Wellspring, social, part-time, good income
Cons: demands self-promotion

LAB TECHNICIAN
Pros: Big Tent, resources, other inventors, stable income
Cons: repetitive, midwife syndrome, requires scientific education

Now that you have read through these lists, how will you use them to discover your perfect job? What elements of your present job are no longer working for you? After Deborah, a writer and video maker, read this chapter, she realized why her day job working as an assistant editor at a fabulous, artsy publishing house was driving her nuts. It had all the bad aspects of the Big Tent: spending time promoting other artists, boring administrative work, and an unsettling feeling that the creativity was going on everywhere *except* at her desk. It had few of the good aspects of the Big Tent. She and her boss shared no special rapport, there was no way for her to use her video or writing skills within the job, and she didn't even have time to *read* the books she worked on. Although eventually she would like to sell her own book to this publishing company, sorting its mail wasn't going to help her write that book. The fact that she knew the editors there might someday be useful, but meanwhile she needed to find a situation that got her excited about her work again.

She focused on finding a job that gave her access to the tools of her trade and offered her the opportunity to practice them—even if it meant working in a less-than-ideal context. She got a job at a local television station as a proofreader. Soon she began writing news features and accompanying the film crews on shoots. When she embarked on making a large-scale video project, her bosses gave her access to the studio's old equipment and editing time at the studio. Although factory fires and convenience store robberies didn't inspire her as much as some of the books whose pages she had counted at the publishing house, the actual work of this new job was far more supportive of her creative life.

Cashing In on Your Bad Habits

There is one last little tool I have used to get people thinking in new ways about day jobs. Use your compulsions, your obsessions, and your plain bad habits. Just as I followed and developed the quirky hobby of asking people about their creative interests into a great day job, you can look into your personality quirks and find wonderful raw material for fashioning a new kind of work.

Michael, a performance artist, loved to do research on bizarre topics. When he "should" have been at work or looking for a new job, he was lost in the stacks of the local library reading everything he could find on Chinese footbinding, the art of dying, or mail-order degrees. Though he had used his researching skills in his performances for years, he eventually realized he could also use it to create an art-friendly day job. He designed and taught seminars that passed on information he thought people might want: grant writing for artists, grant writing for nonprofits, and how to get scholarships for college.

Are you stuck in a day job that's preventing your creative growth? Cash in on your bad habits! Make a list of a few of your bad habits, private obsessions, personality hangups. (Warning: crack addiction, self-loathing, and other unredeemably self-destructive behavior probably won't elicit many good ideas.)

Now jot down one job—real or make-believe—that, in effect, professionalizes each of these qualities.

EXERCISES IN DEVELOPING GOOD DAY JOBS

1. Fill out the following questionnaire.

Work Environment Questionnaire
(circle your ideal choice in each category)

Time

Full-Time
Part-Time   ½   ¾   ¼
Temporary Full-Time
Overtime

Self-Motivation Needed

None (Constant Supervision)
Little (Supervised)
Some (Semi-Absent Supervisor)
A Lot (Absent Supervisor)
Total (Own Business)

Place

Home
Outside
Office
Factory
Studio
Other

Money (Your Absolute Minimum Yearly Income)

5,000	40,000
10,000	45,000
15,000	50,000
20,000	65,000
25,000	80,000
30,000	95,000
35,000	110,000

Responsibility

Little
Some
Lots

Human Contact
Alone
Little
Some
A Lot
Constant

Populations (Those You're Willing to Work With)

Wealthy	Disabled
Yuppie	Children
Middle Class	College Students
Artists	Adults
Teenagers	Immigrants
Elderly	Sick
Working Class	Mentally Ill
Other:	

One Job or Many?
Seasonal Schedule?
What Is the Single Most Important Attribute of Your Ideal Work?

2. Fill out the following questionnaire.

Inventory of the Present
How do you spend your time? In your real life right now, how does the time pass? List the activities that fill up your current life.

Are there any activities you would rather spend less time on? Are you satisfied by how you use your free time? What would you change about how you spend your time in your ideal life?

What are your creative skills? Include concrete skills such as composing music, drawing, and product invention, and more abstract talents like "a sense of color" and "knowing how to create an atmosphere."

What are your technical skills? Include things like typing, mechanical or professional skills, and so on.

What are your innate inclinations? Make check marks where you fall in the spectrum.

Movement . . . . Stillness
People . . . . Solitude
Nature . . . . Culture
Details . . . . Generalities
Product . . . . Process
Routine . . . . Sporadic
Contemplation . . . . Action
Communication . . . . Analysis
Individual . . . . Group

3. List the first ten day jobs you've considered for yourself, based on your artistic needs and your daily needs. If you did an exercise for a specific creative type in chapter 3, use that material in this exercise.

1.
2.
3.
4.
5.
6.
7.
8.
9.
10.

Find an imaginary or real friend to sit with you and talk about the pros and cons of each possibility. Write down the pros and cons for each one. For each job, ask yourself, are there any jobs I can think of that have all the positive traits of this job and none of the negative ones? Create a new list of jobs. Then write down your favorite five in order of what you think you would most enjoy.

1.
2.
3.
4.
5.

4. Personal Homework: Transfer your ideas into your Adventure Book.

5. What did this chapter reveal to you about your present job or lack of a job? What still remains unclear? Do you have any ideas for changing your job in subtle ways to create more of what you need in your creative life?

RAZ KENNEDY, MUSICIAN, SINGER, VOCAL COACH

Through perseverance and a willingness to try many approaches, Raz Kennedy has managed to weave together three threads of music in one interesting life. He coaches singing, performs and records as a jazz, rock, and avant-garde singer, and works as a producer. By now he has sung with luminaries like Bobby McFerrin, Al Jarreau, and Todd Rundgren and has amassed a résumé of experiences any musician would be proud of, but for many years he struggled: through homelessness, alcoholism, lack of parental support, and an endless array of dead-end day jobs.

Although he grew up in a musical household (his mother was an important Motown promoter), in many ways he had to deal with the same familial disapproval other aspiring musicians face. After years, he gave up trying to satisfy his father's expectations that he engage in "real man's work." He made a decision that he would give himself three years to pursue his passion for music. In those three years he discovered that he could bring together all of his talents: as a teacher, composer, singer, and producer. With the Whirling Dervish's* sense of versatility and personal purpose, he simultaneously balances these distinct roles while fulfilling his life's vision.

Q: You do lectures for kids who are interested in becoming musicians. What do you tell them about their expectations in the music business?

A: I try to show them all the different kinds of things they can do—engineering, producing, working in the theater, teaching. There are so many other options that one can pursue in the music business that people don't think about. What I do is bring these kids into workshops and lectures and discussion groups so they can get a grip on how you can really make a living in music and all the ways one can survive. Most of these kids will not be record-selling-type artists. You want to bring them into an awareness of this early. There's the day jobs and then there's also teaching. A lot of musicians find that to survive, as they're working on their craft, they can share what they know with others. Teaching can often be a way to help those coming up.

* For a definition of the whirling dervish, see page 179.

Q: How did you get into teaching?

A: My ex-wife was an educator, she opened up an alternative school for kids from grade school all the way up through high school. I had been playing music since I was eight, but never in a million years did I think that I would have the capacity to teach till she approached me to come up with some songs they could teach the kids. I got in there and started doing some songs, playing some games. Sure enough, the kids got into it and before long I had a regular curriculum there, and that led to me working with kids at a music camp up in Cazadero, on the Russian River. I worked there as a volunteer for a couple years just to be involved. Before I knew it I was working there as an instructor for four years and the next thing I know, I'm codirector.

Q: How old were you?

A: I was in my midtwenties. Met a lot of the artists that are around here, got involved in the music community. A lot of the students I coached are now out making a living as professional artists. I think I played a major part in their pursuing music and finally performing. So one thing led to another. All along I was doing my own music. Of course that and working in the kitchen, washing dishes, making drinks and making pizza . . .

Q: Tell me about some of the day jobs you had.

A: Everything. I went through carpentry—building decks and houses. Working in community centers. I also washed dishes for a fish restaurant, was a buyer for another restaurant in Berkeley. While I was doing that I was also getting little gigs that didn't pay much, trying to put together calls for session work. The day job thing only lasted for a little while because I started establishing this reputation for being very good as a vocal coach.

Q: And you began to teach privately.

A: Yes. Before long I was recommended for a job as a vocal coach at Blue Bear School of Music. Along the way I was establishing myself also as a singer doing mostly session work. And I was getting more inquiries from people wanting me to produce them in the studio. Management agencies and producers started calling me to work with their singers to get them up to speed for recording projects or ready them for tours. Before long my reputation for working with singers in a coaching capacity sort of preceded my reputation as a singer myself. Right now I do perform, but most of my work involves coaching. The other thing you have to be hip to is the whole idea of being versatile and flexible. Sometimes teaching wasn't jumping. One time, for instance, I got a call from a friend who worked for this corporation. He asked me to put together a rendering of the Michael Jackson song "Beat It" to introduce a new product, working off that Weird Al Yankovic song "Eat It." I'd never really organized musicians, or worked with the computer sequencing—but in fact, this is how most of the stuff I've gotten into has happened, by accident. So the corporation calls me up and asks, "Can you do it?" I don't know if I can do it or not, but I tell them sure. So there I am in the studio, trying to figure all this stuff out on the fly, borrowing my ex-wife's computer, bought some sequencing software for it and worked all night long figuring it out. The producer digs it, they try it at the convention, it's a huge smash. So the next thing, they're calling me all the time. Before long I'm doing corporate stuff around the clock and it's actually quite lucrative.

Q: Did you come from a musical family?

A: My mom was not an artist, but she was the first woman and the first person of color to hold an executive position with a major record corporation. She was, in her time, a real pioneer. I grew up in L.A. When I was really, really little, my parents got divorced because my mom decided she wanted to be a career woman in the music business. I grew up listening to music because my mom had music in my house all the time. When I was eight, we'd get milk crates in the garage and set up chairs in the driveway facing the garage and we would play records and lip-synch the records. From that I went to playing the cello in junior high to the guitar. By the time I was twelve, I was in bands. I played all through junior high school and high school. We were very popular, we'd play at parties, community centers, and high school dances.

Q: Did you go to college to study music?

A: For a short time. I dropped out and decided that I wanted to be a monk, so I joined a seminary and I dropped music and started singing in the Greek choir—Byzantine music.

Q: What happened when you were trying to be a monk?

A: I did community service work, worked in a record store, but it was more about studying the Greek and Hebrew texts. I was also into the serious discipline of yoga each day. I was going to move to the Egyptian desert and stay at the monastery there—Saint Sofia. But that plan got thrown out when I started playing piano in the university practice rooms just for fun. I realized I couldn't give music up. I left the seminary and joined a funk band in East Palo Alto. I went to government-subsidized welding school, got a job doing all kinds of welding while I studied classical guitar on the side. Didn't like the people I was working with, though—biker types mainly—so I went back to L.A. and started working for a record distributor and went to music school down there. I left L.A. because I became an alcoholic. I was really ruining myself down there, so I moved to Berkeley and was homeless for a while. You know those people you see on Haight or on Telegraph? I was one of those people. I spent four months riding buses all night, staying in youth hostels when I could drum up enough money.

Q: How did all that change?

A: I ran into somebody on the Berkeley campus who I knew from high school and she said "Damn, man, you're fucked up. You really need help, what's going on with you, Raz?" I had nowhere to stay, no money, no job. But I would go into the dorms and play the pianos in the rec rooms and this one woman said, "You play great piano, I've always wanted to get into music." I said I'd teach her and she said, "Well, you can leave all your stuff in my studio apartment and just come and go as you want." Then this other person who I had met on campus went to the administration and got me a phony ID card, which gave me access to the job placement center which was only for students. I saw a listing for a job painting houses, which I'd done before when I ran away from home. So I got hired to paint houses, which enabled me to rent a hotel room and buy some food. When the woman who I was teaching piano saw that I was making some money, she said "Well, you can stay here and help me pay the rent." So then I'm living in this walk-in closet. Then I went to Tower Records and said, "Hire me. My mom was in the industry, I know all about the music business." So they made me the jazz record buyer. So my buddy who I'm living with in the studio apartment (who's now a big-time record person in LA) suggested we go up to the university and get a job promoting concerts. Our first job was passing out the will-call tickets—promoting jazz—at the jazz festival every year. Next thing you know, I'm turning it out. I know who's coming months ahead of time 'cause we're booking, so I can talk to the record companies at the record store and say. "Let's have a big promotion on this artist. He's going to be in town, why don't we do a big record signing?" So the next thing you know, we're building a market for jazz in this town. We're selling out shows where they could never sell out before. Record labels are approaching me to do promotions, they're giving me payola big time. Soon Bill Graham approaches us and asks us to work for him.

Q: Do you think learning about the business of music and then going back to make music again allowed you to approach it in a different way, with a more professional approach?

A: One thing I realized is I don't want to be a businessman, but because I know how it works, it's a lot easier to maneuver in it. You don't get your expectations up. You understand that it's a very cutthroat business. You have to really do music because you love it, not to make a whole lot of money. For every big star who's making bucks, there's millions out there who are very talented (sometimes *more* talented), who aren't.

Q: What is your work like now?

A: In terms of making money—people love me to do backup work, production work, coaching work. I'm a behind-the-scenes cat. When I've done my own thing, it's been really project oriented, where I can go in, make my statement, do it my way where I don't subscribe to a lot of the jive that goes on in the clubs. I generally work in situations that are conducive to my creative aesthetic. I don't like smoky clubs, so I do things in theaters, in performance art spaces. I've been invited to Japan to do performances there.

Q: It sounds like you've made your peace with the music business by separating the creative work from your skills that pay.

A: Part of it has to do with having been in this community for so long. You have to stay on the scene. I mean, I've been working here since 1978 and it's only been within the last seven years where I can work. Up till then, it's been odd jobs. If you stay in something long enough and you're persistent about being true to yourself . . . Really, consistency is the key to success. You can't just jump ship if things don't work out. If you stay around long enough, you're going to create a niche for yourself.

Q: What does your workday look like?

A: I get up at five in the morning and do floor work, breathing exercises, yoga for an hour and a half. I teach yoga. Then I'll go to the gym for about an hour and a half or I'll do something aerobic like surfing. My style of singing is very dynamic, very physical, involves a lot of stamina. Most of my singers are R-and-B singers, or rock singers, so it takes stamina. Because my work involves sitting around, I need this physical activity.

Q: How long does this go on for?

A: Five or six in the morning till about ten or eleven, every morning except Sunday. Then my workday kicks in around eleven o'clock and that's when I see clients, whether coaching or in the studio producing or on a gig where I sing. That takes me up till about eight or ten o'clock. Then the last part of my day involves taking inventory—checking messages, sending out letters, returning phone calls. Lynn—my lover, my business associate and partner—handles a lot of the scheduling and negotiations and correspondence. And that has been a big benefit because now I can get a lot more done, help out a lot more people and get back to my own music. I write music for a lot of people. I help them put together demo tapes or auditions for musical theater or rock bands, or session work for jingles. I have worked with up to two hundred people in this last year. I give lectures and seminars about singing and how to make it in this business as a vocalist.

Q: What was the most frustrating period for you in getting to where you are now?

A: I was at a place where I wasn't sure that I could do music. I was writing some music and this producer, Andy Norell, said that he'd be happy to help me put together a demo for next to nothing. I never had a good relationship with my father. He always put me down and never accepted me as an artist, but I'd been married for a while and I guess he thought by being married, I was starting to take life a little more seriously, and he made a pitch by saying, if there was ever anything I needed he would help me. I never asked him for anything, but I really wanted to do this tape except I didn't have any money. So I called him up and said that I'd like to do this project. He said, "Come down to L.A. and we'll talk about it." So I go all the way down there to his place and he locks me in the building and jumps all over my case. Says I'm no good, that I'm not worth shit. Just mentally abuses me, tears me down. I leave there completely empty and torn out from the inside. I come back and talk to my friends and say my father thinks I should get a straight job, what do you think? And all my friends except for two say,

"Well, maybe he's right." But two friends say, "You know if you change what you really want to do, you'll look back on this and you'll be so bitter, because you know that you really want to be an artist." If it hadn't been for those two guys . . . I decided to turn it around and really pursue the music. I decided to give it three years: I'm going to give everything I can—I'll be washing dishes or selling fruit at the fruit stand—but every day I'm going to make an effort to further my musical pursuits. If in three years I'm in the same place as I am today, maybe I'll look at another option. My father has been an Achilles' heel in my life from day one—never supportive—and, in fact, I ran away from home when I was sixteen and have been on my own ever since because of his rage and his abuse. Actually, that's why I'd never put a hundred percent effort into music before, because I was always trying to please him. That's why I did welding and carpentry. I was thinking, Well, this is like "real work," this is what "being a man" is all about, but I was never really happy and I'd always come back to music. But I'd never believed in it enough to go all the way. At this point I said, Well, if he's not there for me, nobody's there for me but me.

Q: How did those three years turn out?

A: I wasn't where I wanted to be, but there was such a momentum by that time that there was no turning back.

Q: That's a really common story I hear. People are about to quit, they decide not to and give themselves a certain amount of time, and then they go for it.

A: With music there's few external rewards. You work these gigs, you schlep this equipment around, you're not making any money, there's nobody in the club, you're not getting any compliments. The only thing that's going to keep you there is that you really love it.

Q: What are the elements of your creative process?

A: Where I come from first and foremost is that feeling of the blues [*goes to keyboard and starts playing and singing*]. A sense of alienation and feeling sad, and then I can go toward the joyful. As a coach, I work from both angles—the strictly technical and then the emotional. And one enhances the other. When you're learning good technique, it should be a means by which you're allowed to be more expressive. It should be a vehicle.

Q: If you were to give one piece of advice to someone wanting to pursue a life in music, what would it be?

A: They would have to really do some soul-searching about their sincerity, about how passionate they are about the art. If you love music enough, it doesn't matter what happens.

Q: Did you have any mentors who taught you about what it meant to be an artist?

A: The people I mostly learned from were just people I knew in the neighborhood, people I sang with. You learn a lot more from the guy singing right next to you than from listening to a record.

I learned a lot from June Watanabe, who's actually a dancer. She taught me what it means to be expressive—I did vocal scores for her. Later Bobby McFerrin, who I sang backup for. He gave me a capacity to trust in the moment and to know how to listen. Not only for what's going on out here, but also inside. Most music involves the ability to listen. Even before you can make one sound, you have to be tuning into what's going on. Music is really a listening art, it's not a doing art. When you can really crystallize how you're feeling, what you're thinking, what's stirring, then you can sing.

PART 3

The Design

This is the true joy in life, the being used for a purpose recognized by yourself as a great one; the being thoroughly worn out before you are thrown on the scrap heap; the being a force of nature instead of a feverish selfish little clod of ailments and grievances complaining that the world will not devote itself to making you happy.

—GEORGE BERNARD SHAW

These three chapters will guide you through a step-by-step process of imagining, committing to, and planning your long-term creative vision.

The Long and Winding Roads
Exploring Your Possible Futures

> How could I be an artist and a writer and an organizer and a per-
> former/director, a teacher and politically active person . . . Was it
> right to be all those things, I wondered? And how could I either
> integrate my talents or choose among them?
>
> —JUDY CHICAGO

Imagine standing in the middle of a landscape that stretches out in all directions. To your left, there are snow-crested mountains, to your right, sand dunes leading to the sea, in front of you, clusters of green, rolling hills, behind you, a desert in bloom and a dripping, lush jungle. There are paths leading into all of these landscapes, but for most of them, you can't see past the first twist in the road. From the patch of earth where you stand, you can spot a few well-equipped, feverishly determined individuals ice-picking across glaciers and bushwhacking through rain forests. Which path will you choose?

The task of looking at your life as a series of paths winding out in different directions emphasizes two of the beliefs inherent in this book: first, that there *are* many roads to choose from; you really do have free choice. Second, you cannot literally go everywhere at one time. You can only take one path at a time. Do not take this as an endorsement for a one-career life or even the idea that you must always be focused on a single goal. You do, however, need a direction in order to go anywhere.

How single-focused you are is determined in large part by the terrain you choose. Some paths (such as mountain climbing, directing a feature film, ballet, and writing a book), require a high degree of single-mindedness. Others (exploring a jungle, creating a business, collaborating on a multimedia project) demand versatility and the willingness to do two or more things at once. Still other paths (walking along a beach, doing freelance work, teaching, selling crafts, and bodywork) are more flexible; they can be approached as all-encompassing activities, or they can weather desultory focus, competing interests, and varying levels of intensity.

In this chapter I will invite you to travel down more than one path. Using your imagination, you will think through three possible futures for yourself. The "three paths" exercise was the first element of Life Worth Living and I continue to consider it the most essential exercise in the entire book. Later I discovered that Anaïs Nin had recommended a similar method to the young Judy Chicago when she complained of feeling torn between her art, activism, and teaching.

"Anaïs suggested that I use writing to 'try out' all the paths I could see myself taking and as a method of exploring the many directions for the arts," Chicago wrote. "She said that writing allowed one to 'act out' what one could not actually live out."

Like Judy Chicago, you are going to let yourself experience your possible futures through writing. I have created forms to make the process clear and simple. Though some of my students choose to imagine four or five possible futures, I recommend you limit yourself to three plans in order to avoid getting overwhelmed.

Out of the many ideas and schemes you have unearthed in this process so far, how do you know which to pick for this exercise? Begin by thinking about the primary career plans you have been juggling inside your head. Everyone in transition has them. What are the sources of your greatest indecision? What are your inner voices constantly debating about? Often the three plans express three distinct sides of the individual's personality. One plan you regard as whimsical, another as practical, and the last as saintly or selfless.

If you are already fairly clear about the particulars of your art form or creative pursuit, the three paths may appear to all fall within the same career. Stan, a cinematographer, chose three worlds of cinematography: feature film; MTV and commercials; and documentary film and video. Because Stan was already working in the field, he used

R. J. CUTLER, FILMMAKER, PRODUCER, DIRECTOR

Filmmaker/radio producer/theater director R. J. Cutler grew up in love with drama and journalism. At the age of six he began working on student newspapers and directing his friends in plays. "I've never lost interest in either of these two fields. My whole life I've been trying to bring those two interests together, and it's taken lots of different forms."

First trained as a theater director, Cutler moved into radio, producing *Heat* for National Public Radio, and finally he became a documentary filmmaker with *The War Room* and *Oliver North for Senate*. When I spoke to him he was planning his next project, directing a feature "fiction" film that would use not only his documentary production skills but also his experiences in theater. Nowadays he can see that the arc of his interwoven careers has a certain logic, but back then, in the muck of it, he often faced the disapproval and confusion of his friends and colleagues:

"I used to feel like I was constantly stopping something to start something else. I stopped directing plays to start producing radio, I stopped producing radio to start studying film, I stopped studying film to start making a documentary. But when I start thinking about it from the perspective of someone who has had a little success, it's easier for me to say, All this time I've been laying a foundation for my life's work. I've come full circle. But I can remember very vividly the look on my theater agent's face when I said to him, 'I'm going to stop doing theater and I'm going to produce a radio show.' He had no idea who I was anymore, and that was a common experience: people not understanding why I wasn't more single-focused. It was frustrating, but I just kept pursuing my interests."

When asked whether he is ever so frustrated that he is tempted to quit, he says, "Yes, all the time." Then he quickly adds, "But frustration is inherent to what we do. So today is the most frustrating day I've ever had, but I don't want to judge it because it's hard to figure out. I'm much less tempted to quit now than when I was younger, when I was always asking myself, Am I any good at this? Is this going to get any better? You always ask these questions but you learn that they are part of the process instead of being legitimate concerns. Sometimes you want to quit because you want it to be easier, you want to know the answer instead of only knowing questions. For me, though, this is what gives my life meaning, so I can never quit."

the three paths to explore his concerns about the different directions in which his career could go. Other students have used the three paths to express their attraction to strikingly different worlds of work. Mariana, for instance, felt strung between her scholarly interest in anthropology, her desire to start a wilderness survival course for inner-city youth, and her dream of being a textile designer. Raymond was hovering between writing fiction, inventing low-fat desserts, and starting an environmental think tank and consulting firm.

Though you should aim for specificity in defining each of your three paths, be careful not to box yourself in with overly detailed paths for which you have little enthusiasm. If you must, go ahead and use phrases like "artist/performer," "teacher of something," "freelance consultant in something."

The only requirement is that each path must excite you enough to consider it seriously. If you're in a mopey period and nothing tantalizes, revisit the human cat exercise in chapter 3 and choose the best three lives from your list of nine. Don't discount any path just because it seems impossible. This is just an exercise—you're not signing over your future in blood. If the human cat list doesn't work, sit down with a couple of friends and do an exhaustive brainstorm of all the really cool careers in the world and let your friends pick three they want you to pursue. If you feel disappointed by their choices for you, ask yourself which ones you wished they'd chosen. Then pick three of those.

Sometimes surprising realizations spring from the action of choosing three possible futures. Nick realized that after years of living as a professional performer doing mime workshops for thousands of children each week, he felt constrained by the very idea of professionalism in the arts. He decided to "drop into the underground," to make every moment of his life a work of art and do massage for money. He had a vision of himself as an urban troubadour, sewing his own clothing, doing free performances in parks, and living the life of a true bohemian. Having worked for many years in the world of mainstream and commercial art, this third path allowed him to see how far he had come from his original artistic sensibilities.

Once you have chosen your three paths, explore each one with an equally honest, nonjudgmental mind. Give ample time to each plan. If you get bored with that life, are you bored because of your mood or because the idea actually bores you? Though I often recommend disregarding boredom (it's terror in drab drag), in this exercise I advise you to take your boredom seriously. If you are listless now in this purely imaginative stage, think of the paralyzing stupor that will overcome you when you actually try to undertake the most arduous tasks of the project. On the other hand, if you feel a lot of fear while you are thinking through a given plan, that may well be a sign that you have hit something exciting. If you think, "Oh, this is ridiculous, I could never really do this," please continue with the plan, however unrealistic you consider it to be. There will be plenty of time for practicality later. For now, promise yourself that you won't discard any possibilities based on "the reality principle."

The reality principle is the oft-cited reason people give for not acting on their real ambitions. But the longer I work with people on their creative dreams, the more convinced I am that such claims to realism are dangerous illusions. Often I hear older adults talk about the accomplishments of children and young adults with statements like, "They could do it because they didn't know they weren't supposed to be able to do it. Their naïveté worked to their advantage." But who's naive here? Who's misguided by some apparent notion of the way things really are? When you begin any new path, there is no certainty. If some people (young or otherwise) fill in the chasm of uncertainty with faith and action, then it should be seen not as naive but as simply pragmatic. As people get older they often want some kind of guarantee before they begin—a guarantee of money, talent, success, or happiness. But this desire for guarantees is the shovel that can dig a grave for the most ingenious idea. As we look down several paths toward your possible futures, try to quiet those world-weary voices of realism. In any case, these three trips are entirely in your imagination; they risk nothing but your preconceptions.

Many people feel unable to articulate the path that they want. If someone were to ask you what kind of terrain you preferred for a walk—forest, desert, snowy mountains, jungle—you would probably be able to answer without thinking too hard. Maybe you would want to choose a couple of climatic zones for different times of the year, but generally it wouldn't be a question that created too much anxiety. Instinctively, your body knows what feels right.

As creative people, we often unlearn our instinctual craving for a certain kind of life through the endless arguments convincing us that our dreams are either unrealistic or selfish. Yet without being absolutely honest about what you really want, even the greatest accomplishments may ring false. If you choose a path of lesser interest you might feel like you're really getting somewhere along the way (and, indeed, you are) but when you reach your goal—perhaps a summit of twelve thousand feet—you may find yourself wondering why you didn't take the path that led to the tropical beach. While other travelers surround you, *ooh*ing and *ah*ing at the fabulous view, you are shivering and planning the quickest descent back to ground zero.

A note to those generous souls out there who think they must inhibit or delay their creative dreams in order to help other people (the starving in India, at-risk inner-city youth, a lovelorn friend, or an alcoholic brother): creativity and service are not diametrical opposites. Not only is it possible to integrate selflessness and service into an artistic life, I believe creativity is gift-giving in its highest form. Through your creative work, you concentrate your inner self and manifest it in a form anyone, even a stranger, can understand. This alchemy of good art is one of the best things we can offer the world. Moreover, if you are creatively and personally fulfilled (not the same as obsessed or self-involved) you will actually have more to give to others because you won't feel deprived, jealous, or anxious.

After I graduated from college I worked with inner-city high school students and teenage mothers. Everyone told me I was doing such a noble thing, and at first, I tended to agree. The work was difficult but meaningful, and at the end of the day I came home equally exalted and exhausted. Then slowly I began to sink into a foul mood that increased with each hour of my work. I had other ambitions on my mind. Like a horror movie, the ever-sympathetic counselor gradually transformed into a glowering monster. Inside I was thinking, Poor me, I have a job I don't like. But that thought wasn't enough to get me to quit. Then I realized: Forget about poor me. Think of these poor kids. They deserve better than a counselor who wants to be elsewhere. Initially, I thought I could fool everyone and be who I thought I should be. But I couldn't.

If you have a tendency to drop your personal ambitions in order to fulfill an ideal of selflessness, then resent the sacrifice later, you may need to give yourself a break to realign your priorities. Consider spending a limited period of time (say a week to six months) where you put your goals first. This does not mean you become a selfish jerk (though your neediest benefactors may make you feel like one), but that you make the priorities of your highest dreams take precedence for a while. During that period, try to pour all your generosity into your creative dream; organize your day according to your highest goal. At the end of that period, begin to integrate your altruistic urges into the life you've established.

We are born onto this earth with no clear set of instructions written on the inside of our arms. We can look for instructions in a variety of religions; we can wander the planet searching; we can get a decent job and try not to think about death, purpose, meaning, and other cosmic party tricks. As we grow up we develop various ethical and religious beliefs that can point us in certain directions, but within these belief systems, there are still many choices and so much uncertainty. I know a Christian man who sat at home and prayed for two years waiting for Jesus to tell him what job to take. Though his God had led him rather dramatically to his wife (it involved a rapist, a Sri Lankan jungle path, and a visitation from Jesus), the deity was not so forthcoming on career advice. After two years of praying and daytime television, he was forced to start working in his wife's business. Only years later, after he gave up on getting specific instructions from the Almighty, did he begin to follow his own curiosity and discover his true passion for journalism.

Waiting for an idea from a guru or a God, a career counselor or an older sister, discounts the one innate clue we all are given to our possible purpose in life: our desire. Many of us grow up being told that we have two basic choices in life: Leave behind our desires in order to survive, or risk survival in order to pursue our desire. We may discount our desires and dreams as selfish or impossible (and probably some of them are) but maybe desire is the last trace of the universe's desire for us. Maybe our desire is our only clue to navigate this labyrinth of life, and by ignoring it we have about as much chance of finding the right path as the Minotaur in its maze. If nothing else, it's worth entertaining the notion that desire is not a capricious tick of immaturity but an invitation to action with an elevated consciousness.

EXERCISES IN CLARIFYING YOUR OPTIONS

Before our trip into an imaginary future, let's take one final detour into your personal life goals. Focus on everything *except* your career ambitions. Let yourself look as far into the future as you possibly can. Concentrate on your hunger for a certain kind of life.

I realize that the various threads of our lives—creativity, career, spirituality, and politics—are woven together, and to look at personal goals as separate from career goals may seem artificial. This exercise is more mechanistic than holistic, but it will compel you to take inventory of your desires by articulating those desires that you might never think consciously, much less write down. Even if many of your desires seem to contradict one another, write them all down in an exhaustive wish list.

Personal Goals

What would you like to have in your life within the following years? Consider all aspects of your life *except* your career (romantic, physical, social, familial, material, artistic, monetary, psychological, and spiritual).

One year: Socially confident and
             2 to 3 Girlfriends, couple Friends

Five years: Live in L.A,

Ten years:

Twenty years:

The Three Paths

Now you are ready to begin walking, skipping, flying, and crawling along your three distinct paths. If you are one of those generalists who resists this exercise of developing three single-focused futures because you already know you want to "do it all," please don't skip this exercise. Imagining each of your ambitions as life-consuming pursuits will tell you a lot about where your priorities really lie. It's especially useful for the generalists, multimedia mavens, and diverse desirers out there, because it will help weed out the false desires and give nourishment to the real ones. Even if you do decide you want to combine all three plans, you will be forced to be honest with yourself about how important that single goal is in the overall tapestry of your interests. Think of your plans as the dissected organs of a creature named Vision. Thankfully, our imaginations are a more resilient system than our biology. We can splice and inspect at will and still put it all back into a living thing.

Most students tell me that after initial resistance, they have a blast with their three plans. Giving yourself the leeway to think big can be exhilarating, and diverse imaginative journeys can feel, as one actress put it, "like watching yourself in three great movies."

PLAN 1

If from this hour forward you devote your life to this path and *only* this path, what do you want to accomplish in one year?

Five years?

Ten years?

Where would you need to live?

List the advantages and disadvantages of this life:
Pros   Cons

You are on your deathbed looking back. How do you feel?

What personality traits does this life cultivate in you?

If you were to dedicate yourself to this plan tomorrow, what would be your short-term goals?
One month:

Three months:

Six months:

What are the feelings evoked from writing out this plan right now?

If your plan isn't immediately lucrative, how will you earn a living in the process? (If you don't know, that's cool. If you have ideas, jot them down.)

PLAN 2

If from this hour forward you devote your life to this path and *only* this path, what do you want to accomplish in one year?

Five years?

Ten years?

Where would you need to live?

List the advantages and disadvantages of this life:
Pros   Cons

You are on your deathbed looking back. How do you feel?

What personality traits does this life cultivate in you?

If you were to dedicate yourself to this plan tomorrow, what would be your short-term goals?
One month:

Three months:

Six months:

What are the feelings evoked from writing out this plan right now?

If your plan isn't immediately lucrative, how will you earn a living in the process? (If you don't know, that's cool. If you have ideas, jot them down.)

PLAN 3

If from this hour forward you devote your life to this path and *only* this path, what do you want to accomplish in one year?

Five years?

Ten years?

Where would you need to live?

List the advantages and disadvantages of this life:
Pros   Cons

You are on your deathbed looking back. How do you feel?

What personality traits does this life cultivate in you?

If you were to dedicate yourself to this plan tomorrow, what would be your short-term goals?
One month:

Three months:

Six months:

What are the feelings evoked from writing out this plan right now?

If your plan isn't immediately lucrative, how will you earn a living in the process? (If you don't know, that's cool. If you have ideas, jot them down.)

Analyzing Your Plans

Once you have finished your three imaginary plans, you are ready to put all these emotional, factual, creative ingredients together and boil them in a pot. Ask yourself the following questions:

- If you had to step out onto one of these roads tomorrow, which one would you choose?
- Which one in your dark secret core excites you the most?
- Which one do you feel willing to act on?
- If none of them thrills you singularly, does some combination of the three pique your interest? If so, when you combine these interests, which one is the most important to you?
- Which path would you ideally make your priority?
- Is there a way that one of these plans can pay your way as you develop another more heartfelt path?
- If no combination works for you, are there any insights you can bring to your *not* choosing? What do you gain by not choosing?
- Are you not letting yourself think big enough? Are you thinking so big it depresses you?
- Are you fulfilling someone else's dreams for yourself rather than your own?

Plans for the future often break into three categories: 1) very creative but risky financially, 2) somewhat creative and somewhat risky, and 3) less creative (or less important to you creatively) and more lucrative or financially stable. To see if this is true of your three plans, place them in the following creativity/financial stability pyramid.

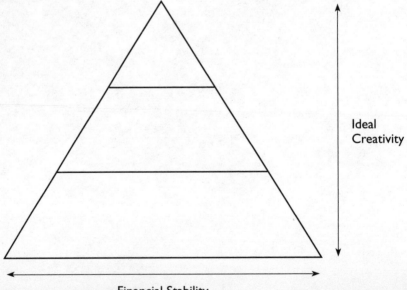

Explore in writing your conclusions and feelings about your three excursions into the future.

1. Personal Homework: Is there anything you can do this week to help you clarify your options? Research, phone calls, visits to certain places? Allow your personal homework to help you elucidate your choices in the three plans.

    Transfer all your new ideas into your Adventure Book.

2. How is your daily action going? Is there a way you can improve it?

3. What did you get out of this chapter? What was missing for you?

LYNN GORDON, INVENTOR AND DESIGNER

Lynn Gordon began as a toy inventor, wending her way through the world of children's product design to discover her niche as an interdisciplinary author-illustrator in the publishing industry. She has designed diaper bags, authored children's cookbooks, and invented activity card decks like "52 Things to Do on Road Trips." While her skills in writing, drawing, three-dimensional textile sculpture, and product design have taken her in many directions, an interest in fun and creativity drives all her work. Her relentless focus on the initial spark of creation coincides with her generator nature, while the inventor in her selects a few of her many ideas to experiment with and bring into being.

Her multifarious work brings together the many-armed actions of the interdisciplinarian* and the changeability of the project nomad†. At various moments of the week, her office/studio becomes an idea factory, a manufacturing plant, an executive office, and a playroom. Like many creative entrepreneurs, her imagination and her business sense have always been married. The problem lay in discovering how she could weave these two threads of her personality into a career that kept her mind stimulated and her body well fed. She resolved this issue by again and again returning to her innate impulse as an inventor, reinventing her process and her career every step of the way.

Q: What does your workday look like?

A: I wake up at about seven, and start to think about everything . . . I plan out my day with my eyes closed. At quarter to eight I pull my phone into bed and start making all the East Coast calls, as the pen leaks onto the duvet cover. Then I'll sit and edit for an hour at home, write, or read. I'm in the office by ten. I recently realized, the more successful I've gotten, the more demoted I've become in what I actually do. I used to do all this "blue sky" creative research and development, art direction. Now I do a lot of intense middle management.

Q: You get farther and farther from the product?

A: I get farther and farther from the original epiphany, the creative epiphany. It's weird. Even though it was frustrating to not know what the future was and to not know how long it would take before any ideas

---

*For a definition of the interdisciplinarian, see page 178.
†For a definition of the project nomad, see page 178.

came to fruition, I was doing an intense amount of creative work. Now I am more of a middle manager; I do not spend much of a day being creative as much as managing the minutiae of running a business and a life.

Q: Do you have a regular eight-hour workday?

A: Sometimes I leave early to take a field trip, or I stay late to catch up on stuff when the phone stops ringing. These days I do the creative stuff on the weekends. I think with this kind of job—it's actually not a job, but a genetic predisposition—the creative stuff doesn't happen in any planned way. Someone once asked me if I sit down and invent. But it never happens like that.

Some weeks are completely devoted to administrative stuff, and some weeks are completely devoted to art direction and writing, while other weeks are creative and I will try to facilitate a creative sphere; I'll get out of the office and do stuff that will take me away from the phone and junk mail.

Q: What about Saturday and Sunday?

A: Sometimes I'm here, because this is also my playroom. I have my art materials here. But I also take the weekends to have adventures and replenish my energy.

Q: What are the different elements of your creative process?

A: I keep many notebooks on different projects. I usually think of something and just let it gestate, unwritten-down, in my brain for a while, and then if it keeps coming up, it'll sort of have its own amoebic life and start to grow, and if it's something that keeps coming back to me, I will write it down and look at it to see whether it fits in with what I want to do. And then I go through the editing, the creative editing, which I almost do more instantaneously these days, as to whether it fits with where I'm going, what my resources and energy and interests are right now, as well as how it fits with my values.

Q: What do you consider the creative part of it?

A: The creative part happens in about two seconds and then it takes a year to go into contract. Seriously. And then it'll be as much as two years before something's actually out in the world. So by the time something has come from that really joyous moment of "Oh my God, I love this, this idea is so weird, this is really neat and strange" to actually being out there, it's probably about three years.

Q: Are there any habits or environments that create inspiration?

A: Financial duress kept me creative for years [*laughter*]. The older I get, the clearer I get that I work better in an environment that is very quiet and low stress. There are all sorts of floodgate controls as to how much stimulation, how much outside interference there is in my life. So there's a certain kind of protection I've created to allow a lot of down-time and a lot of personal thinking. It's like that from seven to ten in the morning. I need that a lot, the quiet. I rarely listen to the radio or watch TV. There's always this incubation environment. So I guess I've done that unconsciously.

Q: Did you always have this process?

A: I always had scratch paper. I have files and files of scratch paper that I've saved since I was little, of clothing designs and toy designs. I always had ways of collecting ideas and validating what I was doing through collecting. When I look back, I've been inventing things since I was very young. I used to sew weird stuffed animals and then go door-to-door selling them. I just didn't know what it was called in the real world. I didn't know it was a job. I'm still not sure it's a job [*laughter*]. But it is an interesting life. It's just taken me a while to understand which industries I fit into. In the book world it's just called authors or book packagers.

Q: How did you go through that? Did you study in college?

A: I have no training in design. I'm self-trained. Since I was little I've just been making things and being really scrappy and trying to sell them. I have a degree in English literature.

Q: What happened after you graduated from college?

A: I started a company. I had always been starting companies, these weird little companies. I had had a company in high school where I designed and made clothing. I was making peasant clothes and selling them at a little boutique.

Q: You sewed?

A: Yeah. I loved fabric. Then I invented a product out of college, which I marketed. It was really interesting, but I realized I was good at coming up with ideas more than developing one thing to fruition and selling it and distributing it and then coming up with a follow-up product. I had a company called FUNdamental Design Group. I knew I wanted to do something with play, playfulness, fun, and psychology. It took me years to figure out what that would be. I moved from New York to California and learned about industrial design; I thought that's what I wanted to do. To work in three dimensions and design products. But then I realized that wasn't necessarily an inventor's role, though it was a very visual role. The main break came when a guy mistook me for a *Newsweek* reporter named Lynn Gordon, and he turned out to be a designer at Fisher-Price. I took that moment to ask him if there were things they weren't developing in-house that they were interested in seeing ideas for. And he said, "Yes, diaper bags." That started me developing products for the juvenile-products industry. I realized it was an unbelievably fun thing to do, and that people would actually pay you to invent things. I developed a whole line of diaper bags, and they ended up optioning one, and it ultimately fell through, but I made some money, and I thought, That was pretty great. Simultaneously I started to create these three-dimensional books for kids and got a lot of offers on them. It became clear to me that the publishing world was very responsive to the kinds of weird stuff I was doing. I eventually signed my first book contract and I haven't looked back since.

Q: Did you have any role models or mentors?

A: I've pieced together aspects of other people's lives. I have files on cool jobs, like this guy who travels the world designing opera costumes. I collect these articles that strike me as wonderful, and somehow I fabricate a mentor from afar. Some people have invisible playmates, I have invisible mentors. I probably would have benefited from having a mentor but even now I don't know people in this area who do what I do.

Q: What kind of support system have you had?

A: I have an incredibly great group of friends. When I was young my parents were supportive, even though they couldn't quite understand what I was doing. I think the hardest thing about what I did was the incredible self-doubt. Year in and year out, when I first started out I thought I was doing something wrong. To go through years and years of . . . There was nobody to say, "Lynn, I've been in this industry for twenty years and it took me fifteen years to get to this point, it just takes time." So I assumed that I was doing something very wrong and I would run and invent something else. That kind of scattered, incredible output of life redesign and professional reinvention was very painful and exhausting.

Q: Because you kept on starting new projects?

A: Always. Which, ironically, is what I'm best at doing. I'm an inventor, so what I'm good at is taking something from nothing. But the allocation of energy, of constantly re-inventing your life and thinking, I really should be doing this, or, I would be successful if I came into work at seven A.M., was grueling. The best thing that my support group, my friends, did was to believe in me. Ultimately your life and who you are is the creative product. It really is about process and not the outcome.

In the beginning it was really rough, and the stress definitely affected my personal life. I've always been so fraught with this sense of having to work harder, run faster. I wouldn't actually wish this on anybody [*laughter*]. But I also don't see that I had any choice, because it was self-birthing. What I do for a profession is very much about raising myself, that's what the process has become for me. When people ask me, "How do I bring a product to market?" I look at where they are in their life and what they're doing and what they want to do, and I have no interest in talking to people who are just out to make a buck, and just want to know how to patent something and license it.

Q: It's a commitment to a certain kind of life.

A: Yeah. It's about designing and inventing a life. It's really not about the making of the money.

Q: Do you have any tricks you play on yourself when you don't feel like working?

A: No. Just the boring stuff. I exercise, listen to music, and try to lay off the sugar. You know, it's more about trying to prevent frames of mind that I know lead to really rocky patterns.

Q: Did you ever have day jobs? How did you support yourself when you first started?

A: For the first three years I temped part-time, because I typed a hundred and ten words a minute and knew word processing programs at a time when other people didn't. Then I did client work for years. I worked with clients like Esprit or Gymboree, or Discovery Toys. So until the last three years my income had come from client work, whereas now it's royalty-based.

Q: Talk about some of your failures and how you moved past them.

A: Well, because the outcome I wanted wasn't happening for years, I kept redesigning the process. Which wasn't necessarily a good thing to do. And I look back and say, I wish I hadn't worried as much, I wish I had focused on other things. But that's really easy to say when you have a certain amount of confidence that's built from a success. So I don't know. The isolation of what I've done has been painful, and I see the amount of pain and self-questioning as being sort of a failure, because I can see that the years could have been more enjoyable if I had had more faith. But how was I to know?

Q: When you talk about reinventing yourself, do you mean the actual work that you were doing, or the daily process, or . . .

A: All of it. It wasn't conscious, I would just pound the pavement with a different pair of shoes. I did an enormous amount of pavement pounding in a number of different industries to try and figure out where I fit in with a zillion different companies. I have all kinds of records of letters I sent out, different promo things, and notes from the number of times that I kept thinking, Well, maybe I should be inventing in children's clothing or something else.

Q: Thinking, maybe this is the right home for me . . .

A: Exactly. It's all one big Wizard of Oz story of trying to come "home."

Q: Have your thoughts on what success means changed since you started?

A: Success for me for the longest time was to be able to pay the rent. And as soon as I was able to do that it was very much about having meaningful work. If I can continue to pick and choose and design work that also integrates my values, then I can't imagine a better life. It is a pretty great life; sometimes I pinch myself and say, Oh my God, I don't believe I get to do this. On the days it works it's unbelievable, on the days it doesn't work, it's the worst nightmare.

Q: If there's one piece of advice that you would give a beginner in your arena, what would it be?

A: Go for what you really want. Don't do what you think you should do. It's important to do something that will pay the rent, while keeping the focus on what you want. And I think that when I look back, I realize that although I didn't have a conscious mission statement, I was very clear. When I talk to people who say they want to do what I want to do, I ask them what's important to them. If security and money are important to them, they should definitely be employed by someone else. If they're up for the adventure of trying to make a living through being creative, then there's truly nothing more exciting. But I think it's important to be clear on your values. When I look back I realize I have had an incredible tolerance for risk, having done this for so many years with such little reward, both from the outside and from my own lack of confidence. But at the same time I was certainly leading *my* life, and I never felt like I was victimized or doing something I didn't want to be doing. In spite of it not having been fun day in and day out, I really feel like I was very conscious every day of the past ten years, and that in itself is gratifying and meaningful.

Q: *That it was a choice rather than things choosing you.*

A: Right. But to make that many tiny decisions about how you spend every moment is pretty intense self-management, and it's really, really draining. I don't think it's necessary for everybody. If other people are really comfortable with the status quo, there is no need, nor any value, in inventing so many aspects of one's life from scratch.

Q: *Where do you look for ideas?*

A: I read a lot. For me, it's kind of the surreal cross-pollination from a bunch of disciplines, from cookbooks to traffic lights to . . . it's just that weird way that I combine unlikely things, and then suddenly realize that I'm looking at something unique.

Q: *So your method is sort of reinventing the wheel every day . . .*

A: Right. I think maybe all those years of searching was preparing me for the process of what it is I do: invention. To always go back to scratch, back to the tabula rasa. And when you look around the studio, even though there are eight projects at different stages of development, I always return to this empty creative space. And that's the process. The toys get put away at the end of the day . . . and the next day, I start again.

Goals

The Art You Give Yourself

To dare is to lose one's footing momentarily. Not to dare is to lose oneself.

—SØREN KIERKEGAARD

Now that you've exercised your eagle vision in all directions in the form of the three paths, you are ready to hone in and set your sights on a specific destination. This chapter will help you carve out and commit to a midterm career goal which reflects your highest desire. Neither too near at hand nor too far away, this goal should represent the first large milestone in your chosen career.

Settling on a goal just the right distance from your present situation can be a tricky task. When Melanie, a young conceptual artist who had never had a professional show of her work, told me that she wanted to have a solo show at the Whitney Museum within a year, I applauded her ambition but suggested that she first focus on a more modest goal—like having her first solo show in a good gallery or being in a group show at a local museum. Though my suggestions were still ambitious for an as-yet-unrepresented artist, they didn't reflect a pie-in-the-sky attitude. Fixating on the apex of your career may put too much emphasis on the future and devalue your important achievements along the way.

In the same light, goals that are too easily attained won't light your way far enough into the future to allow you to see your true path. When Angela, an affluent woman in her fifties aspiring to make documentary films, told me her creative goal was to work as a production assistant for a local film-maker, I encouraged her to make this a subgoal of a more substantial project like finishing her first ten-minute documentary. Because of her independent wealth and ample free time, she had none of the typical obstacles that usually impede beginning artists. Instead, she had a single paralyzing obstacle, the inability to create an ambitious goal for herself.

Often when we arrive at this stage in my workshop, there's a lot of nose wrinkling and loosening of collars. It's as if the room had suddenly been pumped with a hot, foul-smelling gas. One young inventor exclaimed, "I don't believe in goals. They're so corporate." A choreographer nodded, "Yes! Goals give me a headache."

Indeed, for many artists the very idea of a goal casts a dark pall over their creative impulse. There are good reasons for this. The importance of goals has been flogged into our collective mind since infancy. In our status-conscious culture, we often value ourselves and others for what we do rather than who we are. And in this ethos, the goal-oriented individual appears to have the best chance of feeling worthwhile and loved. Ironically, it is this same rushing to the finish line for accolades and acknowledgment that undermines the patience and present-mindedness integral to all creative work. So if you feel suspicious about goals, let me agree with you in advance: Old-fashioned, boring goals stink. But well-crafted, creative goals—that's a different thing altogether. They are tantalizing, provocative, and gorgeous. They are little aesthetic worlds perfectly shaped from your own desire. They are works of art designed and created for a single person: you. You create them for your own benefit, your own excitement and joy. And just like a successful work of art, a creative goal should provoke you to new insights and new experiences.

Before chiseling out the details of your goal, you'll need to think about how you want to approach your career in general. Do you want to have many careers going at once or only one? If you want to maintain two careers, how will you organize them? The following types embody the various ways people organize their many goals in the course of their lives.

ARIEL GORE, WRITER

At nineteen, single welfare mom Ariel Gore never guessed that by the time she hit twenty-five she would be a national spokesperson for poor mothers and the editor and publisher of her own magazine, *Hip*

Mama, an alternative parenting zine. In many ways, she was driven by necessity.

"One of the main incentives for starting the magazine was that nobody wanted to publish my stuff," she told me. "I thought, I'll just publish my own stuff. I can hire a printer, too. I was sending stuff out that totally hopeless way—like they tell you in the *Writer's Market,* which never works. Now *Hip Mama* is listed in there and I can see why this method never works. I have crates and crates full of manuscripts and then I have these poor people calling me and I have to tell them that I haven't read their work yet. Don't use the *Writer's Market!* Then I tried sending out queries and I got only rejections. I just couldn't handle getting those little rejection slips in the mail. I couldn't take it."

Unlike her classmates in the journalism department, Gore knew she didn't have the time, money, or flexibility to fly around the country to those unpaid full-time summer internships at daily newspapers. She needed to figure out a way to stay home and still pursue her writing. She was also disillusioned with the things she was being taught in her journalism classes:

"They sort of expect you to do straight nonbiased reporting and work at a daily newspaper. But I'm not objective. Nobody is. And it's funny because that's one of the things that's made *Hip Mama* success-ful. Now when I help friends who want to start their own zines, I tell them they have to have a point of view. They can't just try to be what other people want them to be."

Though the creation of this very personal project has never earned her any money, it did launch her career as the media darling of welfare mothers, and as a freelance journalist. Based on her radio and talk show appearances and her articles, agents began calling her to see if she had any book ideas. She happily obliged them and wrote several proposals about teen parenting, all of which were rejected. Finally, she understood that what people appreciated about her was not only her radical position on motherhood but her sense of humor. Out of that realization, she wrote and sold a book proposal for *The Hip Mama Sur-vivor Guide,* a mixture of essays and interviews with young progressive mothers. While her friends are out covering fires for the local daily, Gore can now stay home with her daughter and write about the issues closest to her heart. Echoing my exercise of "cashing in on your bad habits," she says, "Whatever is the hardest thing in your life, let it become your PR gimmick."

The Monocled Monk

This single-minded little creature focuses on one career for an entire life. Monocled monks were common in the fifties, when men worked for companies until they retired with a fat pension and a gold watch, and women spent their lives homemaking. During that time most people didn't have alternative careers, they had hobbies. The monocled monk has become less common as job stability disappears and people have access to so many more options.

A fair number of artists still elect the simplicity and purity of the monocled life. Of the people I interviewed for this book, I consider David Lloyd, Jonathan Lethem, and Mary Gaitskill to lead monocled lives since they have no secondary creative careers and their work is single-tasked: either writing or painting. They are all obliged to do other things like teach, give readings, and attend showings, but all those things are related and subordinate to their primary work. The peril of monocled monks is that they may identify so closely with their work that any intrusions feel intolerable.

Project Nomad

The project nomad roams from project to project the way a Berber roams the desert. Each new place demands exploration, a new set of laws, and absolute diligence. This is a model that many artists use to explore distinct aspirations without spreading themselves too thin. R. J. Cutler, currently a documentary producer and director, has been a theater director, a radio producer, and a journalist. He says he just follows his interests but once committed to a given project, he works on it with absolute single-mindedness. If project nomads move from project to project too often, however, they may lose their way and never gain mastery over anything.

The Interdisciplinarian

Like a many-armed Hindu goddess, these hungry souls weave together their many interests into a single project. A performance artist like Chris Wink of Blue Man Group, for instance, must write, drum, act, direct, and conduct the business of his show, though he is working toward one show with one group of people. He needs a variety of different skills ranging from public schmoozing to private contemplation, from writing about new technology to chomping Cap'n Crunch in polyrhythms. In a different context, Lynn Gordon also has the life of an interdisciplinarian. In her work as a product inventor, she thinks up concepts, makes prototypes of her visual and text-based ideas, manages a staff of artists and writers, and sells ideas to companies and publishing houses.

The Tightrope Walker

With two careers always in the balance, the tightrope walker maintains two meaningful kinds of work simultaneously. My student Jason, for example, splits his attention between his teaching and his theater work, maintaining both a theater company and a school simultaneously. All highly involved parents who work must, at least for a couple of decades, walk this dual-career tightrope. Although it is often enviable for its richness and complexity, the life of the tightrope walker is a precarious and demanding path. Not only is it easy to fall into one arena and thereby neglect the other, the energy required to stay in balance may make forward movement slow and difficult.

The Whirling Dervish

This model was created by one of my students who sought to show how her three different careers—visual art, teaching, and documentary film—together led her toward her ultimate political and spiritual goals. In creating this model, Meg realized that she needed to do her three kinds of work in a specific order. For a few months of the year, she painted. This work not only fulfilled her solitary yearnings, it provided her with ideas she used as an art teacher in public schools. In turn, working with teenagers from a variety of ethnic and socioeconomic backgrounds gave her ideas for her political documentaries about education, youth, and race relations. Finally, exhausted from the extroverted, multileveled work of filmmaking, she would again retire to her studio to paint watercolor landscapes ... and so, the cycle began again. The whirling dervish has turned out to be a popular model for many of my students who cannot imagine focusing on less than three full careers at a time. What is important about the whirling dervish is that the three careers are interdependent on one another. They don't pull you in three different directions, they spin you inward!

The Wood Nymph

Like the branches of a tree, the Wood Nymph's career flows from a single trunk but splits into divergent but related goals. For instance, Nina began as a yoga teacher, then began studying related forms of dance movement and bodywork. The dance movement techniques led her to develop a class combining yoga and meditative movement. The bodywork classes led her to organize a consortium of other bodyworkers to start a studio offering training to other bodyworkers and medical caregivers. After twenty years working in the field of movement, touch, and health, she had worked as a teacher, bodyworker, and coleader of an organization, and she was writing a book on alternative medicine.

The wood nymph's life has much the same continuity as the monocled monk's, but their work is manifested in very different activities. Instead of being focused on developing a single craft or action (like writing, painting, or dance), they have devoted themselves to a single subject matter (like the world of alternative medicine) about which they become experts on numerous levels, not only as practitioners.

EXERCISE

Which model do you now use in your life?
Which model would you like to use?

Often my students recognize that the model that they are currently using doesn't work for them. I hear things like, "Right now I'm a tightrope walker, but I yearn to be monocled monk," or "I'm naturally a project nomad but I think I need to learn to integrate all my interests into a more multimedia project like the interdisciplinarian." If none of the models in the previous pages describe your ideal, then draw your own in the space below. Just remember not to create a model that will drive you crazy with multiplicity. (And if it works for you, please send me a copy!)

Now you are ready to begin the process of creating your specific goal. You have excavated many ideas, considered artistic types and day jobs, explored three possible futures for yourself, and decided on the overarching organization of your career goals. Now it's time to hone in on your most essential commitment and mold it into a thing of beauty.

What path, out of the many paths you've considered in this process, do you have the energy, enthusiasm, and desire to pursue today and for the next _____ years? (If you are torn between many career ambitions, another way to think about this question is, which of your endeavors do you want to be on the front burner for a while?)

What event or achievement would represent the apogee of your aspirations? (Go ahead and think big: win an Oscar, earn a million dollars, publish a novel acclaimed as a masterpiece, a retrospective show at MoMA, and so on.)

What achievements would represent the first, second, and third milestones in your career as you have defined it above?

1.
2.
3.

Star the one you think you want to use as your goal.

Use Your Goal, Don't Let Your Goal Use You

The goal is an act of imagination because it is like creating a character with great powers of persuasion. While you need to recognize and respect this formidable figment, you should keep in mind that it is something you have intentionally imagined into being to consolidate and focus your energies. Sometimes the energy of the goal leads to other kinds of work and renders the specific aim of the goal obsolete. For instance, Bill's goal was to finish his first novel. In the process of writing the first half of his book, he developed a writing habit and began to dabble with short personal essays that he sold to the local daily newspaper. He realized that essay writing came naturally to him—much more so than novel writing. He put the novel aside and began selling his essays to national magazines. Though he never set out to become an essayist, it was the goal of writing a novel that ultimately led him there. In this way, the goal need not ever "come true" in order for it to do its work.

Here are the practical parameters of a good creative goal:

It Lies Within the Arc of Your Faith

When you create a goal, remember that you want it to inspire you, not depress you. If you create a goal which you cannot for a moment entertain as possible, you probably won't want to work toward it. On the other hand, if you pick something you can accomplish in the next month or two, then your goal won't help you venture beyond your present situation. Just as artists work from both their conscious and unconscious experiences, let your goal be a mixture of clarity and mystery, light and darkness.

It Is Rich in Visual and Emotional Imagery

The more sensory clarity your goal has, the more power its engine has to move you forward. What does your work space look like while you are working toward this goal? How do you feel when the work is going well? How do you feel on the day of success? Who will you share the joy of your accomplishment with? What sounds, smells, and tastes attend your days of working toward this goal?

Explore the minute images and sensations you imagine on the day you achieve your goal.

If this step was difficult for you, you can develop imagery by reading biographies of people who have walked paths like yours, by surrounding yourself with people whose lives inspire you, by discussing your ideas with friends, and by practicing creative visualization.

IT IS IN THE AREA THAT EXCITES YOU THE MOST

This is vital. If your goal is not in an arena that completely thrills you, eventually you will be disappointed. Even when demanding jobs and other responsibilities prevent you from spending time on your highest goal, having that goal present in your mind can help you overcome obstacles. When essayist Sallie Tisdale was struggling through nursing school as a single mother and had no time to write, she still remembered her ultimate goal. "I went to nursing school to support my writing. That was always clear to me." Though developing a secondary career to support your primary goal can be arduous, understanding your final goal can help you stay focused through all sorts of complexity.

IT'S OBJECTIVE

If you say, "My goal is to be a good drummer," you might never let yourself think you are good enough. Or, if you're feeling indulgent, you can decide tomorrow, "I'm good, I quit." It's better to say, "My goal is to join or form a band of musicians I respect and get my first professional gig." Or, "My goal is to sign a contract with a small record label and produce my first CD."

The more specific you can make the final event or action, the more power it will have for you. For instance, "I want to contribute to the world," is a powerful and admirable impulse, but it won't help you decide what to do when you wake up in the morning.

If you think you need to, make your goal even more specific.

IT IS AN EVENT OR AN OCCURRENCE THAT HAPPENS IN TIME

As an artist you already understand that you don't simply "make art"; you paint, pluck strings, or shoot film on a specific project in a limited time frame. When I hear students say, "I want to build a community center for artists someday," I ask lots of questions. How long do you think it will take you? How long are you willing to spend on it? When would you like to have it finished? All goals created in my class have attendant dates. Sometimes these dates may seem arbitrary, but as long as we are mortal beings, time is a necessary ingredient for every human endeavor. We may as well include time in the equation of our dreams from the very start.

On the other hand, the time lines shouldn't be too rigid. They should not be the only factor in measuring your success. You must hold onto your goal with a firm but flexible grip. Fate, chance, the world, your desires will all affect your goal and how much time you will need to execute it.

Write down the date when you would like to have achieved your goal.

Possible Traps Around Creating Goals

The Dangers of Multitasking

Beware of the temptation to create a goal that is really many goals masquerading as one. The more goals you juggle, the more time you will need to organize and decide what's most important on any given day. Setting multiple goals can be a diligent, neurotic way to avoid commitment.

Callia, a struggling sculptor living in a big city, said her goal was "to start a rural artists' retreat." She explained that she would live at the retreat, working as a full-time sculptor (showing her work in a gallery in the city), and then travel several months of the year as a photojournalist studying the lost cultures of the Amazon. Though I thought her vision of this life was remarkably inventive and tantalizing, I felt like she was underestimating the enormous and ongoing work of running an artists' colony. She mistook the experience of being on a retreat with creating one. Had she already developed a full-fledged sculpting and photojournalism career, she could have maintained these careers while creating the artists' retreat. However, she was a beginner at both. I encouraged her to prioritize her goals and focus initially on the most important of her ambitions. Once she had accomplished even the basic elements of one of these ambitions, the others would become easier. A career as a photojournalist would give her sculptor self valuable knowledge about the workings of the media. Running a retreat would provide her with a community of artists that would help inspire her art, and so forth. The secret that many chronic multitaskers never learn is that expertise in one area opens doors horizontally into others. That's how baseball players get to write books and performance artists get jobs as professors.

If you are like Callie, with big dreams in arenas where you have little background, set yourself free from the prison of eternal possibilities and begin walking toward a single powerful image. Don't set yourself up for failure even before you start by creating a goal that has as many snake heads as Medusa's hair and is just as venomous.

Grass Is Always Greener Syndrome

Sometimes people are tempted to create goals far removed from their experience. One punk rocker told me he was thinking of opening a grocery store chain. A banker explained that his fantasy was to have a life of "pure artistic freedom and survive on eight hundred dollars a month." If you are tempted to create a goal that is radically different from your entire lived experience, you may be suffering from Grass Is Always Greener Syndrome. It's easy to idealize a life that seems to have none of the problems of your own. But remember: Many of the problems you are having now will follow you into very different situations. For instance, you may think that your problems arise from a lack of money, time, connections, or material goods. But chances are, your problems are more related to the ways in which you fail to use what you *do* have than all the things you lack.

Perhaps you want to quit your full-time job in a high-stress office environment because it doesn't allow you enough time for your artistic projects. Suddenly you have a lot of time on your hands, but it's uncomfortable because you are used to other people organizing your time for you. Every time you sit down to do your art, something inside you whispers, "Where's the money coming from?" Your savings are running out, so you begin a job search. The search takes over your life. Once again you are wrestling with the ticking monster and losing. The problem springs from the fact that you haven't yet developed the skills to negotiate the dizzying freedom and financial complexity of an artist's life.

Perhaps you have been scraping by, going into debt but putting your art first. Fed up with the constant anxiety, you decide to get a "real job." But because you never learned to budget your money (how could you budget what wasn't there?), now you continue to live as you lived before, scraping by from paycheck to paycheck, spending three times the amount. You again blame money for your lack of initiative, but money is only the crutch you lean on to avoid the hard work of pursuing your dreams. You've locked yourself into a job for a lot of financial and materialistic reasons that you don't necessarily value.

Caught Between Ambition and a Life

Sometimes it's difficult to create a goal that expresses our whole self. More often than not, goals express our ambitious side, ignoring our personal needs. When creating your goal, think not only about the pinnacles of power, prestige, and mastery you wish to scale but the kind of moment-to-moment day you want to have. If you are a thirty-year-old female who wants four children before the age of thirty-five and a career as a professional dancer, then you may need to rethink these goals and compromise. Would one child be enough? How about choreographing and teaching to take a break from performing?

As you compare your ambitions and your daily desires for leisure, friendship, and recreation, do you see any contradictions between your personal and professional goals?

Creating Your Goal

The basic principles are simple. A good goal usually entails something you can imagine, something you really would love to do, and something specific. Your goal should also represent the first milestone in your most important arena of creative pursuit.

Here are some examples of creative goals developed in my workshops.

Rebecca: A steelworker and mother of four, wants to get into journalism.

Goal: To write and sell my first freelance article for the daily newspaper.

Means of support: To start a handywoman business, doing carpentry, seismic retrofitting, and gardening.

Time line: One year.

Desire (What's at the heart of this goal? What makes me want to do it so bad?)*:* I want to learn to shape my thoughts into a form for the public. I want to develop a job which will provide me an ongoing opportunity to learn.

Images: Running around the city interviewing people, sitting at my desk with my cat in my lap, talking to my editor on the phone ... we're laughing.

Chitra: A former graduate student in English.

Goal: To start a nonprofit that deals in policy issues for international women and children.

Means of support: To work for other similar nonprofits in various capacities.

Time line: Four years.

Desire: I want to create a situation in which I can think about global issues but not in an academic context. I want to be able to travel and work toward the betterment of women and children.

Images: Working with four other women in a sunlit studio. Traveling to India for a conference. Meetings with my board of directors—all interesting women from a variety of backgrounds.

Hardy: A working actor and visual artist.

Goal: To create and perform a full-length puppet show.

Means of support: To expand the marketing of my one-of-a-kind boxes and other crafts in a variety of upscale stores. To begin making beautifully made puppets as gift items.

Time line: Eighteen months.

Desire: I really want to combine my acting and visual arts into a form that I can conceivably take on the road. I want to be a puppeteer for adults!

Images: Performing to a full house of raucous hipsters one night and a senior citizens' home the next. Touring through the Northeast, performing at colleges and prisons. Making puppets alone in my studio as the clock strikes midnight.

Now it's your turn. I recommend choosing a goal with a time line of somewhere between one year and five years. Anything less than a year is probably a subgoal and anything more than five is probably too long-term to get you working toward it today. Most of my students choose goals with timelines between twelve and thirty months. Write your goal, time line, means of financial support, and desire in the spaces below. If you have no ideas about your means of support, then leave it blank. Future chapters will address this sticky question.

Goal:

Timeline:

Means of Support:

Desire (What's at the heart of this goal?)*:*

Images:

Once you have written down your goal, go over it with a friend. Ask them if they think you are underestimating yourself or being overly ambitious. Make sure this friend is someone you completely trust, someone who has no competitive feelings toward you and thinks very highly of your abilities. If you can't trust any of your friends, by all means keep your goal a secret and begin looking around for a person with whom you can cultivate a supportive creative friendship.

EXERCISES IN TRANSFORMING GOALS INTO ACTION

1. Every night as you go to sleep imagine yourself working on this goal.

    Every morning jot down your dreams and any message you might be receiving about your goal.

2. During your daily action, think about the first five steps you can take to embark on the path toward your goal.

3. Personal Homework: Do two of these steps.

    Transfer your new ideas into your Adventure Book.

4. What did you learn in this chapter? What's missing? How can you seek out this information or experience?

LORETTA STAPLES, DESIGNER AND ENTREPRENEUR

As owner and founder of u dot i, a San Francisco–based interface design company, Loretta Staples uses a mix of analytical and artistic skills to run a company, write essays on design, and design complex computer environments. As the only person in her family to attend college, Staples depended upon her curiosity, her confidence, and her intellect to develop her career. When she graduated from Yale, she had no support system or financial security. As an African-American and Japanese-American woman working in a field largely run by white men, she embodies the most creative, defiant spirit of entrepreneurial self-directedness. A quintessential thinker type, her attraction to art, business, and writing all revolve around her fascination with ideas and the joys of conceptual problem solving. Yet she avoids the pitfalls of pointless pondering by being stubbornly goal-oriented and pragmatic in her attitudes toward energy and time.

Since this interview, she has accepted a tenure-track position teaching graphic and interface design at the University of Michigan at Ann Arbor. Without a formal teaching background or any graduate degrees, Staples received the offer based on her work as a thinker, designer, and entrepreneur.

Q: What does your workday look like?

A: Typically I get to the office at eight in the morning. Most of my time is really spent on the phone, or writing E-mail, or writing proposals and managing projects. I still do designing and I still do production, but I actually don't want to do as much designing and production as I have done. I think one of the things that differentiates me from other designers that I know who have their own business is I really love managing and strategizing business. I consider it really creative work. As a design endeavor it's so challenging. It's so much more interesting than designing a poster or a book or even an interface, because there are a lot of interfaces you have to design to make a business work correctly.

Q: What are the internal elements of your creative process?

A: I'm extremely analytical; I tend to be very thorough. I like to think deeply and thoroughly about a lot of things. I also use writing a lot in the course of my business day—my business decisions—to help me clarify my thoughts and my concepts about things.

I've been a designer for a long time, but actually I'm much more of a conceptual person than a visual person, and much more of a verbal person than a visual person. So, for instance, I don't really draw or sketch or do any kind of representational stuff that often. Most of my ideas are carried in my head and then at some point realized in written form, or in some schematic or diagrammatic form.

I'm trying to write more as an endeavor that's independent of my business. It's been interesting trying to fit that into my schedule, because it takes a certain kind of quietude or depth of concentration. . . . Lately it has been hard for me to carve out the space for that. But I have found certain things really useful. When I finished a recent essay, most of the final writing I did at lunchtime, where I'd go and eat a sandwich with my draft spread around, and I'd write for half an hour or forty-five minutes. I did that each day for a week and a half. It worked perfectly. But for whatever reason, I haven't been able to carry through that momentum over this last couple of months. I am trying to figure out how to change my life or restructure my day to make space for that kind of writing.

I also have some sculptures I want to make. I actually have a sculpture I want to make that's a piece of software, and it would require funding because I'd need to hire a programmer to do it, a linguist to work on it, and I'm also trying to figure out how I can fit that in. I don't seem to have enough time or resources to fully realize all the things that are in my head right now. So maybe it's a scheduling problem.

Q: Where did you learn self-discipline?

A: I feel like I'm self-taught in pretty much everything. I taught myself interface design. When I was growing up I was really into crafts, and I taught myself how to knit and do all sorts of needlecrafts. I always read how-to books; I'd go to the library. By the time I was seven, I knew how to make a barbecue grill out of a recycled gasoline can and a piece of galvanized mesh. I knew how to make party favors carved out of peach pits so that they looked like little baskets. I have always been very self-motivated and curious.

Q: Is anyone else in your family similar?

A: None of my immediate family is alive now. But when I was growing up I'd say my father and brother were both very self-motivated also. My brother was a self-taught musician; he played every instrument. He was self-taught in everything. My father was very smart and talented;

he used to build things and he could draw, so there was a lot of talent in my family. My life has gone in a lot of cycles, and my current level of productivity is very hyper; I'm really hyperproductive. I think it's a little weird, frankly, and it's a form of compensation, I think, for the fact that a lot of unexpected things have happened in my life that have been extremely traumatic. The loss of my family being one. The part of me that is aware of the unexpected things that can completely transform a person's life has stimulated in me this kind of counterresponse of wanting to be very specifically productive, and very proactive about governing the parts of my fate that I can. I do think there's a very strong relationship between this imminent fatalism on the one hand, and then this desire to make up for that by really commandeering everything I can toward the ends that I want to fulfill. I think that's where I get a lot of my current motivation.

Q: Do you have a support system of people that help you?

A: I have a circle of friends who are very supportive, but I must say that I find most of my strength and motivation from within. I do often seek the advice of people who are in a position to know more than I do about a given subject, however. When I incorporated the business and hired my first employee, I was definitely experiencing the first of my entrepreneurial growing pains. The first resource I went to was the San Francisco Renaissance Entrepreneurship Center. I had heard about them through the press; they had been written up in local papers. The goal of their class was to write a business plan. That was a tremendous help to me, it really was. It was really helpful for me to be around other small-business owners who were just trying to make their business work.

The thing I really liked about the Renaissance Center was their approach in talking about business. The discussion was always done in the context of one's larger personal goal. That is, the conception of the business was always highly personalized. It wasn't like, "The business is out there." It was like, "This is something that you're making for yourself, presumably to fulfill certain personal goals or needs or ambitions. Be clear about what they are. Because there are going to be times when running the business will be extremely difficult. And you're going to need to know, to remind yourself what you're really in this for." I really liked that. Because I think it's really not emphasized in most of what you read about business.

I am very pro-entrepreneurship, because I do feel it's one of the few opportunities that we have to carve out our destiny in American culture. And I think it's really quite easy to do. I don't think it's necessarily difficult. It can be difficult if you put forth complex business propositions. But it doesn't have to be.

Q: Do you have any tricks you play on yourself when you don't feel like working?

A: I don't let myself feel overly deprived. By that I mean if I don't feel like working on something, I try, at least momentarily, not to work on it. I don't force-feed myself a regimen of what I should be doing. I find that that really helps. So I'm not functioning in this punishing framework, where, "You were supposed to do that and you didn't, so you're bad, and now you have to make up for it by doing double time." I just don't do any of that usual guilt-tripping stuff on myself at all.

I don't try to compete with myself in trying to make something of myself. And I can honestly say I do think it's a real key to success. Something gets unblocked or uninhibited by the fact that it's not a contest. I'm not trying to prove whether I can write or not. I don't know whether I can or can't, but that's not what I'm interested in. It's the writing that I'm interested in, and the process of what engaging in writing means, and what I learn from that engagement.

Q: How did you support yourself before getting a job as a designer?

A: I started out as an insurance policy typist. I fell in love with someone who was college-educated. He was the first person I had ever known who went to college, and he kind of introduced me to this new world. After I graduated, I ended up going to a graphic design program at Rhode Island School of Design for a year. I loved the program, worked like a maniac. And then I moved out here and did exhibit development work for a while.

I wanted to learn a set of skills that I could apply as an independent worker if I chose to do that. I really loved graphic design as an undergraduate. Yale at that time was the premier design institution, teaching Basel pedagogy—the design there was incredibly rich, it was a very fertile environment. I really loved the idea that graphic design was sort of a trade skill. So I thought, it would be nice to go to school in graphic design, and have the opportunity of working for a company, or working on my own.

Desktop publishing started to get off the ground in the middle eighties. And the fact that I had formal design training meant that I had a body of conceptual skills in design that I could apply. So I was freelancing back then, and then ended up working for a design firm called The Understanding Business. It was probably the largest Mac-run design studio in the country at that time.

I ended up leaving them because I wanted to go into interface design. I just quit my job. I had no prospects at all, nothing lined up, no savings, nothing. I had no training. But I was just very clear that I wanted to do that. I was really inspired from my personal relationship with the Macintosh computer. I really was. The Mac was like a really good friend. I did a lot of research, I read all the literature in the field, I joined the professional organization. Fortunately I got two projects that allowed me to do some interface design for multimedia. After nine months of doing that, Apple recruited me to be a designer there. I worked at Apple for two very turbulent years, during which time I was laid off twice within fifteen months. This is after having been recruited by them. After the second layoff, I had an opportunity to interview with the system software group at Apple, but I had already gotten really good freelance projects and I just thought, I can do better on my own.

Q: What was the most frustrating period in terms of development?

A: I think the worst episode for me was in January of 1994. I was in this office space downtown, and at this point I had been in business for about a year and a half. Everything was just great. I had an endless stream of work, I never had to look for work, people always called me. Then, in December of '93, the work started to trickle off, and I thought, Well, maybe it has to do with the holidays. Well, January first came and went and I was waiting for the phone to ring, and there was just no work. So I thought, Well, I'll wait until the fifteenth. Still no work. Now I'm at the very end of the month, and there's no work except for one long-term client who I'd worked with for the past year and a half, but nothing else, and I really started to worry. I have a house, a mortgage, this new office, and I'm incorporated, I have my salary and I have to pay withholding taxes on a monthly basis against that salary. I literally had no savings, nothing. I had no fallback, except a little credit card money. That's how a lot of small businesses work, on personal credit cards.

I used the time productively. I basically used that period of time to develop marketing materials. I came up with a promotional booklet; I wrote a lot about what the business was, defining the products and services, really trying to think of how to position the business in a client's eyes. So I put together some marketing materials, and that was good. I wrote lots of letters reminding people that I was around. It didn't produce any immediate results, but it's always good practice just to let people know that you're there.

Anyway, to continue the story, my mortgage is due in a few days. I don't have anything. I'm really worried. It's very stressful. I had a meeting lined up with my one client. At that meeting Wayne, my client, says—and I think he's joking—"I need to talk with you about whether you would be open to accepting advance payment for your services over the next several months." I thought it was a joke. I thought he'd heard of my situation and was just teasing. And he said, "Oh no, I'm serious. My corporation's fiscal year ends at the end of this month and I have some funds I need to spend. What would you like? How's ten thousand? Is ten thousand alright?"

I was to find that episodes like this would happen again and again. So I think that when you're really clear the world responds with clarity. It responds with the same degree of clarity that your consciousness is operating in. It's very magical. I do think it's a gift from God, I think it's a very cosmic thing. And it's happened to me many, many, many times. It's something I really believe. Because I believe it so strongly, that's why I become so frustrated with friends of mine who have dreams that they don't seek to fulfill. Because I know that if they put themselves out there, and kind of surrendered themselves, that it would work. But they just want to play it safe, or whatever.

Q: Have your thoughts about what success means changed at all?

A: I don't really think of success, per se. I am heavy into goal setting, though. I am the biggest goal-setting freak you can ever hope to be. It's the only way you get anything done in this world. But I don't just set goals, I check myself. When I set a goal, it's always against time, and then I check when the day comes; did I do it or didn't I?

Q: A lot of creative people don't like to set goals because they feel it limits them.

A: And I'm very sympathetic to that, because I do think creativity is a very mysterious thing, but I also think that our culture, and the culture of artists, has a romantic attachment to a certain version of creativity that's hard to let go of. I think that effort, the magic ingredient that shapes human will, can be harnessed or directed. And a lot of the goal setting I do is around where my effort goes. Literally where my energy goes, what are my tasks during the day, how they're allocated. I think those things are really quite easy to structure.

It's interesting though, because I do think there's a kind of aesthetic objection to it. I primarily describe myself to people as a businessperson, so I'm not offended by these ideas at all. But a lot of people I know are appalled by how I describe myself. They see me as an arty person or something.

Q: If there's one piece of advice you could give a beginner in your field, what would it be?

A: To really know the field. Know the area. A lot of times strangers call me and they're interested in interface design and they want to talk with me, and it irritates me. Do your homework. When I decided I was interested in this field, I did my research. I learned what the professional organizations were. I read the literature in the field. I found out what it was about. So I do think really knowing your field is very important, and being motivated enough to find the information out on your own, and being thorough and diligent about it.

The other thing that is really, really important that people just don't think about is: Think about what kind of day you want to have. Literally. Think of how you want your day to be. How do you want to wake up? What time of day do you want to wake up? What do you want to see when you wake up? Do you want to see another person, do you want to look out the window and see the sunshine? When you go to work, do you want to get in the car, do you want to walk into the next room? I find that so often people think of their lives and their careers as a complete abstraction. "I want to go into law." What does that mean? I have no idea. What do lawyers do? I don't know what they do. "I want to go to medical school." "I want to help people." I don't know what those things actually mean; the words are so abstract. I do think you can actually envision how you want your day to be. Who do you want to bump into; who do you not want to see? When do you want to eat? When do you want to sleep? Do you want to be indoors or outdoors? I feel like all of those things are so important in terms of whether or not you're going to enjoy the day.

Then figure out what kind of tasks fit into that day. I think that's a much better way to do it. Because I've met lots of people who thought they wanted to go into law. They went to law school, started practicing, hated it. I think it's so easy to have an idea about what something's like, and realize later that it's not like that at all.

The other magic ingredient—and this is something I'm obsessive about—is communication. It pays a lot to think about how you communicate with the world. Whether it's inanimate objects, or human beings, vendors, clients, whatever it is, what is your communication style and what do you enjoy or not enjoy? Like for me, I'm really a reclusive person; I'm very much a loner. But it's interesting because in business, I'm really quite good at client relations, and I'm very good at presentations and stuff like that. But it's funny because I think that's my one little arena to be public. Otherwise I'm an extremely private person.

I think it's a very important life skill to be clear with other people and with the world about what you want and what your expectations are. The more you know yourself as a communicator, and the situations in which communication takes place, the more you will be able to structure a life for yourself that is optimum for you. If you're a very introverted, shy person, and you go into business for yourself, and you have to get clients and present, it's may be really difficult and painful. It could be very unpleasant. It could be something you might learn to love, and you might develop skills in new areas. But for a while it's going to be really painful. And you should know that at the outset.

So, communication, goals, and knowing what kind of day you want. Those are the three keys.

9

A Map to the Moon

Planning Your Project

> Did you observe to whom the accidents happen? Chance favors only the prepared mind.
>
> —LOUIS PASTEUR

E. L. Doctorow says that writing novels is like driving a car at night: You only see twenty feet ahead of you at any given time, but you can travel a thousand miles. This is a wonderful and useful metaphor for all large-scale creative projects. We never really know what will happen next, and yet we must move forward and maintain the faith that someday we will arrive. At the same time, most journeys never take place without a destination, a sense of direction, and a working map. After the last chapter you should have an idea of your final destination. This chapter will help you make your map.

Your plan will teach you how to break actions down into bite-size tasks and draw the path to your goal. It will also help you embrace a new attitude toward all your creative work, an attitude that cuts through passivity and fear and concentrates your energies on concrete actions.

In the next exercises you will create a visual path from your goal back to the present moment. The mapping style you choose should depend on your own creative inclinations. If you are conceptual, draw diagrams; visual, paint pictures; verbal, write narrative; kinetic, act it out physically. But before you begin deciding on your particular style of mapping your future, first think about what you want your map to do.

Here are my basic parameters; can you think of any others?

- The map organizes the project in time. It helps me see the steps to the goal in the order that they need to happen.
- The map clarifies what I can do *now* to begin my work. It links the distant future with the present moment in a very concrete way.
- The map illuminates my black holes, the parts of my endeavor that seem murky if not downright confounding.

In developing these creative mapping processes, I looked at the planning techniques of different art forms: storyboarding for film, scoring for music and choreography, blueprinting for architecture, clustering for creative writing, and sketching for paintings. Listomania is probably the easiest for anyone who likes lists. Scoring creates a more aesthetically pleasing linear model and helps you visualize the emotional arc of your project. Blueprinting is definitely for the spatially minded, for those attracted to the idea of peeling off lists of small tasks to throw away forever. Storyboarding is for the inherently nonlinear thinker. The tasks are written down first, then organized into families, and finally put in order of their importance. No matter which model you choose, I hope you can use it to create your own planning system that works best for your creativity.

If you use these techniques diligently for a year or so, they will become a natural ingredient in your problem-solving process. Even if you feel ambivalent about the specific goal you created in the last chapter, working through these exercises will still be extremely valuable. Goals are only as powerful as the imaginary paths that they illuminate from the nebulous tomorrow to the concrete today. These planning techniques offer you a chance to practice your creative night vision and see these imaginary paths in vivid detail.

Step 1 (For Everyone)

Clustering: Letting the Compulsive Worrier Run Wild

Often when we are faced with a large project, we are overwhelmed by a swarm of unorganized thoughts. We think of tasks, worries, needs, and secondary goals; we see images both terrible and fabulous; we hear voices that are encouraging, disparaging, and irrelevant. The onslaught is so overwhelming that the very thought of the project makes us jump up to eat a peach, walk upon the beach, call that unemployed friend, shop for the perfect pair of socks, watch three consecutive reruns of *Paramedic Live*.

Clustering, a common creative writing technique, allows you to express these divergent feelings and impulses without organizing or explaining them. When you face the myriad responses to your project, you can let go of your anxiety and begin to think more clearly.

As any woman who has been pregnant will attest, creation is not an orderly, coherent process, but a sticky, painful, and beautiful mess. It is the unfurling of your spirit in the realm of action. Honoring the emotional and logistical complexity of your project will not only enrich the experience a thousandfold, it will allow you to avoid the two quicksands of self-deception: first, that it's easy and you should already know how to do it; second, that it's impossibly mystical and subject to fate, and therefore you have no control over how it happens.

1. Place your goal in the middle of the page in a circle. Then, radiating from the circle, jot down *anything* that comes to mind: specific tasks, problems, feelings, related goals. Just let the storm of your brain wash over the page.

2. If one of the ideas leads to other related thoughts, radiate more stuff around that idea. Let yourself go until you are depleted—until everything that was *inside* is *outside*.

Crazy Cluster

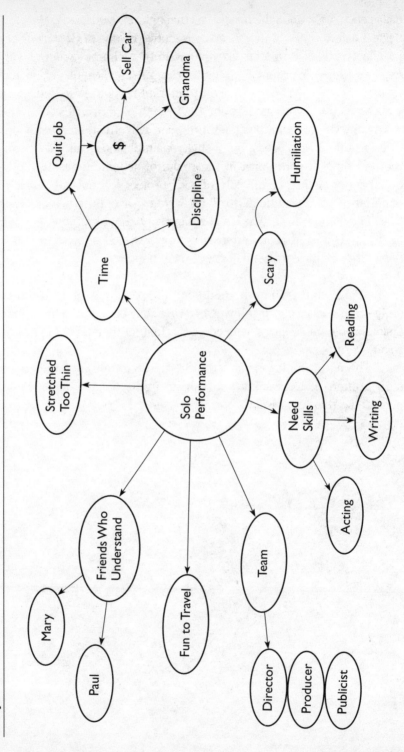

Step 2
Making an Action Plan

On the following pages you will find four models of planning: scoring, storyboarding, listomania, and blueprinting. Choose one of them and use it to chart a path toward your goal. Refer to your "cluster" to remind yourself of all the elements of your project. If one mapping process doesn't work for you, then try another, but don't overburden this decision. Follow your instincts; select the mapping model that seems the most fun and practical for you. If you need simple, elegant lists, choose listomania. If you want to see the concomitant unfolding of a multilayered project, use scoring. If you want a picture of your overall life and how your projects relate to one another, do blueprinting. If you wish to organize a complex project in which you understand the little tasks but not how to organize them, try storyboarding.

If you are technologically inclined, there are a host of "flowchart" CD-ROMs and software that can help you plan a large project. Because flowcharts are such a common planning technique in business and education, I have skipped them in favor of more artistic models. If you want to read about them, *Wishcraft,* by Barbara Sher, and *Organizing for the Creative Person,* by Dorothy Lehmkuhl and Dolores Cotter Lamping, both have chapters on creating flowcharts.

In each of these four planning models, you will probably reach a point where your mind goes blank and seems to suck the whole project into negative space, threatening to implode. These are the places I call "black holes": the places where you know you need *something* but you don't know how to get it. To shine some light on these black holes, you will apply a number of different creative approaches, collaborative and individual.

Planning Model 1: Blueprinting Your Project

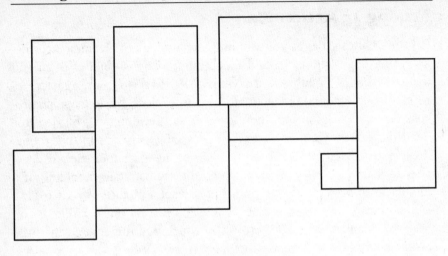

Materials: large white sheet of paper and pieces of tracing paper of equal size, pencil, pen, colored pencil (optional).

1. On an opaque piece of paper, lay out your plans for your project as if they are the rooms of a new house. Use a pencil so you can erase. When the floorplan is just as you like it, trace the pencil lines in pen. For more important areas, give the rooms more square footage. Place related rooms next to one another. It may take a couple of sketches to get the design just right.
2. Write in the permanent "fixtures" within each room. These fixtures represent the ongoing actions for each area of work. For instance, a fixture in becoming a musician is practicing your instrument (See sample 1, next page).
3. Write in the long-term subgoals in each area of work.
4. Place a sheet of tracing paper over your floorplan. On this sheet, furnish your house by writing short-term (one to two months) projects in each of the rooms. Trace the ongoing activities from the floorplan as well (See sample 2).
5. After you finish your short-term projects in each of the rooms, strip off the top layer and create a new sheet of short-term projects, incorporating the next step: the mid-term projects.
6. For those arenas where you don't know how to go about fulfilling your needs, place a question mark in the appropiate room of the plan. *These are your black holes.*

Sample 1: *Same floorplan with permanent fixtures (ongoing actions) and long-term goals*

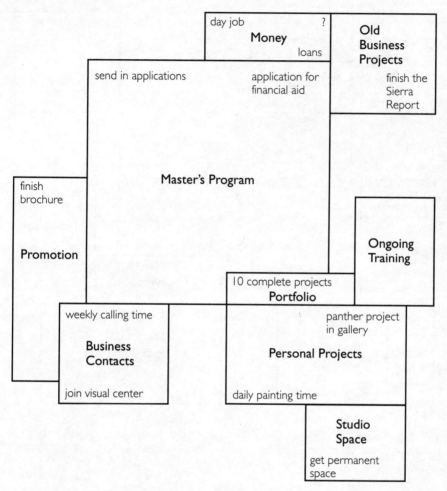

Goal: to earn a living as a freelance designer by 1999 with an M.F.A.

Blueprinting Your Project (cont'd)

Sample 2: *First tracing paper furnished with short-term goals as well as ongoing actions*

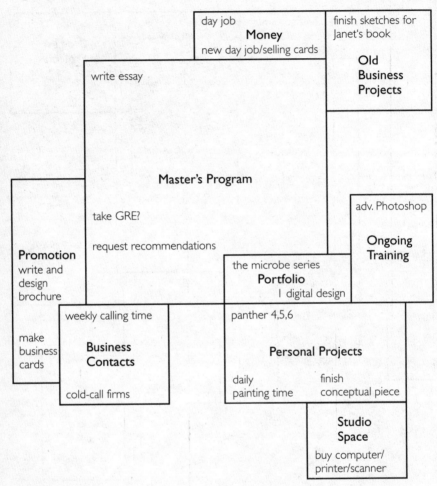

Goal: to earn a living as a freelance graphic designer by August 1999 with an M.F.A.

Planning Model 2: Scoring Your Project

Materials: scoring sheets, pencil, pen.

1. In the five lines in each staff, write the four primary arenas of your creative and groundwork (See example). By "creative work" I mean the very essence of your art. "Groundwork" represents all the stuff that needs to happen to bring your art to the world—the business or the logistics.
2. Count out your project in months, allowing each bar to be equal to a month. For instance, if the approximate time for the project is 12 months, then make sure you have 12 bars in your score.
3. Work by halving. Write in goals at the half marks, then quarter marks, then eighth marks and so on until you have completely filled in your score with tasks and subgoals in each of the arenas.
4. Now read through your score, attending to its emotional flow as you would a beautiful piece of music. Add musical dynamics terms such as *forte, adagio, piano,* and *crescendo* to signal the different moods, speeds, and intensities you'll need at certain times. This is a fun way to express your feelings as the project unfolds—adding a crescendo when you feel the chaos mounting, etc.
5. Remember the lesson taught by all great composers: silence is sometimes more beautiful than sound. To that end, don't forget to score in plenty of rests in both clefs.
6. Now post your musical score and allow it to keep you on track in all areas of your project. Use the score not only to see the overall flow of the project and foresee what is coming next, but to keep time in the present. Use it to focus on the kind of music you are making today.
7. Wherever you are not sure of the way you can succeed in a given area, place a question mark in the appropiate bar. *These are your black holes.*

Scoring Your Project (cont'd) Goal: To create and perform a solo work.

The treble clef represents the purely artistic areas of your project. The bass clef represents the project's groundwork: the logistical, material, financial, and business activities that you must do to fully manifest your work in the world.

TREBLE: The Creative Work

		pianissimo	rough of 1st ten-minute section	rewrite 1st/rough 2nd
script	create writing habit collect 10 fragments		rough of 1st ten-minute section	rewrite 1st/rough 2nd
acting	sign up for class	class	class	
visuals	sketch sets/props			
sound				

BASS: The Groundwork

			deciso	
time	schedule writing time			cut down to thirty hours
space	visit theaters	approach producers/theaters	finalize contract with theater	
publicity				
money	write fund-raising letter	write two grants		

script	write 3rd and 4th section	finish rough script	do reading	do 10 minutes at group show
acting	alexander	play in studio!	interview/hire director	
visuals	three design ideas	get input—choose	design props for 10-minute seg.	final set design
sound	compose songs			

Scoring Your Project (cont'd)

Table 1

time				
space	find rehearsal space			
publicity		sketch posters	do photo shoot	send out press packets
money	plan budget based on income	move to cheaper place		

forte

Table 2

script	revisions			Performance
acting	begin rehearsing	rehearsal four x's a week	Rehearsal five x's a week	Performance
visuals	make props	build set	design lighting	Performance
sound	record music tracks		tech for sound	Performance

Table 3

time	go into overdrive	use sick time?		
space	visit theater			
publicity	hire publicist?	harass press	postering/friend ticket drive	
money	? ? ? ? ?			

Scoring Your Project (cont'd)

TREBLE: The Creative Work

BASS: The Groundwork

Planning Model 3: Listomania   Goal: To finish book project (list for this book halfway through first draft).

ONGOING	PRESSING	SHORT-TERM	MID-TERM	LONG-TERM
walking/yoga	Chapter 8	finish diagrams	weekend away!	finish interviews
writing	Chapter 9	finish models	organize quotes	format interviews
reading	call Mom	Chapter 10	call agents	do rewrites
Lory		Chapter 11	write agent/pub. letter	publish book!!
Rebecca		massage!!	call publishers	
		make Ch. 4 corrections	call everyone for contacts	
		revisit intro	hire editor?	
		revisit 1	write proposal?	
		revisit 2	—synopsis	
		edit 3 & 5	—market research	
		find artist	—table of contents	

1. List all the tasks in their respective categories.
2. Focus on the first two columns until you have finished the "pressing" list.
3. Take the pressing elements of the short-term list, and break them down into tasks for the new pressing list.
4. Create a new pressing list and revise the mid- and long-term list.
5. Wherever you have a sense of a need but no idea how to accomplish it, place a question mark next to the task.
   These are your *black holes*.

Listomania (cont'd)

ONGOING	PRESSING	SHORT-TERM	MID-TERM	LONG-TERM

1. List all the tasks in their respective categories.
2. Focus on the first two columns until you have finished the "pressing" list.
3. Take the pressing elements of the short-term list, and break them down into tasks for the new pressing list.
4. Create a new pressing list and revise the mid- and long-term list.
5. Put question marks after any items you don't know how to approach. *These are your black holes.*

Planning Model 4: Storyboarding Your Project
Goal: to start a food invention company.

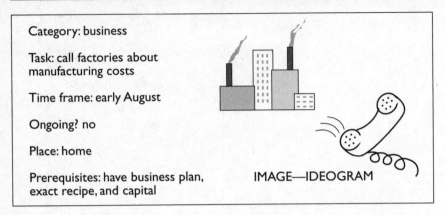

Category: business

Task: call factories about manufacturing costs

Time frame: early August

Ongoing? no

Place: home

Prerequisites: have business plan, exact recipe, and capital

IMAGE—IDEOGRAM

Materials: a package of 3 x 5 cards, a pen, and, if you like, colored markers.

1. Make a list of the various arenas of endeavor within your project. These are your categories.
2. On each card write a task you imagine you will be doing to get this project done. The tasks will range from small ones like single phone calls to big, ongoing activites like weekly meetings with collaborators. You don't need to be organized about this, just randomly write down all the tasks you can think of. You will have a chance to organize it later. If you have a sense that there is a need but you don't know how to accomplish it, place a question mark after the task. *These are your black holes.*
3. Under the task write the approximate date when you imagine yourself doing this.
4. If it is an ongoing action, note that on the card.
5. Mark where this action needs to take place. Home? Office? The far reaches of the Nile?
6. Write this task's prerequisites—the main thing or things that need to take place *before* you can do this action.
7. Sketch a quick image or ideogram that captures the essence of this task for you.
8. Now you have your hefty stack of actions in front of you. First organize them into categories, marking on each card which category the action falls under. In the example above, the budding food inventor's categories were business, cooking experiments, food sources research, tastings, and marketing.
9. Now organize them into time frames: the next month, the next two to four months, the next four to six months, etc. Take the most pressing stack of cards and put the longer-term stacks away in a drawer. Work through your project by stacks, throwing away and creating new cards as the project unfolds.
10. For ongoing actions, write down how many times you will do them per week. Post your ongoing cards in your work area and mark with little hash marks on the card each time you do the action.

Step 3
Playwriting with the Sage

This technique offers you an individual approach to problem solving through the black holes of your project. Your black holes may be emotional/psychological issues or external and logistical ones. For your biggest black hole, lead yourself through a written dialogue between two fascinating characters: you and the Greek philosopher Socrates. For the purposes of this exercise you need no special knowledge of Socrates, except to know that he goaded his students into new insights through posing questions. By engaging the students in a debate with their own beliefs, he pursued his method of persuasion without declaring his opinion or preaching.

1. Socrates begins the dialogue by asking the question, "What is the problem?"

You answer with something like "I want to figure out how I can . . ." You try to define the obstacle as clearly as possible.

SOCRATES: What's the problem?

AMANDA: I want to figure out how I can make a comfortable living while I pursue my acting career. Specifically, I want a part-time, semicreative job which allows me a lot of flexibility but which is stable.

2. Socrates always questions the validity of the question. He might answer, "How can you achieve this goal *despite* this problem?"

Try to answer with a positive response instead of simply saying, "I can't." Try to come up with some positive ideas that do not solve the problem but simply circumvent it.

SOCRATES: How can you have a comfortable life without getting this perfect job?

AMANDA: I could lower my expenses, I could take out an enormous loan. I could sell my car or my body. I could move to a cheaper city. (And so on.)

3. Now let your characters go at it. Remember that Socrates only asks questions, thereby pushing you to discover new solutions and clarify the issue. If the conversation sinks into pessimism and conflict, does this throw any light on your current thinking patterns? Are you closing off the possibility of seeing new solutions? Or are you just in the mood for complaining?

SOCRATES: How could you get the perfect part-time job?

AMANDA: I could focus all my energies on it. Throw away my television.

SOCRATES: Your what?

AMANDA: Never mind. I could get rid of all the distractions in my life and look for the perfect job.

SOCRATES: And what does this perfect job look like?

AMANDA: Something simple—not too multifaceted. I like words. I would like to write horoscopes. I have a friend whose sister does that. She said it was kinda lucrative.

SOCRATES: Have you called this woman?

AMANDA: No.

SOCRATES: Why not?

AMANDA: Because it seems ridiculous. I'm not an astrologer!

SOCRATES: Do you think the woman is?

AMANDA: I don't know. I could call her just to see how she got it. I also would like to write stuff for clothing catalogues.

SOCRATES: How could you find out about that?

AMANDA: If I knew, why would I be writing this stupid thing to a dead man?

SOCRATES: Perhaps I should rephrase the question. If I said I knew of such a job, where would you guess it was?

AMANDA: At the Grope headquarters downtown. . . .

4. Once you have finished your dialogue, make a list of the ideas you have culled and list them in order of your willingness to try them. Choose between one and three ideas to try in the next month. Put them in your Adventure Book.

A Tempest in the Darkness: Brainstorming

One day as I was moping on a park bench, oblivious to the blue summer sky, worrying about my career or money or some other adult thing, I overheard two little girls playing furtively under a palm tree.

"What can we have for dinner, Mother? I'm hungry!"

The older one stroked the younger one's hair, "Don't worry, we'll find something." Then she grabbed two large rocks from the ground. "Look what I found, Sweetie! Granite, your favorite flavor."

"No!" the little one cried. "The witch told me that these rocks are poisonous! Oh, Mama, what will we eat for supper?"

"Oh, dear." The older girl dropped the rocks. "Then I suppose we must eat air. The air is always delicious."

Then both girls ran through the park pretending to eat large portions of the sky.

I watched, wondering what I could learn from these plucky little scavengers. When we played imaginary games as children we were comfortable making up the rules as we went along. In grown-up life, it's easy to forget that most of the rules we live by are also made up. The only difference is that when the imagination has played itself out, adult games must produce real food. These children reminded me that even when problems seemed insurmountable, we can still improvise in the moment and make up a solution out of thin air. Even if the solution is ridiculous, the change in attitude and perspective it brings can help move us into productive action.

In working with adults and their career problems, I realized that I would need to generate the same power of play in our problem-solving sessions. The best method for this is brainstorming. When I ran a theater arts school for children, I developed a brainstorming process that would create whole plays in a few chaotic sessions. While in the adult art world writing a play is considered "hard work" and "serious art," children don't have much interest in theater unless it feels like the imaginary games they play at recess. The class would set a timer for five minutes and begin to spew out ideas. I told them I especially liked evil, illegal, and silly ideas. In fact, I asked them to make sure that they gave me at least one idea that they thought was just plain dumb. I would write them all down. After the timer rang we would go back over our ideas and develop the most promising ones. In transposing the method for adults, I decided to have all of them start by writing down three immoral, illegal, or impossible ideas that would solve the problems. I added the writing step because although many people are familiar with the concept of brainstorming, few people have much faith in it. Beginning with writing bad ideas scares the censor away and allows people to first test their creative mind in privacy. With this method, there's no need to have faith in brainstorming. It works.

Step 4

Brainstorming: Letting Loose the Air-Eating Child

1. The person articulates her problem to a friend or group of friends, formulating it into a question that begins with the word "how."

For instance, "How can I get a hundred thousand dollars to make my first movie?" If she is having trouble articulating this question, she can ask her listeners for help.

2. Each person, including the brainstormee, first writes down three kinds of idea: illegal, immoral, and unlikely. For example: "Extort money from your married boss who is having an affair." "Start a 1–900 number offering advice on how to make a film with no capital." "Call your favorite movie star and ask for a loan." Once these "bad" ideas have been written down, the brainstormers can write down as many brilliant, obvious, practical ideas as they can think of. "Apply for a grant." "Get a job at a camera-rental studio and borrow the equipment." "Beg your parents." "Make a five-minute clip and try to find investors."

3. Set the timer for ten minutes. Then begin the verbal brainstorm, with the brainstormee adhering to two simple precepts: Never say no or argue with your brainstormers. Write down all ideas—without discussion or comment. The brainstormers should say all ideas that come into their heads: the "bad" as well as the brilliant and boring ones. They should not only read ideas from their written lists but throw out ideas suggested by other people's ideas.

4. When the bell rings, the brainstormee has the option to rearticulate her problem or make it more specific if the ideas she is hearing are not addressing her problems. Then the timer should be set again for five minutes.

5. When the bell rings or the ideas peter out or become repetitive, stop. The brainstormee should circle all the ideas she doesn't like or is unwilling to do. She must then articulate what she likes about each idea and what she hates. Then the group asks the following question: What good ideas are lurking behind this bad idea? For example, "The thing I like about extorting money from my boss is that it's bold, fast, outrageous, and would make great publicity. The problem with it is that it might not work, I might get arrested, and it would be too evil." "Can we think of any ideas that raise a hundred thousand dollars in a way that is bold, fast, outrageous, and would make great publicity but that wouldn't get her arrested, or feel too evil?" "How about starting a 'mock extortion campaign' in which you teasingly approach all your friends, family, and acquaintances—especially the more affluent ones—with a letter pretending to extort money from them for outrageous reasons?"

6. The brainstormee writes down all the new ideas that the group generates.

7. Finally, the brainstormee chooses her favorite ideas from both lists in order of preference. She picks the first idea on that list and puts it on her list of goals for that week.

When your problem is being brainstormed, let your friends get goofy. Crude, illegal, impossible, and dorky ideas break the veneer of intelligence that stifles creativity. Even if the idea is totally useless, it may make people laugh, an important tool of group creativity.

LIST SOLUTIONS GENERATED BY YOUR BRAINSTORM

Choose the best of them and put them in your Adventure Book.

MARGARET JENKINS, CHOREOGRAPHER

Margaret Jenkins's evolution as a dancer and choreographer is an old-fashioned tale of the making of a professional artist. She began studying dance at the age of four to be like her older sister. By the age of thirteen she had made the decision that dance was her life path. By twenty-four she was living in New York City and had studied under a number of historical figures from Martha Graham and Jose Limón to Gus Solomon and Viola Farber. As a young choreographer, she was part of the vital experimental scene known as the Judson Church Group, often credited with the creation of postmodern dance.

In the beginning, Jenkins had to patch together a living from waitressing and artist modeling like her fellow starving dancers. Soon, however, she used her creativity and resourcefulness to escape her ordinary host of day jobs. By offering noon exercise classes for office workers long before the words aerobics and jazzercise had been invented, she managed to quit all her other jobs and survive exclusively on her noontime gig, becoming the envy of her friends. "It was a little germ of an idea that was taken to a pretty extraordinary place," she says. She also became Merce Cunningham's substitute teacher and rehearsal director, which paid her a small stipend. When she moved to San Francisco and started her own company, she survived partly with the support of her attorney husband. She readily acknowledges that between her moment in history, her lunchtime class, and her husband's support, she has been very lucky. Yet in addition to her luck, fifty-four-year-old Jenkins has the steely-eyed determination that makes many young choreographers admire her. "She's in it for the long haul," said one of her dancers. "She's pretty amazing."

When I ask Jenkins about what she has that has allowed her company to continue when other dance companies are folding like card tables, she admits that her success "has something to do with administrative acumen."

But even with talent, luck, and the capacity to organize an office, Jenkins has not come by her success easily: "I work seven days a week, often from eight-thirty A.M. to eleven—but I don't brag about it. There's just no way out of it. There's so much that needs to be done. Money's always an anxiety. It never changes. Even today. I make the same salary I did thirty years ago. So what has to propel you is the necessity, everything else is secondary."

For her the motivation for making art is more about what she doesn't know than what she does. "Mimes have an expression that you have to go back to zero position in order to fully embrace going forward," she says. "I think you have to be willing to admit that you don't know anything. Robert Rauschenberg said something wonderful many years ago: 'Being an artist is the capacity to function passionately and thoroughly in a world that has a lot more to it than paint.' That's why it's necessary to come back to what drives you—which is the necessity of the work."

For aspiring dancers and choreographers she tempers her encouragement with caution: "First of all, it's one of the grand things to do with a life. Second, after identifying the necessity to be an artist, get yourself a good job. Let the art define itself. I think the biggest mistake is to think that there's some model of success out there. There's no such thing. You have to define your own model based on your own ethics. So as much as one can, you identify on some primitive level that you need to do this, and then you figure out the ways to do it."

EXERCISES IN CHARTING NEW TERRITORY

1. Clustering

2. Choose and do one of the following action plans:

    blueprinting your project
    scoring your project
    listomania
    storyboarding your project

3. Playwriting with the sage

4. Brainstorming black holes with friends

5. Personal Homework: How about one or two of the new solutions you came up with in the playwriting or brainstorming process?
    Transfer your new ideas to your Adventure Book.

6. What was the most useful thing you discovered in this chapter? What still seems murky for you? How might you bring more clarity to this issue?

CHRIS WINK, PERFORMANCE ARTIST

Cofounder of the New York–based Blue Man Group, Chris Wink never set out to be a performance artist. But when he began weaving together his strange mixture of interests, he uncovered his idiosyncratic medium. With the restless, active mind of a generator, and the visionary energy of a leader*, he also discovered that he needed other artists to work with. In retrospect, he now sees that his cofounders Matt Goldman, a maker/inventor[†], and Phil Stanton, a classic realizer[‡], are the perfect partners to help manifest his ideas.

He lives an interdisciplinarian's[§] life: integrating enormously divergent activities into a single show. In the satirical, mystical rituals of the three silent men painted entirely in bright blue paint, Wink gets to drum, comment on contemporary culture, and catch marshmallows in his mouth. In his workday, sometimes he works alone—writing, conceptualizing and problem solving—and sometimes he works with others: playing, rehearsing, and meeting with his cofounders and company. Like most devoted collaborators, Wink understands that his work is only as good as the group he is working with. To that end, he continually expresses a sense of awe, gratitude, and respect for both his collaborators and the process they have discovered.

Q: Did you always know you wanted to be some kind of artist?

A: No. People talk about following your bliss, which is wonderful if your bliss happens to fit into a neat category like, I want to be an evolutionary biologist. Of course it's great to hear that term, "follow your bliss," because it doesn't occur to a lot of people. In fact, it didn't occur to *me* for a long time. But I couldn't follow my bliss, because I had *blisses*. And so I had to pick my bliss.

Q: What were some of your blisses?

A: Geology. I was a DJ at the radio station. I was doing African drumming. I liked art history, film . . . When I graduated, I continued my American Studies major by doing this job where I synopsized American magazines for a Japanese company.

---

*For definitions of the generator and the leader, see pages 75 and 77.
[†]For definitions of the maker and the inventor, see pages 65 and 79.
[‡]For a definition of the realizer, see page 70.
[§]For a definition of the interdisciplinarian, see page 178.

Q: Is it true that you almost studied business?

A: That was my lowest point. I actually took the GMAT. While I was at this job, I became interested in the new ways Japanese management was developing a humanistic style—that was sort of a new topic in the early eighties. I was addicted to the New. I couldn't wait to see what kind of cultural iterations were spewing out. At night I would look for things to be interested in, and in the day I was at this company, and I was also in a band. I had to deal with how to live, how to survive. It seemed there was always this tacit pressure to specialize. So I picked drumming for a while, but got depressed cause it was too narrow a bliss. Eventually I left that job with the Japanese company to figure out what I wanted to do. It seems to me that it's a very dangerous and tricky path—every artist goes through a huge search. I think about all the things that could have kept me from being an artist.

I didn't know that I wanted to do performance art till I was twenty-six, and I really suffered up until that point. It wasn't an easy answer for me because I don't have any skill as a fine artist; I didn't find myself attracted to the theater department. It was only after a couple of experiences performing that it hit me like a two-by-four. At a certain point, I made my brain a secondary organ and listened to my gut: "Find a way to combine all your blisses, and who the fuck cares if you're a waiter?" I had to rid myself of my immaturity, insecurities, or societal this or that. I had to develop my own self.

Q: What happened just preceding your making this decision?

A: Total depression. Actually I think there were two decisions. I finally rejected trying to have a real job. I came out as a bohemian. This was preceded by a year of What-am-I-going-to-do? I mean saying you're a performance artist isn't exactly narrowing it down. I could catch things in my mouth, drum, say something funny, make an art history reference, a science reference, and that's the show. So I found some friends, and we started developing a salon atmosphere, a little community . . .

Q: You started inviting people over?

A: We'd have a Sunday brunch: "Come over, we're going to have a Show and Tell." People would come over with just about anything from really high art to really lowbrow culture. We were aware that having a salon is kind of pretentious and we were a little on the defensive about it. Then at some point, we asked ourselves, "Why isn't this a normal thing, why isn't everyone doing this?" We were all so hungry for community. There just weren't enough ways to connect. So we began these outings to Central Park. It was just following your interest, and bringing what's unique about you. We talked a lot about what we didn't like. For an artist, being dissatisfied is a really good place to start, because by being dissatisfied, you elbow your way into a space where everything can come from an original place right from the start. You need the perfect blend of dissatisfaction with decision and optimism. We had no idea what we were going to do at first. One thing that galvanized our group was not that there was something exciting, but that something was missing from our lives, from our culture. So we developed something called "Funeral for the Eighties." It was so simple: "We know what we don't like. Let's all get a big coffin together and throw a bunch of symbolic effigies into it." And little by little the form implies what you do like, even though the content is implying what you don't.

Later on when we formed Blue Man Group, it was the same dissatisfaction we were working with. We were interested in a character that expressed a little bit of our own feelings of isolation and frustration with the numbing and overwhelming effects of information overload. A character that needed the other two all the time—sort of anti-hyperindividualist—a kind of communal persona. Again, just through form, not through words. The form makes the point, if there's a point to be made.

Q: Did you start out as a three-person group?

A: When we did "Funeral for the Eighties" there were about eight or nine men and women; it was just an invitation to come to Central Park. One woman was an accountant who moved to Bali, and gradually we ended up dwindling down till it became the three of us. Blue Man Group is not a democracy, it's consensus. Sometimes it's just us three, sometimes it's everyone who we collaborate with.

Q: You told me that the process writes the piece, you don't write the piece. What do you mean by that?

A: If you're going to create something, the first step isn't to start creating something, it's to create the *process*. We approach our work on a more interpersonal level. We have to look at our relationship, how we're doing, before we can have a successful creative meeting. Then you get into more specifics . . . like who's going to do what. But tending to the vessel and shaping it into what it's going to be is really important.

Q: Do you have any structural elements that integrate that?

A: It permeates the way we set things up. As soon as we take on a new project, we ask ourselves what is our system, our process, our structure. It feels like we have a unique configuration. We're ordinary people with an extraordinary relationship. The rewards of collaborative work so far outweigh solo work for me. I was walking around with the idea for Blue Man for two years before Matt said, "Well, what the hell, let's do it." And Phil said, "Why don't we build some cool shit?" Phil's the builder. Matt's the guy who takes ideas from nothing: words, social constructs. I think that's what strikes people who know us: our fortunate synergy.

Q: What does your day look like?

A: It's cyclical. When we were in the show, we did twelve hundred shows in a row, which meant for three years at eight o'clock you do a show. We'd plan a show, generate new material, work on it, build it, perform it and back to building again. During the run, it was about tweaking it. So there's been no single season that's the same. It's kind of hard to describe my day. Today, we took turns putting on this clown nose for a few hours. Then it's off to the theater for a company meeting—nothing glamorous about that. Then at that point there's a semirehearsal.

Q: Do you ever not want to work? Do you ever have trouble with self-discipline?

A: I'm definitely convinced that there's no such thing as a lazy person or a hypercommitted person, because I've been both in different contexts. I've been on certain jobs where I'm dead.

When you're dealing with trying to get muses to show up, I tend to give up real quickly if it's not happening, I never try to discipline the real sparkle in your eye. You're either into the flow or you're not. I don't see any point in disciplining the flow. But I feel a certain amount of discipline in terms of the brass tacks.

Q: When you started out, what was your idea of success?

A: When I first became a performance artist, my idea of success was to have some work we liked and to have some people come and see it. It was really nice to have such a low, doable ambition. Now, my definition is simply how to hold onto that.

There's no person on the planet that doesn't want to be respected by his or her peers. But you've got to follow your muses rather than try to solve the social wounds of your adolescence. And then there's a certain point where you need to let yourself enjoy the success that comes your way. It's that thing that everyone gets nervous about—that if they enjoy the success, they might ruin how they got there.

Q: Did you ever get nervous about that? Was it distracting when you started getting a lot of attention?

A: Yeah, it became an issue. You've got to keep your eye on the ball. But there hasn't been a huge lifestyle change; because we're not like movie stars or rock singers. No one can recognize us on the street. Our situation is continually humbling, and that's a good thing. As soon as we think we've figured something out, we try something new.

Q: If there was one piece of advice that you would give someone in your field, what would it be?

A: Our story doesn't create a new piece of advice, it corroborates resoundingly advice given already: to have the courage to reinvent. I look back now and see that there were little moments along the way, but you don't listen to them till later. I had a moment when I was running up on a mountain, and that moment made it so that I could never really go to business school, because I knew I wouldn't have that feeling there. It kind of haunts you. It was a "leap" moment.

So my advice is this. Harness the anger, the angst, and the passion, and make your work really fucking good. We've lost a generation of people who are dealing with their environments by retreating. By going into therapy. So instead, you go to open mike at a crummy tavern and you perform your art. Rather than being introspective and constantly working on your shortcomings—get angry, get excited, get social. And make your work and then make it good. Our generation has attention deficit disorder—they don't wait around till the third draft, much less the seventh or eighth. I get offended by all the first-draft work I see: "This is me, so that's good enough." There's no quality to anything anymore. But if you have the patience to stick with your work—it's like that phrase by Pasteur: Chance favors the prepared mind.

PART 4

The Doing

You must be the change you wish to see in the world.
—MAHATMA GANDHI

These three chapters will help you institute new daily and weekly structures into your present life and keep you working toward your ultimate vision.

Magic at Work
Designing Your Daily Process

> Writing is like making love. Don't worry about the orgasm, worry about the process.
>
> —ISABEL ALLENDE

> To see a world in a grain of sand
> And heaven in a wild flower
> Hold infinity in the palm of your hand
> And eternity in an hour.
>
> —WILLIAM BLAKE

Up until this point we have been basking in the expansive views of "eagle vision": identifying dreams, setting long-term goals, and making plans. Now it's time to return to the world of the squirrel, where all the real work gets done, step by step, day by day. You have created a goal and developed an action plan, now how will you bring the project to fruition? In this chapter you will explore those increments of moment-to-moment effort that transform ideas into reality. Through a holistic, systematic investigation into your daily life, you will set out to recharge the very battery of your imagination: your creative process.

If you have continued to use the daily action as a tool of self-discipline and inspiration since chapter 1, then you probably are already engaged in this process of daily change and self-reflection. If, for whatever reason, the daily action has fallen by the wayside, then this chapter will help you understand why and allow you to institute a new working model for your creative process.

Practicing most art forms usually means learning a very simple action such as ballet pliés or piano scales, and then doing it many, many times, usually every day. Though this kind of practice might use little in the way of equipment or cash, it draws from an even more precious resource: the deep reservoir of self-directedness and devotion.

With the same emphasis on simplicity and repetition, I designed the daily action as a tool to prepare the self for the creative life. The daily action is just one tool—a tool I hope has served you well in working your way through this book. But now it's time to develop your *own* creative process. Good creative processes are as individual as artists themselves. Don't be satisfied with a secondhand model, discover the practice buried within you.

By creative process I mean both your method of conjuring the invisible world of your dreams and the way you manifest it in doable actions and concrete events. Creativity is a little like alchemy—it's equal parts fact and fiction, pragmatism and mysticism. What's bizarre is that it's often through the most repetitive, simple, seemingly mindless actions that the magic of creativity erupts. For a writer the banal action of sitting down and putting pen to paper every day creates the occasion for inspiration. For an entrepreneur, the act of writing a business plan prompts a whole new level of creative ideas. For the singer it is the return to simple breathing exercises and scales that maintains a voice that can burn with passion. For the choreographer, walking into an empty space and experimenting with movement is the first step to innovative dance. Echoing Blake's vision of the world in a grain of sand, I would say that all art resides in a moment of practice. And by practice I don't mean virtuoso technique, unless that's what your goal is. By practice I mean practicing the art itself in its simplest form with patience, humility, and compassion. What amazes me is how many creative people (including myself at times) live in denial of this one terrible, beautiful truth. This is why you shouldn't consider your daily process an afterthought, an indulgent New Age ritual preceding the real, important work of making art. How you wake up and prepare your mind, body, and spirit for creation is *the* vehicle by which you will transport yourself to the place of your dreams. It may feel irrelevant when you give it time in your hectic life, but the truth is that if you continue to return to your daily process (whatever that may be), your creativity will burst forth in all sorts of unforeseen ways. You will learn to be in the present, wait for ideas, appreciate your daily life, and feel the adventure you are living now (not when you are famous, successful, or dead). You will learn that the struggle—quiet and small as it is—is really the greatest reward of all.

Let us now open up the invisible laboratory inside you to discover the emotional, intellectual, and physical alchemy of your creative process. When you were digging up your past and analyzing those moments when everything worked as if by magic, you were searching out clues to this process. Now the time has come to do a little experimenting.

Your creative process is a mixture of four elements:

1. Your Routine

Ideally, these daily routines and weekly activities represent the optimal way of using your time and appreciating your life. Your routine includes when you choose to work a day job, when you do your art, and when you play. A good creative schedule takes advantage of your most creative hours of the day and diminishes the negative voices that interrupt your thoughts.

For some artists, the creative schedule is their first step in committing to their art. Novelist Jonathan Lethem declared his need for "lots of time to write" even before he was writing very much or very well. Even now, as a developed artist, his daily schedule is the primary thing he refers to when he is discussing his creative process. He talks about his schedule, his getting up in the morning and writing at eight or nine A.M. It seems stupefyingly simple and, at the same time, the mark of a brilliant mind. Although it contradicts the stereotype of the relentlessly spontaneous genius, the profile of the schedule-centered artist is quite common. These artists developed a rigorous routine even before they fully mastered their motivation, their goals, or their subject matter. Even if you feel hazy about the exact content of your creative work, building a healthy daily schedule now will help you develop the self-discipline you will need later.

What kinds of routine do you need for your creative work? (This might include a daily practice, particular sleeping or eating schedules, creative schedules, exercise routines, weekly activities.)

BETH CUSTER, COMPOSER

Avant-garde clarinetist/composer Beth Custer has worked in a wildly eclectic variety of settings and styles, as both a solo performer and a collaborator. As a founding member of three groups—Club Foot Orchestra (a jazz collective renowned for its original scores for silent movies), Trance Mission (a world fusion group), and The Clarinet Thing (a group comprising five clarinetists), Custer has patched together a life devoted to composition and performance.

Her Wellspring day job is composing for dance companies and local theater productions. She also privately teaches a few clarinet students. Her willingness to compose for other art forms has balanced her unwillingness to pursue a more conventional job like teaching music at a university. This whirling dervish approach has allowed her to live her passion and at the same time stay alive. With her national reputation building, she is now beginning to reassess her many-tiered pursuits in favor of a simpler, more monocled monk existence.

She has stacks of glowing reviews and a growing reputation as a musician, but when she went to graduate school to study music, she didn't find the support she had hoped for: "Graduate school was disappointing. I didn't feel very encouraged there. In the very last lesson this teacher said to me, 'You should really go into teaching.' This was after I had finished my performance degree and had given a recital. It was totally out of line." After graduating, she sought out a teacher who not only taught her about playing the clarinet but also about pursuing her dreams: "He's a clarinet guru, and a renaissance man. For four years, I commuted two and a half hours once a week. He taught me a lot of things besides clarinet—mainly do what you want to do in your life. Follow your heart and take the scenic route. There are ways to follow your own path. You just need to know what it is and stick with it."

While her daily process once included lots of restaurant food, caffeine, and workaholism, she now has a routine that gives her the calm and stability she needs to be creative. "I get up about seven or eight," she says. "On a good day I do an hour of yoga, drink some coffee; sometimes I work on the computer for a while or do a lot of phone calls to get more bookings. Then I go down to the studio and bang away down there from noon to six. Then I come home and do some more work on the computer or take a walk on the town. I do a lot of cooking, hang out with friends, read. I don't take regular days off; I would say it's a six-day workweek."

Along with her new routine she has a new creative work space: "My studio is in a navy shipyard. My baby grand stands in a meat locker with metal walls and two windows with bars on them that face the ocean, surrounded by these decrepit buildings. It's a really desolate place. Very inspiring. I sit at the piano, and I play and sing. I record everything I improvise. I have to bang things over and over again, it must be horrible to listen to. For me though it's almost like meditating with a mantra. You repeat the same thing over and over and then something else evolves out of it." With a place, a routine, and a method for developing her work, Custer has grown less and less enamored with all the external rewards of success. "When people say they want to 'make it,' well, that usually means material accumulation, and I only want the simplest of things," she says. "I don't want ten houses and I don't want to be hugely famous because I don't like a lot of attention from the media. To me the fact that I can go to my studio and play music every day is success."

Custer's advice to would-be composers and musicians is encouraging: "Go for it. Throughout my life I had people saying to me, 'You really should get a teaching job in a university. You really need to have some security.' But I never in my life said I wanted to be a college teacher. I think teachers ought to be people who *want* above all to be teachers and if you want to be a performer or if you want to be a composer, just do it, and do it absolutely all the time. But make sure that's what you want to do."

2. Your Attitude

These are the little nuggets of emotional and intellectual wisdom we hold fast to. Despite tantrums and manic fits, depression and elation, we know underneath our melodrama that our creativity springs from a source deeper than our moods. Your ideal creative attitude neither glorifies nor negates your feelings, but it does allow you to act on difficult tasks, attack challenges, and dream schemes with minimum frustration and maximum delight.

Though they may incorporate much-touted principles such as calm, singular focus, enthusiasm, and a sense of humor, ideal attitudes don't necessarily read like a to-do list for reaching nirvana or mental health. Some of your ideal attitudes might mean respect for your particular form of madness, a sense of urgency, giddiness, darkness, or melancholia. They may also reflect quirky bits of self-knowledge or superstitions, like "I can only create when I sleep with my head to the north," as well as more intellectual notions, like "Assume nothing. Everything must be questioned."

Performance artist/composer/choreographer/filmmaker Meredith Monk spoke of many attitudes she tries to live and work by: that her creativity moves in cycles and sometimes she simply has no ideas, that movement and voice and character are not distinct disciplines but facets of the same art form, that success is a double-edged sword because it can encourage you not to take artistic risks, and that she shouldn't be distracted by praise or criticism.

Ideal attitudes are as varied and complicated as human beings. What remains essential is that you know yourself and live by your own beliefs, not anyone else's. Most creative attitudes are neither bad nor good except within the context of a given artist's personality. Your velvet love seat may be a fellow artist's bed of nails. When Ingrid, having just finished composing her latest opera, dances around the room chanting, "It's going straight to the Met," her girlfriend Jill shudders. For Jill the very idea of declaring her work's greatness would be tantamount to creative suicide. She tries to avoid thinking about her work as a finished product at all. Though both women share similar routines, aesthetics, and motivations for their music, they maintain entirely different attitudes toward their creative work.

Here are a few examples of some attitudes about creative work that may or may not ring true for you.

- Positive thinking is always good.
- If I know exactly what I'm doing, I'm on the wrong track.
- I look at the truth—this is usually painful.
- I need to stay calm.
- Many projects feed my energy.
- I'm not responsible for my work's meaning; I'm only responsible for making the work.

What do you think are the attitudes that best nourish your creativity?

3. Your Motivation

Motivations spring from many arenas: intimate relationships; a desire for fame, money, or respect; a sense of historical purpose; a sense of community or individuality; a reverence for God or some other deeply held belief.

If you have a thorough understanding of the things that motivate you, you put yourself in their service to challenge yourself and your art to new heights. For instance, Tim, who had sung in many choruses, had always been afraid to perform solo. He knew his voice was good enough, but he had a terrible fear of being alone on stage and going blank. One day a friend who was working on the AIDS Names Project asked him if he would sing a song at a large showing of the AIDS quilt. He said yes, still not knowing if he would be able to overcome his stage fright. On the day of the performance he was terrified, but it was too late to bow out for such a large and important cause. When he got up onstage, his fears dissolved when he saw the quilt laid out before him. He knew why he was singing and who he was singing for. Having tapped into his purest motivation, he suddenly could do what he had never been able to do before. Tim was lucky. He had his motivating moment foisted upon him like a gift from the heavens. Most of us need to think about what motivates us and how we can create in the service of that impulse.

If you are more likely to work hard for someone else or some greater cause, figure out how to make your work a direct gift to a person or community. If you are motivated by privacy and mystery, avoid showing your work before it is finished; lock your writing in a box; practice your art alone. This clear sense of true motivation may be the key you need to unlock a sense of intensity and courage surrounding your work. If working in collaboration with others inspires you, then build a collaborative structure like a support group or class into your daily life, even if your art is an essentially private endeavor.

Too many people discount the joy of the act itself as a source of motivation. A wonderful dancer I worked with said she had ceased to enjoy dance because she had become so fixated on the results (applause, fame, a beautiful body, respect). She had lost touch with her original motivation: the sheer pleasure of the spinning room, the bodies, the music.

For some artists, keeping in touch with their original impulse to create is the dominant aspect of their process. For instance, when I asked R. J. Cutler about his creative process, he returned again and again to being motivated by the political content of the work and the idea of telling stories that reflect contemporary culture. These two principles have been the guiding threads that wind through his multifarious careers in radio, theater, and film. He never mentioned routine except to say that he works a lot and he held few "attitudes" about his creative work. Artists like Cutler prescribe no set routine and their attitudes toward their art are constantly shifting, but their motivation remains the single most stable force in their work.

Here are a few examples of some creative motivations that you may or may not find reflected in your heart.

- My work springs from a desire for political justice.
- My work comes from a desire to express myself.
- I want to work when I think of my grandmother.
- I want to work when I think of my imaginary audience.
- My work springs from the joy of making something beautiful.

What are the most powerful motivating factors in your work? Remember they can be broad universal issues, very personal attachments, or political perspectives.

4. Your Emergency Plan

When crisis hits, and your perfect routine and healthy attitude disintegrate, what do you do? What releases stress and refocuses your spirit of play? Is there a certain person you can call or a place you can escape to? Is there a treat you can give yourself like a trashy matinee or a favorite food? Do you fast and wear a black Elvira wig? Do you feel it's best to wallow or keep working, reach out or retreat? Whatever the case, the emergency plan is as important as your daily routine because *chaos happens,* and when it does, we need to know there are things we can do to soften its blows.

Young or developing artists often lose the momentum of their creative progress at the slightest intrusion from the outside world. Having convinced themselves that they must always maintain a perfect routine and mental attitude, they leave no room for contingency plans. When they stop working for a few days or a few weeks, they become paralyzed by feelings of doubt and despair: "Why me? Maybe it's a sign I'm on the wrong track. Why can't anything go right for me?"

No matter how much you want to create an ideal process for your creativity, the emergency plan reminds you not to be too rigid or perfectionistic. Marty, who had always struggled with self-discipline, finally got himself on a schedule that was working well. He composed music every morning and stopped going to bars on weeknights. Then his father died and he lost his will to get up in the morning and sit down at the piano. In addition to mourning his father, he was beating himself up about how lazy he was. "I never could keep to a regular schedule," he remarked to the bartender one night after one too many. "I try every day but the most musical thing I can create is the ding on the microwave. Even the idea of music depresses me."

Marty thought that his process was a "finished" product and that now he had "lost" it. In his mind he gave no allowances for life. He couldn't legitimately "take time off" or go away for a while. He had no emergency plan. This absence of flexibility in his creative process not only made him feel like a failure, but didn't allow him to take necessary steps to heal from his father's death.

What are some of the emergency plans you would like to keep in mind while developing your creative process?

How to Begin

For a very small group of artists, evolving their process comes easily or is inherited from a mentor. For most of us, however, we must do the work all by ourselves. Like all personal change, putting a new creative process into action can be hard work. Processes evolve slowly. What works for you this week may feel naive and contrived next year. Conversely, just because a certain routine or attitude seems impossible today doesn't mean it won't feel natural and healthy next year. Finally, you must remember that your creative process is never "finished," it is in constant flux.

There is no single, right way, but many, many viable paths to a creative working process. There is no single wrong way either, but many roads to drive yourself crazy. If you feel like the process you've got now is broken or nonexistent, don't give up too soon—it can take a few years (!) of trial and error to discover your ideal daily process and integrate it into your life in a way that feels both exciting and natural. Of course, sometimes pernicious habits masquerade as healthy ones, and vice versa.

For instance, Jessica, an aspiring animator, started the class with the opinion that she "couldn't possibly work creatively before sundown." Since she worked a night shift in a restaurant, she had ruled out the possibility of having daily time to work on her cartoons. After some effort at her "new process" she realized she *could* work in the daytime. This creative attitude was just a way of avoiding the difficult work of being a committed artist.

Peter, on the other hand, believed that he was just "lazy" because he couldn't paint for more than three hours a day. His "new process" entailed long hours in the studio. After a couple of weeks he noticed that the long days were no more productive and a good deal more exhausting than his old three-hour stints.

Initially, it's difficult to discern when your assumptions about your process are true or not. Sometimes I find it's useful for students to borrow someone else's process and then gradually alter it to make it their own. Other times the only way to test your assumptions is to experiment with them.

Strong daily processes greatly influence the work, so whatever you choose to emphasize in your process will find its way into the content of the work itself. Rigor begets rigor; patience begets patience; energy begets energy. As Chris Wink of Blue Man Group said, "We create the process, and the process creates the work." Wonderful work is the outcome of a healthy process.

As you begin playing with your process, remember to be both patient and persistent. Don't feel reined in by other people's prescriptions. There are too many people out there who want to tell you how to live your life. When you're in a state of self-expansion and experimentation, you will be especially vulnerable to lifestyle ideology: Be calm, be irreverent, eat seaweed, sleep in a hammock. Remember, the only definitive test in a process is whether or not it works for you.

Step 1: Tracing Your Work Pattern

The following profiles illustrate four distinct methods of approaching a large, multifaceted problem. There are many more methods, probably hundreds. Our work patterns give us essential clues into the actual machinations of our creative process. As you read the following four profiles, imagine yourself in similar situations and how you would behave.

Active Distraction

When Rhoda cleans house, she doesn't clean one room at a time: She starts in the bedroom, moving on to the kitchen with a water glass. There she sets about washing the dishes, only to find the house plant she was watering still draining in the sink. She returns it to the living room, where she finds a stack of books that need reshelving before she can begin dusting. Then there's that pile of gym clothes that she carries to the bedroom and dumps in the laundry. On and on she goes, circling through the house in spirals of small interlinking action. She feels a little disoriented and not very productive, but she's not bored. Halfway through the cleaning, nothing is completely finished. In fact, the house looks worse than when she started because all the furniture has been pulled out from the walls to vacuum. If she finishes, she has a supremely clean house on all fronts. But sometimes she gives up, because the more dirt she wipes away the more dirt she notices. . . .

Deep Delay

When Rami writes a paper for school, he spends weeks reading every possible article or book related to his topic. He passes long, languorous hours in the library, reading, taking notes, and daydreaming about how great the paper will be. These days seem precious to him and essential to his process because they produce such a wealth of detail and ideas. As the due date for the paper draws near, he feels compelled to read a few more books before he can dare write a word. He has begun to dread the inevitable shift from reading to writing. The research stage is comforting and feels natural. When he reads, he feels smart; when he writes, he feels that he is being forced to "witness his own stupidity." At the last possible moment, he begins to write. By now he feels rushed and anxious—just as he had feared. He turns in the paper five minutes before the office closes on the day that it is due. He regrets not giving himself more time to rewrite; he knows how much material he left out to get the paper in on time. . . .

Perfection Pending

Louise loves to paint, but whenever she begins, something comes up. The phone rings, she remembers an errand she has to attend to, she realizes that she needs one more essential supply. Sometimes before she paints she has a vision of herself going into her studio and going mad with spontaneity, but when she gets there she just wants to "get other things out of the way" first. She cleans; she returns phone calls; she shops with fabulous efficiency. Tomorrow will be perfect, she tells herself. The next day, incredibly, something else comes up. How she resents these interruptions! One day she ignores all her "responsibilities" and decides to devote herself to her art. The morning begins well. She arrives at the studio and begins to work in a giddy frenzy. She becomes absorbed in one painting for a whole hour, then she realizes, "I am getting lost in this! Wonderful but not perfect. I need something. Caffeine." At the café, there is a newspaper with a profile of the latest senator-turned-sex-offender. She reads the entire article, and gets really riled about the state of politics today. It's depressing! She buys a brownie to soothe her ruffled emotions. She carries it back to her studio, scolding herself all the way: "What a loser you are! Your mind is everywhere but on your painting!" Back in her studio she works a little more, but she can't really concentrate. The coffee has kicked in and suddenly, it seems, there are a thousand errands screaming for attention. Halfheartedly, she begins a new piece that she immediately decides is loathsome. She feels like an "artist automaton," not really present or imaginative, just slogging away. As she walks home she begins to think how perfect tomorrow will be. . . .

Single-Pointed Obsession

When Trevor is working out a design project, even his baby daughter screaming in the other room can't distract him. He thinks only about one thing over and over. When his partner comes home and they have dinner, Trevor cannot concentrate on the food or conversation because the problem of how to fit a lighting fixture underneath a glass pool so it shines through the glass but not in the eyes of the swimmers is turning over and over in his mind. At night he lies awake for hours trying to figure out the problem, jumping up to scribble notes on a pad. His family is annoyed by his obsessiveness, but he secretly believes it is the only reason he is successful. When the plan is presented, the client says, "It may be a little over budget." Trevor sinks into a depression and refuses to get out of bed for a month. . . .

These profiles illustrate just how important work habits are in your creative life. If you develop healthy, stable habits, you will accomplish a lot. If your work habits undermine you every step of the way, then you might be more productive in situations with a ready-made structure. Understanding your work patterns is the first and most important step in reengineering your creative process. Though you may consider these patterns to be integral to your personality, with persistence and effort, you can gradually develop new patterns of behavior. Training yourself to work in a new way may be rather arduous, but it is essential if your current habits don't work. Even people who have the talent, the desire, the opportunity, and the vision may fail if they have a process that thwarts their creative action. In fact, the majority of my students are artists with tons of talent, intelligence, and ideas—and crippling work habits. So, even if you think your work habits are suctioned to your soul like barnacles on a whale, at least give yourself the chance to change. Any adjustments in your daily process can reverberate a thousandfold in bringing you closer to your dreams—simply because these adjustments will happen every single day!

Exercise

Diagram your work pattern. Draw your path of action as you work toward a multifaceted, nonstructured goal. Look at how you deal with obstacles, procrastinate, split or narrow your focus, and use your "eagle vision" or your "squirrel work" to propel you forward. The following examples are some diagrams created by previous students.

Orbiting Moon Artist Model of Work

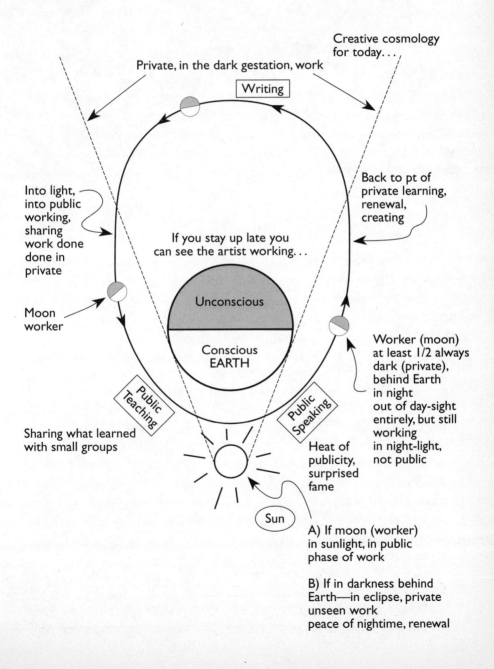

Creative cosmology for today. . .

Private, in the dark gestation, work

Writing

Into light, into public working, sharing work done done in private

Back to pt of private learning, renewal, creating

If you stay up late you can see the artist working. . .

Moon worker

Unconscious

Conscious EARTH

Worker (moon) at least 1/2 always dark (private), behind Earth in night out of day-sight entirely, but still working in night-light, not public

Public Teaching

Public Speaking

Sharing what learned with small groups

Heat of publicity, surprised fame

Sun

A) If moon (worker) in sunlight, in public phase of work

B) If in darkness behind Earth—in eclipse, private unseen work peace of nightime, renewal

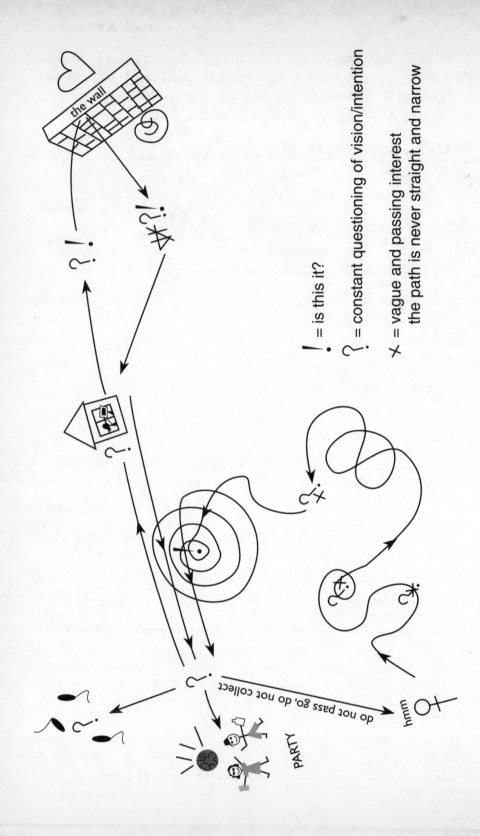

the wall

¡?⚔!¡

!¡

¿:

do not pass go, do not collect

PARTY

hmm

! = is this it?

¿. = constant questioning of vision/intention

✕ = vague and passing interest
the path is never straight and narrow

Now look at your diagram and ask yourself which parts of your pattern you take particular pleasure in. Vow to keep these even if they feel indulgent or inefficient. The idea is not to turn yourself into a machine but to begin untangling and separating out those patterns that you don't enjoy and have had little use for and that you consider self-destructive. Which parts of your work method feel inherent to your creativity even if you don't completely enjoy them? Which parts of your work method do you loathe and wish you were free of? Which parts would you like to tweak just a little bit?

Keep this diagram of your actual working method in mind as you consider, in the next section, some common process ailments.

Step 2: Process Disease Checkup

Before you dive headlong into the specifics of your new process, it's useful to look at some of the common ailments that afflict artists with unhealthy processes.

1. Ambition Virus

You have trouble with procrastination because your ambitions seem so overwhelming. When you're on a discipline kick, you go all out: getting up early, working long hours without breaks or meals, trying to make every minute count. Even at the end of a hard, productive day, you still admonish yourself that you should have done more. You feel that your reading, conversations, and thoughts should *always* be instructive and furthering your goals.

You feel you are playing catch-up with time. You've wasted years and now you have to make up for it by reaching the place you're "supposed to be" in relation to your age group. You have a lot of regrets.

The more successful your new disciplinary kick is, the more tempted you are to push it farther. Then one day you sleep in past your appointed waking time, past your first appointment—you lie in bed thinking, I'm tired! Screw it!

Then comes the voice of Judge No-No booming in stereo: "Failed again—can't blame anybody but yourself," and it takes weeks before you come up with another brave new plan for "doing it all." This has gone on for years, and though you have accomplished many things along the way, they fall far short of the things you thought you "should" have done.

If this describes your pattern, then you may be suffering from an ambition virus. This common illness allows ambition to grow outside the areas where ambition has a necessary and healthy function.

When you are dreaming, goal setting, and creating a vision, ambition has an extremely important role to play. It clarifies passions and energizes your self-image. But in your everyday work process, rampant ambition will drive you to madness, exhaustion, and sickness and, in fact, prevent you from doing the work that will allow you to attain your dreams. Like that old slow-moving tortoise, the people who figure out a deliberate but sustainable daily process will do more with their talents than those like the quick-witted hare, whose energy flows directly from their lust for speedy glory.

For the ambition-driven, try the following in creating your process:

- Move away from a creative process that relies heavily on motivation for fame or success and focus on developing a simple but strict routine-centered process that you can depend upon—no matter what happens.
- Actively rein ambition in. Set weekly goals at half what you think you can do. Tell yourself that your new motto must be "in search of mediocrity."
- Take time to play and rest. Ambition can create low-grade, constant stress, which, in the long run, is debilitating. Don't make your playtime dependent on whether or not you get your "work" done. Play is essential to the creative process, no matter what field you work in.
- Focus on the *enjoyment of the act,* and try to see your ambition as something that interrupts your pleasure in the present.
- If you compare yourself negatively to your peers, try to turn the idea around and instead derive inspiration from them. "If they can do it, then so can I. I just need to keep working at my own pace."

2. Successful but Unsatisfied

You have worked hard to develop the skills and discipline to accomplish fascinating, creative projects, but you haven't paid enough attention to your desires. If you have become successful in a field you don't care for, or pursued an artistic style you don't respect, you may be suffering from the syndrome of misplaced motivation. Sometimes in the rush to become successful and professional, people leave behind their original creative ambitions. Steve, who always wanted to be a writer, found himself neck-deep in the world of advertising copy, earning a hefty six-digit income before he realized that he wasn't happy. When he first got into the field he congratulated himself at making a living at writing, but somewhere along the way he shelved his creative aspirations entirely.

This unsatisfying success breeds a strange sense of disorientation. "But I should be happy" is the plaintive mantra that echoes across the years. Often this person has developed an extraordinary panorama of skills through practicing his craft on a daily basis, but he has lost track of what all the craft was for. If you feel like you're one of these unsatisfied success stories, then try the following in creating your own process:

• Even if you make no money at all from your creative work, make it a daily part of your workweek. Steal back some of those precious hours you have devoted to your career and practice your art every day at the same time. I recommend morning or at least before your job, so that you can reorder your priorities symbolically by putting "first things first" every day of the year.

• Make a list of the motivations that drive your creative work and a list of these motivations attached to your professional career. Compare them and decide which ones you wish to foster in your life.

• Explore your artistic attitudes. Are there any that are currently undermining your ability to pursue what you love?

3. The Selfless Gene

You can be extremely focused, hardworking, and ambitious, but only if the work clearly benefits someone else. You need to find a way to harness your motivation for helping others to your own personal dreams. Making art for friends, dedicating books, teaching, counseling, and collaborating with people who you want to help as partners and peers are all ways that altruistic artists can tap into their generosity and help it fuel their art.

If you think you were born with the selfless gene, try the following in developing your process:

• Don't put yourself down for being "codependent" or other such nonsense. Link your art-making to a source of motivation.

• Remember that the notion of art as a useful gift to a real community of people is a very ancient one that has only in recent years fallen out of common discourse. Study the attitudes of other cultures that value artists as community workers rather than as hyperindividualistic geniuses.

• Make a weekly practice of doing exactly what the artist in you wants for two hours. Though you don't want to rid yourself of your concern for others, you also may need to strengthen your selfish instincts.

- Don't give up. The world needs artists who are not so self-involved! You are a precious commodity.
- Be careful that you have not used an idea of selflessness to avoid the very difficult work of following your own heart.

4. Freedom in Shackles

You have no serious financial or time constraints, but you still can't seem to get yourself organized enough to follow your desire. Drifting on the sea of Potential on a ship called Desire, you suffer from a lack of structure, stimulation, and education. You need a job to anchor you to the world. Because you live such an "easy" life, you feel confused about the fact that you can't make any headway. For the privileged developing artist—whether you're an affluent painter/housewife or a trust-funded grunge rocker, an old-fashioned job can teach discipline, provide community, and give a sense of necessity to your life.

A job in a serious, conventional work environment can also help artists mature in a way that their whims will never teach them. When essayist Sallie Tisdale discusses her first career as a nurse, she talks about the work with reverence and gratitude: "In many ways, working as a nurse made me a more mature person. And maturity made me a better writer." Returning from the real world with real experiences, the artist can devote herself to her creative work with a new sense of clarity.

If you feel like you may be living with too little structure in your life, try the following in developing your process:

- Institute a strict schedule for your artistic life.
- Look for a job—even part-time or volunteer—that ideally you can go to five days a week.
- Look for a job that will teach you the skills or personality traits you need to develop in yourself as an artist. (Do you wish you were bolder? Find a job that requires public speaking. Do you want to learn how to deal with life-or-death situations? Work in medicine or mental health.)
- In the meantime, try to form or join any organization that can offer some structure for your work.
- Seek out a mentor figure and see if you can do volunteer work for them. There are few better ways to build internal structure than alongside someone who has mastered his own process.

Step 3: Planning a New Process

Reading about process is about as useful as thinking about breathing: It's all extremely abstract until you do it. So don't let this chapter hover in the realm of theory. In the final exercise in this chapter you will identify the elements of your current work habits and write down a plan for a new working process. The following is an example of how one woman redesigned her creative process.

Julia is a bright, effervescent filmmaker who has never completed a film. She works hard once she gets started on a film but then "something better always comes up" and she finds herself shelving project after project to make way for new ones. Finally, she quits, concluding that she's burnt out and needs a break. She craves spontaneity. She's thirsty for leisure. After two weeks or two months she has the horrible realization that nothing is getting done! She dives back into all her old projects, newly committed to finishing *all* of them.

Any of Julia's friends would say that she's a hard worker and even a disciplined one. But she's created a process that never allows her to finish or have any time off. When she doesn't take these needs into account in her daily process, they become looming hungers that finally engulf her.

Of course, even with a process that schedules in "playtime" and focuses on one project at a time, she may discover that she is actually *afraid* to finish her films. But then she could see these fears for what they are—emotional issues, not exhaustion, failure, or overweening ambition. In planning her new process, Julia first looked at all the elements of her current work patterns and beliefs.

Julia's Old Process

Routine: Work from 8:00 A.M. to 8:00 P.M., with a fifteen-minute break for coffee and a sandwich. Monday through Thursday work at a camera-rental house from 12:00 to 5:00. All other daytime hours on her film projects. 9:00 P.M. to 1:00 A.M.: make phone calls, watch television, go out with friends, and worry.

Attitude: "I have to finish it yesterday. I'm in a rush. This is so important, it doesn't matter whether or not I enjoy myself. I'm so excited I can't think." Or, "I want to quit. I hate this project. I'm so exhausted I can't think."

Motivation: Fame, respect.

Emergency Plan: Quit art. Alcohol.

Julia's New Process

Schedule: 8:00 to 9:00 A.M.: Walk, clear mind, plan day, breakfast

9:00 to 12:00: Work on *one* film project

12:00 to 5:00: Day job (eat lunch there)

5:30: Dance class or bike ride or something outdoors

7:30: Dinner (plan with friends)

8:00 to 10:00: Going out with friends or working on fun elements of film project

No working on Sunday.

Sell television. To bed with a book.

Attitude: "It's great, but don't get too excited about distant future. Have fun now. Don't jabber about film with friends."

Motivation: The challenge of finishing one film. Following curiosity. The political content of film.

Emergency Plans: Drive out of the city to national park and be *alone*. Get a massage. Go to a matinee on a weekday. Turn off phone and call in sick!

EXERCISES IN CREATING YOUR PROCESS

1. Write down the elements of your old process.
   Routine:

   Attitude:

   Motivation:

   Emergency Plan:

2. Now write what you would like your new process to be.
   Routine:

   (Did you include a daily practice?)
   Attitude:

   Motivation:

   Emergency Plan:

3. Personal Homework: Transfer your ideas into your Adventure Book.

4. What did you learn about your process in this chapter? What do you still wonder about? How can you learn what you need to know to get your process working?

JONATHAN LETHEM, NOVELIST

The first ten years of Jonathan Lethem's career as a writer are a testament to the great power of clear creative priorities. When he dropped out of Bennington at the age of twenty, he struggled to carve out a life that would support his long-term dream. He helped found two writing groups, worked at a bookstore, and surrounded himself with like-minded artists. As the son of a painter, Lethem grew up with a knowledge that being an artist is a job like any other—demanding time, energy, and focus.

Through the years he has developed a rigorous, schedule-centered process. Though he collaborates on screenplays, teaches workshops, works on the occasional CD-ROM project, and performs spoken-word pieces with jazz musician John Schott, his fiction writing takes precedence over all other endeavors. His typical day is structured around the solitary work in the morning and then attending to business in the afternoon. He lives a simple life—full of books, music, and art. During the first ten years of his career, he kept a singular focus on his goals. He traveled little, pursued few hobbies, and owned no car.

It might seem that he has been blessed with early success, since at thirty-two he's already publishing his fourth book. In fact, he exemplifies the principle of day-to-day squirrel work far more than inexplicable good fortune and precocious talent. For seven years he wrote and submitted dozens of short stories without so much as a personalized rejection letter. He claims that when he first began sending out stories, he often received up to seven rejection form letters from a single journal before he received a personalized, encouraging letdown from the editor.

As the interview reveals, he gave his creative process ample room and time to grow. This strong process created a life in which his creative work reigned at the top of his priority pyramid long before it paid his rent. He is the author of three novels, *Gun, with Occasional Music; Amnesia Moon;* and *As She Climbed Across the Table;* and *The Wall of the Sky, the Wall of the Eye,* a collection of short stories.

Q: What does your workday look like?

A: The best days are the ones where I remember what I have learned and what I have to keep learning again and again. The more directly I get to the deepest work right away, the more I'll get done. Other kinds of activities like letter writing and phone calls are always possible later in the day, but the best chance for real writing—adding to first drafts and going into my most inspired half-unconscious meld—is going to happen if I get to it directly, before I've gotten jarred into the world of human interactions.

When things are going well, I get up, drink coffee, read the paper relatively quickly and get right to it either by carrying my computer to a café or switching off the phone for the first few hours.

Q: What time do you usually start work?

A: Well, if I can, I get up at seven-thirty and get to work by eight. It sounds silly in a way, but usually the reward for that is that I've done substantial work between eight and ten. It doesn't mean that I won't write anymore that day, but I don't have to. It's also an opportunity to go well into the black and have another good session later on. The state of mind created by having done one substantial two-hour session before eleven is invaluable. If I try to work with any other structure for the day, I'm secretly playing catch-up, trying to eliminate distractions to get back to my work.

Q: Do you schedule your entire day?

A: I'm usually still at my desk at eleven or eleven-thirty or even twelve, though the work isn't as substantial after a third hour. Then I break for lunch, try to do some exercise—and then it depends on what's more important. Sometimes dealing with correspondence is more important than writing again, or if there's some deadline, I'll take a deep breath and write for the rest of the afternoon. It's costly and it's not good to do that for too long. But I can write all afternoon, or take an earlyish dinner, have a big cup of coffee, and write in the evening.

I don't really take weekends. I view each day as identical. I feel really irritated by holidays and weekends—I thrive on the rhythm that every day is a workday. Now, there are days when for one reason or another that doesn't happen; I'm awakened by a phone call that's distracting—good news, bad news. Starting later in the day is always a little harder. You fall into the psychological traps of "I should have written already." The self is most alone when you wake up before you flower into the social world and the desire for it. Before you start to yearn for company.

Q: How did you develop your creative process?

A: So much of forming a—I hate the word discipline—forming a self that's rigorous is a projection or bluff. You declare it to yourself before anything is substantial. I decided that I was starting my writing for real in the middle of my first year of college. I started stinting on my school-work and stealing time to work on this first novel and I was terribly susceptible to distraction. I wrote very infrequently, really, but what I cultivated first was the feeling of shame or guilt that I wasn't working. I gave myself a lot of shit and I had very little to show for it. It was as though I was holding myself to a standard that I had never demonstrated my capacity to do. I declared that I wrote often even though I didn't, and I felt bad about it when it wasn't true.

Shortly after that I did something that, looking back on it ten years later, turned out to be very unusual. At the time I had a lot of romantic notions about writing and I was very influenced by Kerouac and the Beats, so I had this idea that you retreated off into the wild and cut off contact with people. I've ended up a very social, urban person and very reliant on stimulus—seeing three movies a week and so forth. But ten years ago I got an opportunity to house-sit for eight months at the top of the Berkeley hills in a house that didn't have a phone. I didn't have a car. I had very few friends. I wrote postcards, I took long walks, and I wrote. I wasn't particularly efficient. If I had eight months in isolation now, I would write a whole book, but then I was cultivating this concept that I worked every day and making the opportunity unavoidable. I accomplished enough that I felt that I could go back into the world of people and not be kidding myself or them when I said, "I need a lot of time and space alone to write every day." I hadn't learned all the things that worked best, but I quickly uncovered what's been a really important wisdom for me: There's diminishing returns after three or four hours in a session. Marathon writing is not where it's at.

Q: How did your day job affect your work life?

A: I was lucky that my day job, working at bookstores, always involved some day shifts and some night shifts and so I got to taste writing early and writing late. It gave me different shapes of a day to experiment with and it forced me out of any voodoo that I can only write at X o'clock.

My day job was compatible with my ambitions. I was obsessed with books and specifically with old books. I was working as an apprentice in little used-book stores in Brooklyn and Manhattan when I was fifteen, sixteen, so I was kind of a prodigy as a bookseller. I can market myself as an expert with old valuable book knowledge. I was an autodidact, I never really learned much in school. I always learned a lot by reading, so I loved being surrounded by books and devouring big chunks of knowledge in raw form. But also I wasn't writing in my day job. I didn't go into advertising or become a scientific writer and I think that's better. It would have been hard for me to go home and write if I spent my day writing at my job. It would have muddled my sense of what that was for.

I resented work immensely. I loved being a bookseller, I resented being a clerk. I don't thrill to retail environments and I was in them for ten years straight. I always cheated—I always considered time more valuable than money. As soon as I was in a position to have a three-day weekend, I'd take it. And as soon as I could, I dropped down to working three days a week so I could write four.

Q: Did you have any role models or mentors for your creative process?

A: I read the *Paris Review* interviews. There's a tremendous amount of information about the process of writing because writers always want to talk about writing. It seems superficial, but at the same time you have a ravenous appetite for information about the particulars—like what kind of pencil someone uses. Even now, with my own biases and entrenched habits, I never skip the part when writers are confessing their rituals.

Q: How did you make the commitment to becoming a writer?

A: My father was a painter, so I was tremendously encouraged from the start to be a visual artist. At the same time I was always a little bit of a covert writer. I loved books more than I loved paintings and I read voraciously. I identified with writers' lives and read their biographies. My painting got very narrative and toward the end it incorporated a lot of words.

Q: What kind of support system do you have?

A: My support system is enormously important and it's very multi-plicitous. A safety net works best when it's anchored to a million different trees so when one tree goes down, it doesn't matter. I have two different writers' groups I show writing to, though I don't really need them both. Even if you're not talking about process or being supportive in some overt way, it's really fraternity that's important.

Q: Do you have any tricks you use to get yourself to write when you don't want to?

A: Absolutely. There's a whole list of them, and they're all banal but they have their place. One is calling a bunch of people when I know I'm going to get their answering machine and say, "I have to talk to you today." I leave ten messages like that and then sit at my desk; I'm stuck in my house because all my friends are going to call me back and I work in between the returned calls.

Another one is going to cafés and kidding myself that I'm in the world when, of course, what I'm really doing is working. But just a modicum of eye contact can mimic some other kind of space in the world.

Also I turn my computer on and then read my paper and drink my coffee sitting at my desk. I do as much as I can to clothe the nakedness of the start-up. It's subtle, but it can help a lot.

Q: Have you ever had any failures around creating your working process?

A: I had a major crisis when I was married to another writer. It was the biggest challenge my work had ever faced. It was a very difficult period in the growth of my process, but it was one that forged the strong process I now have. It involved a huge failed enterprise of trying to work in tandem with someone else in the same space at the same time. Trying to synchronize our desires to write was a long miserable failure that was really hard to let go of. After that I knew that my writing was an individual need that had to have its own individual care and couldn't be made dependent on any other system.

Q: Is success a motivating force in your work?

A: Visualizing success and visualizing acclaim is a big part of day-to-day incentive and it's the easiest thing to hold on to and the most obvious thing to focus on. But I don't think it's at the heart of why I'm doing what I'm doing. I think I'd probably be trying to make my mark in some other way if I was doing something else, so it's also the most generic motivation for what I'm doing. I have stories in me and feelings about the world that can only be expressed in books. Initially there's the yearning to communicate and it's relatively raw and amorphous, but the more you work, the more you discover the meaning of craft, and every sentence becomes the opportunity to test your craft and the involvement at the level of syntax. You fall in love with the making, the formal questions, and the formal issues. And if you write seriously you become more a formalist by exposure to the materials. Initially, you're a guy who carves giant chunks of marble out of the mountains and drags them back to the village. Then you become more and more involved in shaping them on the way down to the village and so by the end you're bringing less of the mountain but more finished, intricately carved pieces.

If I weren't so polite about saying what I think in day-to-day life, I might not be as driven to write but it's the most polite way I can think of to say how crappy I think everything is all the time.

Q: Do you have any advice for beginners in your field?

A: Finish things and start the next one.

Building a Bridge You Can Jump On

Support Structures

> Listen attentively, and remember that true tales are meant to be transmitted—to keep them to oneself is to betray them.
>
> —Anonymous

As a creative person, you are a bridge. You connect banal reality to an imaginary land and you allow people to visit this land. It is hard work being a bridge—no one likes being trampled on day and night—but you do it willingly to see the looks on the tourists' faces as they return from your dreamscape.

Like a bridge that needs to be anchored to the ocean floor and connected by great iron cables to the shore, creative people need multiple support structures so they don't float away to some distant professional reef like life insurance or thumbtack distribution. Your will alone cannot keep you in place. You need support systems to help you.

When I explain my bridge metaphor, my students nod with the gratification of finally being understood. Then one of them adds, "That's why I need an agent (or gallery or client or grant). I need someone to support me." I shake my head: "The key to persevering in your art is to build a strong enough structure so that you're creative and happy *without success*." I get a few deadpan stares, a squinted glare, an exasperated sigh. I know what they're thinking: "Isn't success the whole point?

What sort of career counseling is this, anyway?" For many ambitious artists, as most of my students are, happiness is contingent upon success rather than the other way around. I think they secretly fear that with too much enjoyment in the present they will become lazy and never achieve their aims. From my many years watching artists build their lives, I have come to the conclusion that a healthy support system is often the only difference between the artists and the ex-artists. It isn't nobility, heroism, or talent that makes a working artist, but a whole network of helping hands that give the artist the support to keep going.

There are three kinds of support you have been building through the Life Worth Living process. The day job is like a house: It provides basic necessities, and offers shelter while you are slowly building your career. Your daily process is like your bed: It needs to be firm enough to support a strong backbone and soft enough to allow you to fall into deep, gorgeous dreams. Finally, your support system of real and imaginary friendships, family, colleagues, and mentors is a suspension bridge that connects you to the world and raises you above stretches of dark water. The columns of the bridge root you to the ground while the catwalk allows you to sneak high above your troubles. This chapter deals with a handful of bridge-building techniques, starting with the crucial one of partnering.

Partnering: The Basic Technique

Making art or starting a business often involves many hours of isolation. While being alone can bring great clarity of mind, it can also distort our perceptions. If we are in a particularly dejected mood, we see a steel vault where there is really just a sticky doorknob. When this happens, having a kind, intelligent, enthusiastic friend to talk to may mean the difference between a little slipup and a long downhill slide.

Partnering is a formalized friendship that you set up with one other person to keep you focused on the best, most important parts of your life. The primary activity in this relationship consists of meeting with a person once a week to plan out your goals for that week and sometimes for that decade. I like to think of it as a staff meeting for all the projects that don't have a staff. During these meetings you will set goals, brainstorm through obstacles, complain, strategize, and celebrate. Regular partnering meetings can help you navigate through projects that feel impossibly treacherous or complicated. While partners should not try to influence each other's goals, they should encourage each other to pursue their ambitions in a healthy, active manner.

Your partner can help you break down larger tasks into more manageable pieces, provide deadlines, and point out if you are stalling on one of your projects or biting off too much work per week. Most of all, they can give you encouragement when no one else in the world seems to care.

You and your partner can also discuss issues of daily process, like "I don't know why I can't seem to get to my studio by eight o'clock." If you feel yourself slipping into old habits that no longer work for you, these little discussions can be a great preventative measure in catching yourself before you fall into a slump. The partnering meeting will build new resolve in tackling difficult issues and refocus you on the coming week ahead.

Choosing a Partner

The ideal partner is someone who has your best interests at heart and who does not feel competitive toward you. You understand and respect each other's goals, though there's absolutely no reason why you need to be involved in similar fields. Mutual respect and genuine interest are the only rules.

If you are tempted to pick a spouse, a lover, or a new infatuation, please reconsider this urge. It may work for a while, but sooner or later the love relationship will be more important (or more horrific) than the partnering one. Of course, there are great historic examples of lover/partnerships—Jean-Paul Sartre and Simone de Beauvoir, for instance—but these are the exceptions, not the rule. During this difficult journey, it's important that you don't overburden yourself by choosing a route that leads directly through an emotional minefield. For similar reasons, I don't recommend that people choose artistic collaborators as partners because of the intensity and complexity inherent in most collaborative endeavors. You want your partnering to be a clean space where you can see your life with *more* clarity—not less.

Beware of choosing partners with goals too similar to your own. Not only can competition arise, but your partner's project may be so interesting and exciting that you'll get distracted. Seek out someone you like and respect but not someone who threatens the boundaries of your own private vision. Finally, don't rush to try out just anyone; you'll frustrate yourself, waste lots of time, and sour on the idea itself.

The partnership is founded on a relationship of equality and mutual agreement. The ideal partner can listen to you without judgment, ask questions, and guide you in thinking through predicaments in a clear, new way. Good partners need your support and input as much as you need theirs.

This may sound unrealistic if you are someone who specializes in complicated relationships. But remember, the partner doesn't need to be a close friend. You can start partnering with someone who is a stranger and let the relationship grow out of the hours you spend helping one another.

To begin your search, make a list of all the people you know who you believe have good partnering potential. Then narrow it down to three possibilities.

1.
2.
3.

Approach your first choice with the knowledge that if it doesn't work out you can stop the process and move on to the others. Explain to your potential partner that you will be starting a partnership of practical and emotional support where both of you can use each other to achieve your goals, clarify your long-term vision, and develop and maintain a well-balanced creative process. The commitment consists of no more than a weekly meeting for no more than an hour and a half. If the person is grappling with creative career issues, they probably will immediately recognize the need for a very simple ongoing place to think about these issues. If they are avoiding these issues, then the partnership may provide them with a little time every week to begin dealing actively with their dreams. It may take a couple of months to see if the chemistry and scheduling are really going to work. If you cannot imagine partnering with any of your friends or family, then consider acquaintances whom you have always wanted to get to know. You also might try putting a notice in a neighborhood bookstore or café, or an advertisement in the local newspaper.

Whether your partner is a stranger or your best friend, the partnering relationship can change the way you think about your dreams and schemes. Suddenly, they will feel more concrete and more realizable. Why? Partnering draws on another person's faith in you and thereby refuels your belief in yourself.

Scheduling the Partnering Hour

Most sessions will naturally include the following four steps. Before you go to your partnering meeting always give yourself thirty seconds to ask yourself, What do I want from this meeting?

1. A general check-in on both sides. How was your week? How are you feeling?
2. Going over your accomplishments, problems, and plans for the past and coming week. This entails scheduling, brainstorming, and goal setting.
3. Going over your partner's accomplishments, problems, and plans.
4. Talking about long-term directions, goals, and dreams.
5. Confirming the time and place of the next meeting.
6. Social time.

During the partnering hour, it is important not to flip-flop back and forth between both people's plans. Focus on one person at a time until you are finished. For especially eager tongues and tight schedules, it may be helpful to time the meetings so that each person receives equal time.

Unlike many kinds of meetings, I've found that partnering is actually enhanced by food or fun or garden sun. It helps if both people look forward to it as a reward as well as an integral part of their workweek. So, if you can manage, make it a Friday lunch date or a Sunday brunch or a garden tea. Make it something that feels like a treat yet will not distract you from the work of the meeting.

- First meeting: Go over the partnering sheet and talk about scheduling and commitment. Set goals for that week.
- Second meeting: Teach your partner any methods you want to use from this book. (And buy your partner a copy of this book!)
- Third meeting: Hold the first regular partnering meeting and set long-term goals using the Five-Arena Calendar (in chapter 12).
- Fourth meeting: Talk about the partnering process. How can you improve your methods? Is the process working for you? How does it affect your workweek? Make a commitment to continue for another three months and then reassess the process.

One-Way Partnering

You can engage in one-way partnering in numerous ways. You can barter or pay someone to be your partner in return for something like a back massage or a nice meal, money or some other in-kind service. Sometimes your partner will offer to do it for nothing and become a sort of mentor to you. This can become problematic if you don't feel comfortable asking for what you need. Coaches are great if you can afford them, but for most people this isn't an ideal long-term situation. Also, because they constitute "professional" help, the relationship does not, I believe, foster the sense of autonomy that you want to create.

The More the Mightier Theory

Why not develop a whole support group? If one person can give you support and great ideas then couldn't six people give you more? Certainly support groups can work, but only with leadership or a very clear structure. I teach classes with up to ten people in them; the diversity of people and perspectives spawns more ideas and energy but it also demands more time. The larger the group, the less time there will be for each individual's issues.

While groups can provide a great forum for brainstorming, I believe two-person partnerships are less prone to difficult dynamics. Because you're looking for low-maintenance, long-term help, partnering offers a more reliable, stable source of support. If developing, scheduling, and processing a group becomes its own time-consuming task, then the group is probably interfering with at least one person's individual goals (unless his or her goal is to facilitate a group).

Long-Distance Partnering

If your only imaginable partner lives far, far away, it is possible to work through E-mail or phone lines. In general, I would recommend the phone over the computer because of its immediacy. On the phone, you can have the meeting of minds necessary for a good brainstorming session. It also demands a specific time and therefore can function as a deadline.

If you are someone who likes these tools, E-mail or fax partnering can work, but guard against using technology to avoid or delay your interactions. Moreover, if you already have a day job that requires long hours talking on the phone or staring at a computer screen, adding one more hour a week of long-distance communication may make the partnering feel like a burden. The partnering relationship needs to feel fresh and distinct from our daily drudgery.

Self-Partnering

Okay, so you've become a hermit and your closest potential partners are those crazy triplet brothers Bob, Bob, and Bob forty miles down the road. In that case, you probably should self-partner, but first you must spend some time creating an image of who you would like your partner to be.

The next exercise will help you discover the part of yourself that can offer help, guidance, and support and the part of yourself that is willing to *ask for and receive* help. In poet Lynn Emanuel's book *The Dig*, she describes this dual sense of self that leads her toward a limitless world:

> *I will study her longing for far, for everything*
> *to be more*
> *must travel by eye and she*
> *that more distant I*
> *will set no limits . . .*
>
> *Oh, my own far self, I know you are there,*
> *leanly watchful and at ease.*
> *The far is alert, like you, like me.*

Even with the most ideal partner, if you can't articulate and receive the support you need, the relationship will remain purely logistical, offering little real sustenance. In these cases, this self-partnering exercise can prepare the mind for the real partnering relationship.

The Second-Self Exercise

First imagine a mirror image of yourself. This benign doppelgänger looks exactly like you, possessing all of your good qualities. There are no exceptional differences in personality or body except that this person might be a bit older. This person lives exactly as you do on your best day, following the crystal-clear trajectory of your desire and purpose. Can you imagine how he or she dresses? Talks? Walks? Works? Describe him as he walks into a room and interacts with people, then as she works on something alone.

Even though he or she resembles you, try to see this person as a distinct entity. Scrutinize his or her behavior, smile, and body language. Now look at yourself. What elements of your own personality have you accentuated in your imaginary mentor? Which characteristics have you diminished or erased? Let yourself explore these differences a bit on paper—drawing, writing, or listing as you will.

In the current fashion of therapy, the focus remains on the aspiring self. This makes sense in many ways, since it represents the part of us that is giving us trouble. Goals, then, become things we must reach for beyond ourselves. If we concentrate on developing a stronger image of our perfected self, we can stop fixating on our mistakes and begin to take the lead from the part of us that *already knows,* the creative creature who is always watching and hoping for the best of us.

Now imagine yourself in the following scenario.

You are scrambling up a rocky volcanic slope with bloody fingers in order to reach this magnificent, impossibly perfect place on high (your goal). There is no one to help you anywhere except for some people high above you who either ignore you or throw rocks down on you each time you get close to the top. Others sneer at you from below, ridiculing your foolish attempts to scale new heights. You fall down the craggy cliffs into a churning, ice-gray sea. At the bottom of the cliff you look up, farther away than ever.

If you feel this sense of frustrated striving in working toward your goals, then try to imagine the following: bring back the image of the mountain with all its dangerous precipices, rocky paths, and scowling onlookers, then imagine this perfected being, who is you, already sitting on the top, working away quietly. From the top of the mountain you can see a little energetic you down there in the fog, shivering, being lapped at by a murky ocean, perhaps pecked at by some malnourished birds. The "you" on the mountain reaches out a long, graceful hand, which stretches all the way down the mountain. The "little you" takes the hand. The higher being does not pull you up to the top in one flying leap, but leads you step by baby step to a secret path between the rocks (one you would have never found otherwise) and you begin to climb slowly but steadily. You have a hand to lean on and an understanding that you are following a part of yourself that already understands the journey.

In the same manner that writers talk about "getting out of the way" to let their characters speak, we must make conscious room to allow the more self-assured, intuitive side of ourselves to take the lead. To explore how your second self might take the lead in an everyday way, let's consider a somewhat banal situation—not profound like writing a poem or painting a canvas, but something as simple as making a difficult phone call.

A woman you met last week at a party expresses interest in your work. The next day you realize who she was—an important something-or-other in your field. Your first thought is, Oh, well, she'll never remember me; there were so many people at that party. Then a few days later in the shower, you realize: You could call her and offer to help on her upcoming project. In the shower, it seems easy. Your doppelgänger has seized control, basking in the hot water and confidence. You have two ways to respond to this spurt of motivation and inspiration.

1. Step out of the shower and call the woman, naked and dripping on the living room floor. Treat the moment as you would a song lyric sent down to you ready made: It's divine inspiration. If the woman doesn't respond, you can chalk it up to a brilliant experiment in spontaneous living.

2. Put it on that list of things to do and wait for the time when the little tentative you, not your presumptuous doppelgänger, is "ready." After three months of preparation and procrastination, you call.

What are the possibilities if you choose the second option?
- She says, "Yes! Great idea!"—in which case you could have called before.
- She says, "Great idea, but I wished you'd called me two months ago; the opportunity has passed"—in which case you should have called before.
- She says, "No, thank you"—in which case you shouldn't have wasted your energy worrying for three months.

Treat every idea or spur to action you receive as a guiding hand from this elusive doppelgänger. When you self-partner, you need to maintain the idea of this self as a separate entity in order for it to continue to help you. In this way, you don't have to raise your self-esteem before you act on your dreams. You can count on your imaginary partner to help you.

The Logistics of Self-Partnering

Plan a meeting time once a week just like you would with a real partner. Write down your goals for that week and then imagine this second self looking at your goals, asking you what you really want, making sure you're not trying to tackle too much or too little, and suggesting a priority for these goals.

Additional Support Structures

In addition to the partnering relationship, artists need to develop a variety of ways of getting support for their work. As you read the following descriptions, ask yourself which of these kinds of support you would like to nurture in your life.

Sweet Family of Ghosts

Almost all artists derive succor from the dead. The dead continue to give willingly when the living won't return phone calls and refuse to remember your name. Holding fast to your creative heritage is a way of building an impassioned support system without dealing with anybody! This might include people you respect for the way they lived their lives or for the integrity of their work. Having a deep love and understanding for the men and women whose work has inspired and influenced your own can create a spiritual family which has just as much power as a living friend.

In offering advice to young writers, Jorge Luis Borges wonderfully captured the way our beloved ghosts help transform us, as artists, into ourselves:

> He should begin, of course, by imitating the writers he likes. This is the way the writer becomes himself through losing himself—that strange way of double living, of living in reality as much as one can and at the same time of living in that other reality, the one he has to create, the reality of his dreams.

To develop your family of ghosts, read biographies, peruse bookstores, visit museums, write them letters—and make friends with a few dead people. Know their lives and their loves; become intimate with their creative process, their beliefs about art. Love them for what they have given you and they, in turn, will begin to live within you.

ADLAI ALEXANDER, GUITARIST

Born and raised in a lower-middle-class black neighborhood, Adlai Alexander learned his appreciation for music and art from his parents, who loved to sing and tell stories. When Alexander was a teenager he had the same dream as a lot of American boys: he wanted to be a rock 'n' roll guitarist. During his senior year in college his father died, and Alexander dropped out to seek his fortune: "I realize now it was the wrong approach for me to make my life as a musician. I didn't know what it meant to be a musician at the time. It was more for my self-esteem than it was creative. I didn't cherish it, and I wanted the results of fame. I just didn't realize why I was playing music." After years of disappointments, he decided to get a straight job and make some money. He worked his way through the computer industry, ending up as a project manager at Sun Microsystems, where for many years he led a double life: as a corporate team player by day and jazz musician by night. During this period he settled into a period of intense study. Every evening after work, he devoted himself to practicing his guitar. It was then that he began to build his expertise and a deeper appreciation for the craft.

He began studying with jazz guitarist Tuck Anders: "I was really lucky because I think that it's important for a mentor to understand what you're trying to do. People give advice without really understanding your specific situation. It's nice to hear encouragement from your mom, but when you hear it from someone you admire, you have to take them seriously." He developed a unique technique of playing chords and walking bass lines and simultaneously singing. One day he showed it to his teacher, who told him, "Nobody else can do that! You should quit your job." On Monday he went into the office and gave his two weeks' notice.

From there he began the scary but exhilarating transition from steady corporate job to artistic self-employment. Ironically, now that his guitar skills are refined and his attitude matured, he has a remarkably easy time developing his career as a guitarist and composer: "Not only did I go about it from the artistic point of view but from the publicity and business point of view. And I found that it's not that hard." He used his business skills to plan and keep track of his projects and his self-promotion—setting up a database and a computerized mailing list and making phone calls.

When I ask him about his day now, he says, "It's so wonderful, I almost feel guilty about it. When I was doing the corporate job, getting up and going to work was just horrible, but now I look forward to my work. I don't have to answer to anybody. I can take breaks any time I want and I'm alone. That helps a lot. I'm not consumed with a concern that is not essential to my well-being. I was totally willing to get into the corporate cult, but at the same time the work wasn't important to me. Now everything I do can relate to what I'm most passionate about."

His advice for aspiring musicians is to focus on their craft in the beginning and not get distracted by the allure of easy fame. "It's important for artists to develop their skills rather than relying on a dream like I did in the beginning," he says. "I used to lie in bed and hope that one day I'd be as good as Miles Davis. The way to do that is to get out of bed and open a book and with no reward other than that, learn your scales. I used to think this thing cynically: 'You become an adult when you realize that your dreams aren't going to come true.' But, in a way, that phrase led to a turning point. I realized that the dream, in itself, is nothing. It's a thought. It's necessary to motivate you and give you direction, but without putting together the building blocks that will create a dream that's actually tangible, it's not going to come true. You can't become a great guitar player unless you do what the other great guitar players did: Sit there all by themselves in the dark for a year or two and just practice, practice, practice."

Scene Making

Professional communities, clubs, on-line communities, organizations, and social groups can be a great, fun-filled way of receiving support for your work. When you are part of a greater community, your work will feel less arbitrary and less lonely. People will know what you are working on and ask you about it. When you talk about particular struggles or successes, they will actually know what you mean. While the right "scene" can provide an almost inexhaustible source of love, help, and support, few scenes remain untouched by competition and jealousy. Sometimes these groups will support you; sometimes they won't. That doesn't mean they can't enrich your life, only that you need to be very careful not to give them your full weight. That's the irony of graduate programs. Often people enter them hoping to find a ready-made support structure that will nurture the baby artist into adulthood, only to find a den of hyenas hungrily ripping up the carcasses of the young. Practically speaking, you probably won't know what kind of atmosphere presides in a given program until you enter it. In choosing a graduate program, weigh all the variables and do your research. Visit the schools, watch the teachers teach, research their careers and artwork. Try not to go into debt! Be careful before you entrust any institution with your creative children.

Peer groups offer a more organized, controlled place for support. Common artistic peer groups include writers' groups (to read and critique one another's work), artists' groups (to share and critique work), dance collectives (to share and collaborate on choreography); musical groups; and actors' workout groups to practice scenes, improvisations, and monologues. Sometimes these groups also take the form of reading and discussion groups related to the particular art form or creative work.

These peer groups are easy to organize (usually through word of mouth or a poster in your local bookstore or café). They're also a wonderful structure for developing and maintaining friendships with other people in your field. Unlike those of less organized clubs or social scenes, these group discussions usually stay focused on the *content* of the creative work rather than degenerating into shoptalk or professional gossip.

Career Advisory Board

This uses the model of a board of directors (which advises the president and staff of nonprofit and for-profit corporations) and applies it to the individual artist. This model is particularly useful for the creative person who is already committed to pursuing art as a profession and has developed a fairly substantial body of work.

The career advisory board is made up of a diverse group of individuals (three to seven people works best) who love the artist's work and want to help. Ideally, each advisor provides a different point of view. For example, a young female performance artist I knew gathered together a wise elderly woman who had been an actress, a friend in public relations, a businessman who was her most avid fan, and a retired theater critic who had always loved her work. But the group doesn't have to be ideal in profile; they just need to be enthusiastic and resourceful.

Most career advisory boards meet with the artist once every two months over a meal. After the artist reports on the business of her career, the group offers guidance and new ideas. Then together they map out a plan for the next two months.

Whether you choose to build a support structure from dead masters or the old woman next door or a hepcat scene at the local art bar doesn't matter. Creativity springs from a ferment of connections and ideas. So, in addition to your private vision, your rigorous creative habits, and your practical day job, don't forget that you need fellowship connecting you to the world.

Partnering Worksheet

What do you want out of this hour?

   Date:
   Time:

GOALS OF THE WEEK

LONG-TERM GOALS

ONGOING PROJECTS

   How are you feeling about the partnering process?

SAMPLE PARTNER DIALOGUE
   How was your week?

   What's the most important thing you want to get done this week?

   How much time do you have?

   What do you have the most energy for?

Here's how I would prioritize these things:

Is there any ongoing problem you are struggling with?

Star the most important goals for the week, give yourself a treat and make a date with yourself next week.

Date:
Treat:

EXERCISES IN DEVELOPING SUPPORT STRUCTURES

1: Set up an initial partnering meeting with your partner or your second self.

2: Make a list of the most inspiring and supportive people in your life and make a date with one of them to talk about your projects and have fun.

3: Are there any classes, clubs, groups, or scenes that would bring you together with other people with similar creative interests? If you are not a joiner, brainstorm on how can you derive a sense of community support for your work. Is there anything you can do privately to build your internal sense of support (reading certain writers, watching certain films, collecting stones, going through old love letters from high school . . .)?

4: Attend at least one event related to your creative work. Make an effort to get to know someone at the event—not for the purposes of schmoozing but to find kindred creative spirits.

5: Design your own ideal support system. How is it formed? Who is in it? How often do you meet? How does it work?

6: Personal Homework: Transfer your ideas into your Adventure Book.

BILL RAUCH, THEATER DIRECTOR

When director Bill Rauch and playwright Alison Carey started Corner-stone Theater Company, a national community-based theater company, they were fresh out of college. What they lacked in the way of money, professional experience, and reputation, they made up for in passion, determination, and idealism. Equal parts realizer and healer, Rauch uses his directorial creativity in the service of higher goals: staging classic plays in specific communities to foster communication between diverse groups and build a grassroots theater. From the beginning, Cornerstone's goals were not only about community work but about making good art. Before the company settled in Los Angeles in 1992, they spent five years working in rural communities throughout America: from Native American reservations to a small town in Mississippi to the Kansas farmland.

With the many-faceted responsibilities of the interdisciplinarian, Rauch now works as both a nonprofit administrator—organizing events, making community liaisons, and grant writing—and as a theater director, casting, rehearsing, reading plays, and conceptualizing new works. In all of his work he depends upon the collaborative nature of the group—a process that he has come to appreciate and trust as much as his own perspective. Perhaps this is why Rauch speaks with as much pride when he is talking about the internal process of the company as when he talks about his individual directorial experiences. He knows that the conception and making of the company is, in itself, a great creative accomplishment.

Q: How did you start Cornerstone Theater?

A: Most of us who started the company went to college together. Where we went there was no theater major—Harvard-Radcliffe—although we all shared a passion for theater. We shared a frustration over what a narrow segment of the American population goes to theater. We hungered to perform for and with the ninety-seven percent of the population who don't regularly go to the theater, both because we believed in creating for an underserved majority and because we had a hunch that we would become better artists in the process of collaborating with audiences who didn't have strong preconceptions about what theater should be. And that has proven true in ways that we never could begin to have guessed; we have been changed as artists forever.

We talked throughout our years in school about doing what we called "truck theater"—the idea of getting in a truck and driving around the countryside and performing for people. Slowly the idea evolved into not only performing for a community and then taking off the next morning, but maybe staying longer and involving people from the community in the show.

Q: So you do a lot of grant writing?

A: Exactly. We're very grant reliant, very reliant on our individual donors. But we've been really blessed and managed to hang in there. Some of our older professional colleagues thought it was really crazy to go out there and invent the wheel instead of trying to succeed in the avenues that existed. I forget sometimes how scary that was.

Q: To go against everyone's advice . . .

A: Yeah, and just go for it. To start something that didn't exist— make up a name, make up a mission, and send out literature about it— it was incredibly exciting and scary. We were very, very lucky, because what initially got us off the ground was that my parents at that time lived in Virginia and we approached the Virginia Commission for the Arts. They said, "Well, we can't give you any money if you haven't done anything yet, but if you want to work in the school systems, we'll give you money, because we have an arts in education program." We wrote all one hundred and fifty school superintendents in the state of Virginia and then called them all and we ended up having about sixty school systems that were interested, and from that we narrowed it down to four that applied to the Virginia Commission for the Arts for matching money to bring us in and all four were fully funded. So in one day, we suddenly had ninety thousand dollars' worth of funding, which of course could not happen today. That was in the eighties.

Q: Did you study directing?

A: Formally, no. I directed twenty-six plays as an undergraduate. But I had incredible teachers. A woman, Joann Green, was my mentor at Harvard. She taught me that everything and everybody is precious and important. Every moment in a play, every prop, every costume piece, every crew member, every actor, everything matters a lot.

Q: I want to talk about your process as a director.

A: I guess if there's anything to say about my process it's that I'm very reliant on collaborating. Cornerstone is run by consensus. Every time I'm on the verge of getting frustrated with that system, something really dramatic happens that reminds me that had I been in a position to make that decision myself, had I been a dictator, I would not have made as good a decision. I feel pretty good about not making the wrong decisions by consensus.

Q: What do you think are the most common misconceptions about Cornerstone?

A: That we're giving to the community, that it's charity, when in fact we're getting so much. That somehow the community needs us. And I think a corollary to that is that the art must not be very good. It's not real art. The worst moments are when you hear a friend from college saying "Oh, they have so much talent. It's very nice what they're doing, but it's so sad." We won Los Angeles's highest theatrical award over a hundred and ninety other productions for a show we did in Watts with a cast that was three-quarters nonprofessionals. Yet the show won best production of the year. It was an extremely gratifying moment, because even though awards are very silly things, it was amazing to have our professional peers judge the quality of our work as not only competitive with the best professional theater but, in fact, the best.

Q: Were you supported by your family when you set out to do this?

A: At the time, I was working with the director Peter Sellars. I lived with my parents the year we put Cornerstone together. My dad was extremely disappointed, concerned, and negative about the idea. A year later, when we had our first fund-raiser to celebrate our first year of work, my father was in the front row and was very moved, and that in turn moved me. Even though my parents didn't agree with all my decisions, I felt supported to do what I thought was right. We got our first NEA grant the year that the Helms obscenity clause existed, but because of the consensus of my colleagues, we decided to turn down the grant based on that clause. Of course, in the end, it was one of these fairy tale stories. An individual and a foundation replaced the full amount of the grant and then it was found that the clause was unconstitutional, so the NEA actually turned the grant back over to us before the end of the year. We ended up making three times the amount of the original grant. When I told my dad we turned down the grant, he said he thought it was a bad decision, but said that he had thought founding Cornerstone had been a bad decision, so maybe he could be wrong about this too. For any parent to say, "You think differently than I do, but I respect you," is an amazing gift. So that's a very long answer for yes. Plus various members of all our families have flown all over the country to come see us.

Q: What does your workday look like?

A: I teach at University of Southern California part-time to supplement my Cornerstone income. I teach at eight A.M., then go work for Cornerstone at ten and on a day when I'm in rehearsal, I have a meeting or do office stuff from ten to one, and then I'm in rehearsal from one till ten. Over the dinner break I have meetings with designers or funders or whatever. So they're really long days. When I'm not in rehearsal, they are still often twelve-to-fourteen-hour days, but it's not as intense. I don't teach every single day. It's theater in the nonprofit sector, so you work too hard, for too little money.

Q: Do you have tricks that you use when you don't feel like working?

A: I try to use a system of rewards—if I push through and get this particular thing done, I'll go to a movie.

Q: What do you do about getting creatively blocked?

A: That's part of why I appreciate deadlines so much. Having a deadline forces you to make a decision and as you make a decision, you are creating that way. Because Cornerstone is a nomadic company, one of our real difficulties is never knowing what space we're working in. It's completely abstract and you never get anywhere, but I'm always amazed at how one piece of specific information can lead to creativity. I have to say, if I'm really stumped as to how to develop a scene, one of the great things we've developed at Cornerstone is jamming sessions where the professional actors in the company and I will get together for an afternoon and throw out ideas and the actors will stand up and try stuff. It's brainstorming on our feet. This gives me an unbelievable amount of ideas I can bring into the evening rehearsal with the community-based actors.

Q: Have you ever experienced failure related to being a director?

A: In 1991, we didn't produce for about eight months, and during that time I was hired to direct a play for En Garde Arts, an off-Broadway company that does site-specific work in New York City and is very critically successful. To make a long story short, I directed their first critical and box-office failure. It was really painful. It's not like I base whether I think something is a success on what other people think. But in the conventional sense, it was a failure. To put another spin on it, I would have to say everything we do at Cornerstone is a failure—because every single thing we do is reinventing the wheel and is really ambitious on some levels and doesn't succeed on others. I hope we don't get to the point where we're constantly doing something we've "perfected." So much of it means redefining what one means by success or failure. Ultimately I ended up with some of my best collaborators from that project, so it wasn't a failure at all. It was a failure in some external world, by some conventional definition of failure.

Q: Have your thoughts about what success means changed?

A: We set out to do something impossible, but it was really exciting to try, and the fact that we've done what we set out to do is really amazing. Now it's a matter of not resting on our laurels. In Los Angeles, so many of the relationships we have are with artists who are making obscene amounts of money, so that's kind of unsettling and confusing. You just have to refocus on why what you're doing matters to you. You also never want to fall into the trap of thinking that what you're doing is more important than what someone else is doing. I used to be more defensive about "We do art, it's not about social service." I have definitely become more sensitive to the relative importance of whether or not a child has eaten dinner before rehearsal over whether or not we get a line right in a scene. So that measure of success has really shifted.

Q: You probably see other talented friends who have wanted to direct their own companies and haven't. Do you think there's anything that you have a sense of that they don't understand about what it takes to do this?

A: No, I think it's all about determination, sticking to it. With Cornerstone, it's about the people who have done the work, our respect for each other and faith in each other and the community we've made. The culture of our community is one that respects longevity and rewards loyalty and all these touchy-feely phrases, but it's true.

Q: If a young person came to you and wanted to carve out some life in the theater, what advice would you give them?

A: You kind of answered the question for me. Don't sit around and bitch about the system you're trapped in. Remake the system. Start from scratch. Whenever we complain at Cornerstone about the problems we're having with money or the limits on our time, we have to remind ourselves that this is our reality. If it's an unfortunate reality, remake the reality. I would hope to charge those young people with the sense that it really is within their power.

Q: What if they really want to make something happen, but don't know how?

A: Be really systematic and thorough. When we started Cornerstone, I'm sure we would have failed if we only wrote to three superintendents and then gave up. But we wrote to all of them and called all of them. We were so tenacious. I'm a firm believer in the old adage that genius is one percent inspiration and ninety-nine percent perspiration. I can't tell you how many times we've sat down with funders who told us, "We will never fund you," and then a few years later we got a grant from them. You can't give up just because someone tells you no. When somebody rejects you, don't take it personally. It's not like, Well, they're right, I'm worthless. They just don't get it yet. So you have to find another way to convince them.

Swimming in the Darkness

Pursuing the Creative Life

I was in love, then, with monsters and skeletons and circuses and carnivals and dinosaurs and, at last, the red planet, Mars.

From these primitive bricks I have built a life and a career. By my staying in love with all of these amazing things, all of the good things in my existence have come about. . . .

And the trip? Exactly one half terror, exactly one half exhilaration.

—Ray Bradbury

Foolish then to search for wings? Inhuman even? But I dream of flight not to be as the angels are, but to rise above the smallness of it all.

—Jeanette Winterson

These bits of advice speak to the core of this process. Through daring to act, you can learn things you can never learn by waiting, holding off, wondering, and wishing. This last chapter will introduce you to a final tool, offer some parting thoughts on the creative process, and set you on your way to jumping into your new life *today*.

Five-Arena Calendar

The final tool in this process gives you a simple framework for mapping out five distinct areas of your life. It is a tool not just of organization but of commitment. Though this calendar will not do the work for you, it can help balance your efforts, remind you of long-term deadlines, and organize your goals. It will ground you in the world of real actions in time. By using this structure along with your new daily process and your weekly partnering meetings, you will have built a complex web of security. It also allows you to see your life in a more holistic way rather than as a series of tasks leading to a single, specific goal.

I encourage my students to list their arenas of endeavor in order of their long-term creative importance. The first arena should be both the one you feel the strongest about and the one you are afraid you will neglect in the whirlwind of necessity and whim. Usually people choose the creative work that they feel most passionately about: an art form, a long-term business or invention project, or some other dream that they really want to begin to put first, even though there may be many obstacles in the way. Your action plan from chapter 8 can help you in charting out your first and possibly second arenas as the central creative projects in your life. Use your action plan to remind yourself of the larger milestones and goals of this project.

In every class I teach, I encounter students who won't allow themselves to put their first love in their first arena. Kelly spent the whole class talking about her love of cooking and writing, then said that for her first arena, "I'm going to take a computer class and try to learn desktop publishing."

"What about cooking and writing?" I asked.

"It just doesn't seem practical," she said, blushing. When it came to writing her priorities down into a real calendar, she froze up. Making your most intense (and therefore frightening) passion occupy your calendar's first arena is an important first step in structuring that endeavor into your life. Let the first arena express what is really hidden in the secret corner of your basement.

The second arena usually becomes home to a secondary creative goal—perhaps another art form or project, or a more commercial project. For Lana, her first arena was starting an on-line art gallery for tattoo artists. Her second was marketing herself as a freelance web designer. Janice made poetry her first arena, Brazilian dance her second. Sometimes the first arena is so huge and multifaceted, it spills out into the second arena. For instance, Bill realized he wanted to make an independent feature-length film. The project had two parts: the creative development of the film and the business of making the film happen. His first arena comprised the creative work of writing and making the film; the second arena encompassed the business of raising money, working with producers and distributors, and so on.

I encourage students to use the third and fourth arenas to deal with finding or creating practical, transitional situations. For these two areas people often choose day jobs, housing and financial issues, or more commercial creative endeavors. For example, singer-songwriter Tom made his first and second arenas songwriting and the business of promoting himself as a singer. In his third arena he developed freelance work as an environmental editor. In his fourth arena, he concentrated on activities that would lower his expenses: cooking, finding a new place to live, selling his car.

The fifth arena is a place for an activity that balances out your other pursuits and helps you maintain your sanity. Marianne, a poet, chose dance classes as her fifth arena because she wanted to become more physical and spend time every week with people who were *not* talking. Keith, a clown and juggler, felt that he needed intellectual stimulation, so he created a reading group. Spiritual practices, physical exercise, social life, excursions into nature, traveling, or a purely fun, ambition-free art form often find their way into the fifth arena. For artists in the throes of struggling between their art and their livelihood, the fifth arena provides a place for hobbies, play, and recreation. These simple, pleasurable activities teach us again and again the beauty of doing for doing's sake. If you are not yet making a living from your art, you may consider yourself undeserving of playtime. I believe hobbies are an essential element of a healthy creative process. Without unfettered play, we lose perspective; without perspective, we lose a sense of the complexity of life; and without that, how can we really be creative? The fifth arena insures that you will attend not only to your future but also to your present. If you worry that this mapping of goals is a recipe for a grim world of tireless striving, use your fifth arena to crack that idea wide open.

Once you have decided on your five arenas and discussed them with your partner (in your third session), begin to fill out the calendar. Concentrate on larger goals rather than daily or even weekly tasks. Make sure you keep each of your goals lined up in the column underneath its arena. This way you can look at the months ahead and see where your energies will be focused.

Post the calendar near your creative work space and use it to keep yourself aware of deadlines before they creep up on you, and to get a feel for the arc of your progress. After two months, bring your calendar back to your partner and fill in as much of the next few months of goals, deadlines, and aspirations as you can.

Six Tips for Staying in the Process

1. Embrace Inspired Procrastination

When you are really pushing yourself to accomplish your ambitions, you will sometimes be struck by ideas of divine procrastination. While it would be a mistake to welcome all of these ideas, some you should act on with impunity. If you are plagued by procrastinitis, you may as well follow your inspiration to action—even if you know it's a kind of detour. Since these little acts are done in a moment of spontaneous abandon ("What the hell, I can't seem to focus, I may as well do this!"), they can allow you to be much more courageous than if you tried to do the same task from a place of method and will.

Anna, a conceptual artist, was stalking around her apartment, drinking coffee, and worrying about an installation she was stuck on. In a fit of procrastinatory zeal she sat down and wrote a letter to a world-famous conceptual artist who she had always considered a kindred spirit. In the letter she explained how the conceptual artist's work had touched her and how it had dovetailed with her own ideas about art. The famous artist was moved by the letter and wrote her back immediately. This became the foundation of a correspondence between the two women which lasted years and developed into a friendship. Had the young woman never been possessed by this inspired procrastination, she might have never had the guts to write the letter. In this way, if you are seized by the urge to do "something crazy" while you are procrastinating on your "serious work," honor that urge. Who knows what fruit it will bear in the long run?

2. Roll with the Punches

Let the momentum of your creations carry you. There won't always be a direct path to your goal. Though Bob always wanted to be an inventor, his first invention—a new kind of flashlight—was so successful that it turned into a business. During those years of running a small company, he complained that he never wanted to be a businessman—he longed to get back to more "high-tech" inventions. In the meantime, he was learning to do things he never dreamed he could do. Eventually he sold his company and, with the money he had made, set up his dream laboratory. Had Bob rigidly decided that he was an inventor and only an inventor, he might never have earned enough capital to focus on his invention full-time. By the time he sold his company, he had capital and invaluable business skills. Going the long way to his dreams was the path that proved the smoothest.

3. Accept Your Stubbornness

Sometimes you just don't want to do things. You don't want to schmooze your neighbor who works in film, ask your mother for a loan, charge friends for your newly invented brand of bodywork, or intern for free at the local theater company. Maybe you should; maybe it would "help your career." *But you just don't want to!* More important, you won't. Maybe you will eventually. But right now there's no way in hell!

Knowing what you're willing and unwilling to do is crucial. Spending hours wringing your hands over how you loathe to network or how you're just not comfortable "selling out" is a waste of precious time. Accept that you are just not willing to do certain things to promote your career. Focus on what you *are* willing to do and then get to work.

4. Don't Dis Your Opportunities

It is easy to devalue the opportunities that avail themselves to us. When we look at other people's situations, we immediately see the advantages of their particular circumstances: "Her father's in the music business—she has so many connections." "He is a loner with no responsibilities, how can he *not* focus?" "She knows so-and-so; I don't know anybody." "He grew up in three cultures; everyone wants to hear bicultural stories these days, he's a shoe-in at the festival." But what opportunities do other people recognize in *your* life? Whether these "opportunities" are friends you can call on for advice, innate talents, a loving family member, or an unusually difficult life experience, do you really see them as the great resource that they are? Or do you shrug them off and focus on analyzing the great advantages that everyone else has? If you do recognize your opportunities, do you take full advantage of them, or do you let them slip away one by one?

It is the rare individual who can see and make use of all the opportunities life offers him or her. This, however, is an essential ingredient in the lives of most successful creatives. This is the true definition of resourceful: seeing resources where other people can't. I see so many people get stuck waiting for their "big break," not realizing that their big break has come and gone many times and they have not had the presence of mind to notice.

List any opportunities that you now see you missed in the past:

Now list the opportunities in your life right now:

Now ask each opportunity: Am I willing to act on you? Cross out all the opportunities that answer with a resounding no. Post the rest of the opportunities in your to-do book and begin to incorporate them into your action plan. If you're like most people, these opportunities are more than enough to fill up your to-do list for the next two months.

5. Relish Confusion

Yes, the creative adventure will always be confusing, but you will learn to realize that confusion is part and parcel of the creative adventure. Unlike your friends with stable, predictable jobs who answer "same old, same old" to your question of what they have been up to, you will always feel a degree of delirium, wonderment, and yes, dismay. Sometimes it will manifest as anxiety and neurosis, other times as giddiness and playfulness. If you follow the heart of your creative passion I can guarantee you this: You will never be bored.

6. Ward Off Panic with a Profane Mantra

When you are seized by the natural fear that comes from doing what you feel certain you cannot do, fight these feelings with sheer irreverent repetition. Create your own profane (or sacred) mantra and repeat it to yourself while you carry out the abhorrent task—whether it be sitting down to your novel or calling an important agent. By silently chanting "Y'all are worms" or "Blessed be" or "Sweet stinker" (or some stronger language), you can cut through the paralyzing panic of anticipation and move forward. Your irreverent mantra will occupy your conscious mind while you let a deeper part of yourself take over and do the work. Just as an actress suffering from stage fright might quell her fears by imagining that the audience is buck naked, your profane mantra can demystify even the scariest of situations. Just don't speak it aloud!

JOE GOODE, CHOREOGRAPHER

Choreographer Joe Goode grew up in a lower-middle-class home in the prefab projects of Virginia with his crazy, dispossessed Yankee family. Despite his father's liberal leanings, Goode's interests in dance and theater were not encouraged: "It wasn't okay for me to be a dancer, and it wasn't okay for me to be a fag—both of which I was hell-bent on doing. They would have much rather seen me direct my intelligence toward doing something that would make money." After college Goode moved to New York and split himself between the world of modern dance by day and experimental theater by night. "My twenties were very schizophrenic—moving between Cunningham's very faithless and intellectual dance and raw-nerve experimental theater," he says. In his late twenties he became disillusioned with dance, its superficiality and its false heterosexual context: "Here I was trying to be a gay man with a little bit of dignity, and every day I had to go to work and act like a heterosexual. That was true both in the theater and dance worlds." After following a boyfriend to San Francisco, Goode decided he wanted to create his own work. "I wanted to create something about the gay experience which isn't about 'beefcake' or sucking dick, but about living this other way," he says. "I wanted to write, to act, and to make big, dangerous movement. It was my last-ditch attempt to make theater and dance work for me."

His greatest time of frustration and disenchantment led to the discovery of his artistic voice: "I was really disillusioned, but it was my last attempt. I feel so well served by not caring what people think. I didn't care if I was going to get a good review. I really just wanted to see if I could make work that I found meaningful, or if I had to get out of the business. Then, for the first time, I started really enjoying the work and I started listening to the people I was working with and that's when my work improved."

He also learned that his creativity flourished in a collaborative rather than solitary art form. "When I worked solo, it was excruciating. I'd go into the studio alone," he says. "The day-to-day was too lonely, too alienating. I don't do that anymore. I work with people with the same interests: a way of partnering, a way of colliding material, of colliding sound. Now the challenge for me is about how to negotiate with people, how to make the work environment jovial and electric."

When his work began to get attention and develop a following, he handed the entire five thousand dollars of his NEA fellowship to an administrator to set up his company as a nonprofit organization. His background as a professional performer in New York served him well in the business of running a company: "I was coming from this very aggressive New York scene where there were three hundred people at a casting call to this extremely laid-back environment where just a tenth of that energy would take me as far. I wasn't afraid to say to people, 'This is my idea, it's unlike anything else you have here and you need it and people are lining up outside the door to get it, so you better give me a grant or a show or an opportunity.'"

Now Goode divides his time between teaching, rehearsing, performing, and the administrative work of running his company. Touring and university residencies often take him out of town for weeks at a time. As a daily action, he practices sitting meditation and modern dance techniques.

As a teacher, Goode often has aspiring dancers and choreographers look to him for guidance on their careers, but often the advice he offers isn't what they expect: "There's something I say to students and they always look at me like I have three heads. 'Approach the experience of working as the point of pleasure. This is it. This is as good as it gets. Right now. Being here in this workshop and deciding how to put it together. This is as vibrant as it's going to get. Doing it in Europe or at some prestigious little downtown loft theater doesn't change that very much, if you're not vibrant and alive and aware. If it doesn't please you, if it doesn't engage you, then it's never going to. That fifty-thousand-dollar paycheck at the end of it is not going to make you happy.'"

Goode thinks that young artists often make their art without taking into account the experience of the audience. "I'm pretty realistic about theater as a place where you go to learn, but also to be titillated, thrilled, exhilarated," he says. "A lot of people are offering up stuff that is really bland. It's not really an edible kind of food. Feels kind of staid and studied and academic. You have to imagine your butt in that seat and ask if you'd really like to watch this. Is it better than what you can get on cable? Artists are not asking themselves what the experience is like. They end up editing themselves in strange ways—taking out the good stuff, the spontaneous stuff that reveals something particular to them, and leaving in the skilled stuff that everyone else is doing."

He also sees young choreographers misstep in terms of their careers by setting their goals too low and not strategizing enough about how to reach their ideal audience: "If you only make one show a year at some group theater, you're not going to have the momentum. You also need to strategize: 'I want to talk to women in their childbearing years because that's my issue, so where am I going to find these women? How am I going to say "Gals, this is for you"?' A lot of it is context. There are so many specialized groups; why not insert yourself into that setting? It only takes one person who does the programming. I think as dancers we limit ourselves in terms of the scope of where our work might really resonate. We don't think of content enough. Am I talking about something that could get out of dance and relate to some other community? It takes some strategizing, but I think it's doable. Keep asking yourself the questions, Who am I in this? Who cares about this? There are a lot of curious, intelligent people out there who are willing to support your work. You will find each other."

Finally, like many of the successful artists I interviewed, Goode expressed a faith in the ability of any artist to create a life around their creative work: "This is where I'm a little Pollyanna, but I really believe it. If you really devote yourself to something and approach it with honesty and pleasure, then there will be a life in it. It's really that simple. That's not to say you might not have to work at a restaurant on the side. It might not come to you in a paycheck with a pension, but you will be able to do it."

Glimmers in the Granite

In my workshops I have witnessed the magic of people reorienting their lives toward their creative work and I have seen a multitude of creative types secreted away in the most unexpected places. Artists are embedded like secret jewels throughout our society: on downsizing lists in corporate boardrooms, in suburban kitchens mixing up strange new brews for warts, in retail shops redesigning the window displays, in reception rooms across America writing songs to the beat of the Xerox machine, in classrooms, in unemployment lines, in heavy labor jobs.

Sometimes I hear people say, "Everyone thinks he's an artist, but real artists are, by nature, a rare commodity."

This widely held belief has always struck me as particularly odd. Certainly being a committed artist is a difficult thing to do, but so are a lot of pursuits in life—like being a good parent, for example. Isn't being a truly creative person at least as variable and open-ended as being a good parent?

Imagine the following conversation:

"So you want to be a good parent."

"Yes."

"Well, that's pretty ambitious, not many people are really great parents."

"Yes, I know it's a difficult job."

"Well, the world works against you, there are no rules or guarantees and so many disappointments. Don't you see how much you'll have to sacrifice?"

"It's always been a dream of mine—"

"It's everyone's dream. But being a good parent isn't something you can learn—you either have it or you don't."

"Oh."

"And how much money can you make being a good parent?"

"You're right—I guess I should give up."

Do you hear how bizarre this conversation sounds? It sounds weird because we don't see excellent parenting as a limited resource—too demanding and difficult for most people (though maybe we should). We see good parenting not as a zero-sum economy but as a limitless spring ebbing and flowing with people's understanding, desire, and will. Why can't we approach creativity with the same open-ended definition?

"It's an economic problem," you argue. "Our economy can only support so many artists."

Why? Are we somehow cosmically or genetically destined to support international furriers, car companies, bomb factories, and the multibillion-dollar industry of advertising instead?

Yikes, an ideologue! You may be tempted to cross your fingers to ward off the utopian vibes coming off this page. But the purpose of this rant is not to convert or convince but simply to ask you—if, indeed, you are yearning for a life of creativity—what is stopping you? Is it really the outside world?

Though the professional arts have fallen on hard times, signs of a grassroots movement of creative action are springing between our toes. Nuns in Massachusetts are teaching Julia Cameron's book *The Artist's Way* to inject their congregation with a sense of creative exploration. In Oakland, a master's program in creative spirituality teaches creativity as a spiritual rather than professional pursuit. All around the country, extended learning courses in creative writing, art, and theater are springing up, responding to a growing need. Independent film is booming; poetry is experiencing a renaissance. These grassroots movements respond to a growing sense that many people feel the need to create art, not just read about it in *Vanity Fair*. I believe we're poised on the edge of an era in which creative action will become what fitness was for the latter twentieth century—a sweeping popular trend that touches millions of lives. Like the fitness craze, creativity will suddenly be recognized as a necessary ingredient for a well-balanced, healthy life. This groundswell of creative play will celebrate the extraordinary actions of everyday people. Not only will this movement enrich the lives of the creatively reborn, it will create a society that values, appreciates, and—finally!—supports its artists.

Until that day arrives, though, the creative souls of this world must strategize on how to keep their bodies nourished and their minds alive. *You must not quit!* Not only for yourself but for the world. As playwright Romulus Linney wrote:

> No one religion can console this enormous country. No single philosophy convince it. No therapy relieve it of its burdens. No legal system comfort its injustice. No medicine deliver it from pain. No government give it joy. Art does all that. Claim that discipline, belong to it—you will give to the America I hope you love gifts its government cannot imagine.

The Art of Incorporation

How does one integrate creativity into a career? How can you make a living *and* be an artist? How can you take creative risks within your job? Whether you're a starving artist seeking stability or a quagmired professional sprouting creative wings, the project remains the same: incorporating these new needs into your life without discarding the elements of your life that are now working well for you. The task of incorporating old and new patterns is difficult because most of us have been taught to think in diametric opposites.

For the sake of experimentation, discard your hard-knocks philosophies and suffer-to-gain theories; rethink your either-or models of decision making. Cast away feelings that if only you could be more perfect, more positive, then everything would be spiffy. Instead, for the next year, when feeling pinched by two opposing forces—say, money and creativity—don't ask yourself to choose *between* them, ask yourself how you can incorporate *both* into your life. Ask strangers, people you admire, people you love, people who respect you. Ask the good listeners; ask your journal; ask your dreams. If you get answers or ideas, play with them on paper and in action. Follow where the actions take you in an active and open-minded way. Don't settle for amputating one of your limbs when the world deserves nothing less than your whole self.

Once this discerning but open-minded voice takes root, you will begin to see problems in a different way. You will not need to primly translate the word "crisis" into "challenge" to keep yourself optimistic. You won't need to mumble halfhearted affirmations between shots of espresso. You will be interested in experimenting with solutions to the problem. The process will become a game you want to keep playing rather than a punishment you suffer. Faith won't mean "thinking positive," but an evolving understanding of creative questing.

Sure, you need to act in relation to a real world with real limitations, but when you have lost your internal compass, how can you know which way is forward? In this day of ever-increasing technological advance and individual mobility, there are more and more possibilities and at the same time fewer and fewer obvious career tracks. As with modern love, most people don't marry the first career they have a crush on, they have numerous relationships which may or may not end up in a permanent bond. While this situation does create new instabilities, it also creates a wealth of new challenges that artists and innovators are particularly well suited to tackle, because you are by nature curious people. I like to think of your curiosity as a coded message which, like a secret password, will someday unlock your future course. You may not know how to decipher the message now or what doors it will open, but if you continue to play with it, you will eventually break the code. However, if you lose this message, you won't know what to do even when you come upon the right door.

I end with a final piece of advice. Throw away your creative process, your plan of action, your grand organizational systems and healthy habits, but do not forsake your curiosity. For without it, all the techniques and ambitions, timetables and tantalizing aphorisms are powerless to help you on your journey to a creative life. Follow the torch of your interest: Use the ideas and tools in this book when the flame grows dim or flies too far ahead, but keep your eyes fixed on that eternal inner spark—not of ambition or duty or talent, but of your greatest and most precious gift: your burning curiosity.

EXERCISES IN LAUNCHING THE LIFE

THE FIVE-ARENA CALENDAR

1. Pick your five areas of focus—from your art to your job to your life. Fill in the goals and events coming up in each of these arenas. Don't write out all the little steps, just the major actions. Fill in as much as you can and post the calendar. In two or three months fill it out again with updated actions and goals in each of these areas (see next two pages).
2. Meet with your partner for the second time. Brainstorm with each other.
3. Using free association, define the following words in your own terms:

    Career:

    Job:

    Work:

    Art:

    Plan:

    Goal:

    Now look back to the last page of the introduction and compare your definitions before you began this process. What changed for you? Do any of the new definitions reflect a new attitude about your future?

4. Create your profane mantra for moments of fear.
5. List three ways you will celebrate your embarking on this journey. Congratulations!

    1.
    2.
    3.

Life Worth Living Calender: Five Arenas of Endeavor

Month / Weeks	Storytelling	Storytelling business: classes in schools, performances for elderly	Freelance videography	Multimedia work	Dance
January					
1	sign up for Teisha's class			call Fernando, ask for internship	Take class 3x a week
2			xerox more posters		
3					
4	finish lizard series by Jan. 31	rough draft of brochure	poster five hours		
February					
1		call schools & other contacts		go to library, see what's been written	ask Maria about trip to Brazil
2	Start new story about Nubis	call retirement homes	poster five hours		
3			send to galleries and art schools	join organizations	
4		finish brochure			
March					
1	finish nubis	do mailing—40 brochures	shop for new camera	Network! Call everyone and offer barter in exchange for training	
2	begin long piece about my mother				
3					
4			poster five hours		
April					
1					
2					
3					
4	apply for grant				
May					
1					
2					
3				get part-time work in the field	street performances
4					

Weeks

arena

Life Worth Living Calendar: Five Arenas of Endeavor (cont'd)

Month	arena			
Weeks	1 2 3 4	1 2 3 4	1 2 3 4	1 2 3 4	1 2 3 4

Life Worth Living Calender: Five Arenas of Endeavor (cont'd)

Weeks

1 2 3 4 | 1 2 3 4 | 1 2 3 4 | 1 2 3 4 | 1 2 3 4

MEREDITH MONK, COMPOSER, CHOREOGRAPHER, FILMMAKER, PERFORMER

Over the past thirty years, Meredith Monk has created pieces in numerous media, from vocal music and performance art to dance and film. While the scale of her projects ranges from bare-bones solo performances to three-act operas, Monk sees all of her work as part of the same exploration: discovering the hybrid forms between traditional genres.

Monk's life combines equal parts solitude and interaction. Sometimes she works alone in her studio, "keeping up her instrument" and developing her creative material. Once a project gets under way, she often works with large groups rehearsing, planning, and performing. Although her work demands the communication skills of a leader* and the singular focus of a maker,† she is a classic inventor‡—driven to create as a form of investigation. Her work explores new ways of mixing voice, movement, image, and strands of narrative: the nonverbal oratorio, the postapocalyptic cabaret, the non-narrative epic. Open, unaffected, and remarkably humble, Monk has managed to escape the rollercoaster of fame and adulation by viewing success with suspicion and staying focused on her artistic intentions. She is living proof that following the path of your purest curiosity gives you the means to discover what you can best give the world.

Q: You've worked in so many media—did you have a vision early on of being so interdisciplinary?

A: I don't see them as many different media. I see them as all a part of one thing. Music composition was a strong part of my growing up. At Sarah Lawrence I studied dance in a combined performing arts program. Already in school I was trying to figure out how to combine music and dance. I was doing a lot of work with very cinematic structures. I was also in the voice department at Sarah Lawrence, doing opera workshops and singing every day. In school I began to glimpse how I could create a form which combined music, movement, and images. I wanted to use all the rich and various resources of the performer. The more I

---

*For a definition of the leader, see page 77.
†For a definition of the maker, see page 65.
‡For a definition of the inventor, see page 79.

thought about that, the more I realized that Western theater was really the only tradition that did not naturally integrate all of these elements.

After I graduated from Sarah Lawrence and came to New York presenting my own pieces, I started vocalizing every day. One day I had a revelation that the voice could be like the body, in that it could have the same flexibility and range that the body could and that I could, in fact, find a vocabulary built on my own vocal instrument, just as I had on my body with movement. So that was how I started working with my own voice.

Q: When you graduated from college and moved straight to New York, how did you make a living?

A: I did art modeling and I was teaching children dance classes out in Brooklyn for the first year. But in those days it was fairly easy to get along. There was very low rent.

Q: Did you have any mentors?

A: At Sarah Lawrence, I had a wonderful teacher, Bessie Schonberg. She was a real guide for a lot of us in that she was able to see each of her students as an individual. She always encouraged me to follow my own path and really follow it to its limits. I really needed that encouragement at that point. As a teenager I already had a glimpse of wanting to create something, but I didn't know what exactly. So she was very important to me as a guide.

Q: What was the most frustrating period for you in your development as an artist?

A: Oh gosh, I don't think I can think of one particular period, it's more cyclical. Sometimes I have real outpourings of creative energy and sometimes I have the feeling that it's the desert and I'll never have another idea again. I have to live through those periods. It always comes out that the energy is renewed again, but during those seemingly empty periods I'm always miserable. I realize more and more that it's a normal part of the process, though, so I'm a little more used to it now. I have more faith.

Q: Is there anything you do if you get blocked?

A: I try to keep my instrument going. I keep my voice going; I keep my body going; I try to practice piano. That's just basic physical maintenance. But it often gets my creative energy going. I also read a lot, which is really enriching for me.

Q: What are the elements of your creative process? Some people talk about their daily routine, others talk about what motivates them. Others talk about a real ephemeral transition from a dream idea to something that's manifested in people or paint.

A: It's a little bit of all of the above. When I'm lucky enough to have a routine, at an artist's colony or somewhere I can really concentrate, the routine itself is very generative for me, because it means hours of exercises and from there I can go on to creating. I'm not always able to do that because of demands made on me, like if I'm on the road or in New York with responsibilities taking up my time. The other part is that if I do get an idea, it starts to generate its own energy, that begins the process. I always think that the creative process is like throwing seeds into the ground. You keep waiting to see which ones will sprout. You might follow all the seeds for a while, but eventually some will grow and some won't. Part of it is a certain kind of patience; going through the process of working on the material and seeing where it will go. The beginning of a piece for me is really just flying blind. It's like jumping off a cliff voluntarily. It's painful, but that's what you have to do because otherwise you're basically repeating yourself. For me, the excitement is the process of discovery.

Q: When you make each piece, do you have different generative arcs depending on the medium of the project?

A: Yeah, it's also a matter of which medium is the most appropriate. Would it be better live or in film, will it be a musical piece or a music theater piece? A lot of my creative process is figuring out which form I'm working in, because each piece is a different balance of many elements. I'm always trying to find a new way of working between the cracks of the different forms. It's like the last piece, *The Politics of Quiet*—it took me the whole process to figure out exactly what the form was. It turned out to be a kind of nonverbal oratorio. *Turtle Dreams,* a work from the eighties, was based on the cabaret form—halfway between music and theater. Exploring forms is essential to my investigation. I realize that investigating is part of my pleasure. Even though it can sometimes be very painful not to know the answers at the beginning.

Q: Could you talk about any of your failures and how you lived through them?

A: What I've found over the years is that when I think a piece is a failure, usually the next piece is the one I was going for in the first place. I was thinking about a piece called *Small Scroll* which I did in the seventies. I was trying to work with a musical form that had elements of narrative, so it was between abstract and nonabstract. And it just didn't quite work. Sometimes when I'm really stressed about something, it gives me energy to find what the next thing's going to be. The next piece after that was *Quarry;* that was a piece in which I felt that all the elements were really woven together and balanced. The difficulty is knowing when to push through and when to let go.

Q: Did you have support from your family?

A: My mother was a performer, so there was always an understanding of my life choice. And yet her world was very different; she was a commercial singer. She did jingles and was on the radio. I'm not sure she completely understood the idea of pursuing your own path rather than getting the gratifications of the commercial world. But I think that both my parents were very supportive in the early days.

Q: I've seen the Peter Greenaway movie about you, and what struck me was that your style of direction looked so easy and, well, unauthoritarian. Was developing that style a struggle for you?

A: When I was a younger artist, it was a much more obvious dictatorship. I've been trying to work more on people knowing where all the decisions come from so that there is a sense of participation. For example, *Atlas,* commissioned by the Houston Grand Opera, was a huge project, and I was creating all these elements: composing the music, working on the scenario, performing, directing. I was working with people that I hadn't worked with before, so a lot of that process was first of all familiarizing the cast with the way I work. I had completed a lot of musical material going into the first round of rehearsals, which I taught to everybody, so that people wouldn't know what roles they were playing. In a sense I wanted all the material to be imprinted on their voices and bodies. When it came time for somebody to do "this" part of the material, but not "that" part of the material, it didn't become, "Well, I'm only in charge of this" and "How many lines do I have to sing?" I was really trying to avoid that hierarchy as much as I could, because I find it really oppressive; it makes for a lot of pressure. Trying to soften up is something I've been working on for years. I can still be extremely impatient and sharp when I'm not paying attention—I come from a traditional dance background where everything was based on fear; where you felt like you got something out of somebody by scaring them half to death. At one point I realized how unnecessary and pointless this approach was. Now I try to start with a sense of respect and from there keep in mind that people are very vulnerable as performers.

Q: Have your thoughts about success changed over the years?

A: I think I've always had a lot of caution about it. I've wanted my work to speak for itself and I've never wanted to be in a situation where there's so much hype that it has nothing to do with the work. My goal has always been to just be working my whole life. I've found that sometimes when fame gets out of hand, it starts to take over and have a life of its own. You tend to get further and further away from the source of your work. That's something I've been very wary of. In a certain way I've had my foot on the accelerator with my other foot on the brake, so that I could take my own time, to let it come in its own time.

Q: When you started, were you motivated by the idea of success or fame?

A: I had a lot of drive, but it was tempered with caution. I saw people who were playing to the media and were just ground into hamburger meat and never came out of it again. Their work ended up getting destroyed. Sometimes it's hard, but lately I've tried to let praise as well as criticism roll off my back and take neither of these things that seriously.

Q: Do you have any tricks that you play on yourself when you don't feel like working?

A: Get out the old black coffee. Sometimes I'll say to myself that I can do something after I finish working and I can't do that unless I finish the work. It's difficult sometimes—dealing with inertia; dealing with the resistance. But it's also a matter of acknowledging that the resistance probably takes more time and energy than actually doing the work. Which is hard to remember.

Q: Describe the transition from young struggling performance artist to making money from your work.

A: There were a lot of years where it was hard to keep my head above water. It's still hard. I never did this work thinking that I was going to make money. There were no grants in those days. So there was no expectation. I really think everybody was working out of love. Nobody got paid to do anything. And then in the late sixties, the National Endowment for the Arts started its grants program and we started going out on national touring programs and doing wild environmental theater pieces, making site-specific pieces in each place we visited. We did that for a couple years and people got paid a little bit. It was really hand-to-mouth for years and years. I didn't start doing okay financially until my late thirties. Since about 1992, it's been really hard with the NEA cutbacks. I'm going out as a soloist now because organizations can't pay for a group to tour. But I've been very lucky because I'm flexible.

Q: Did you feel that when you started the organization, you knew what to do?

A: No. On-the-job training! I had no idea whatsoever.

Q: What do you think of the current dance/theater scene? Is it supportive of younger artists?

A: Even though there's not a lot of funding, I think things are changing. The field in New York has opened back up in an interesting way that comes from not having the financial support. In the eighties there were people who had gotten their manager before they had done their first piece! Big business entered the field, but that's not happening so much anymore. Now people are sharing—there are performance spaces that are opening up and people do collaborative concerts. You have to be around to know what's going on. What's interesting is that now there are all kinds of exciting places to be other than New York, like San Francisco and Minneapolis. We just toured to Ann Arbor in the fall and that's a pretty exciting town. So there are cultural centers all throughout America.

Q: When you look at other talented artists who haven't been able to carve out a life based on what they do, what do you think you have or understand that they perhaps didn't?

A: Sometimes I'm not sure exactly. Sometimes I think it has to do with luck. For me, I feel I was in the right place at the right time. I had a lot of drive and I would never take no for an answer. It was just a certain kind of will during a particular period. Now I'm trying to learn how to let go of that will, a little bit.

Q: Have you been active as a mentor to any young artists?

A: A lot of the people who have worked with me end up going and doing their own work and I always feel good about that. Early on, I realized that another performer could not be totally satisfied all the time by doing my work exclusively. I can barely satisfy myself! You realize that people have their own things that they need to explore. They can explore a lot in your work and find balances to what they need themselves, but your expression is never going to be totally fulfilling to somebody else.

Q: What kinds of projects are you working on now?

A: I made a service for the Union Theological Seminary in July of 1996—it was for the American Organists Guild—and I designed a nonsectarian service. It made me think a lot about how to make a form that's more direct than theater. We had a great time. I used a lot of my choral music from over the years. It was performed in a beautiful space, a chapel with all the seats out. We had people singing from all over the building.

Q: Was it accompanied by a sermon?

A: No, we just used short texts from a lot of different spiritual traditions—a little Zen poem, a line from Rumi, from Martin Buber, Hildegard Von Bingen, a crazy wisdom Buddhist text, a Native American women's prayer. I wove these together with the music and a little bit of movement. We'll continue doing it through 1999. We're going to teach it to groups from all over the world and one day in 1999 we're going to perform it simultaneously. The texts come from the entire millennium and even before, so it seems like a great thing to do in 1999.

Q: Do you do any kind of daily practice?

A: I do a Tibetan Buddhist sitting meditation practice called Shambala. It's what they call the homeowner's practice. The Shambala practice appeared thousands of years ago in a lot of different Asian countries like India, China, Japan, Korea, Tibet. The legend is that there was a kingdom called Shambala which was ruled by an enlightened king, and he brought the Buddha in to teach him how to maintain an enlightened kingdom. The Buddha didn't let his monks come with him, because it was something that was only going to be for citizenship, not for monkhood or going into a monastery. It's really very simple, very fundamental. It's about enlightened citizenship, and how to be compassionate. I've found that vision to be extremely helpful. It's a very expansive vision and simple, to the point. No bullshit at all. I'm not able to do it every day, but I carry it with me in all situations.

Q: If you could give one piece of advice to a beginner in your field, what would it be?

A: Take courage. Follow your vision.

Selected Bibliography

Not only is this not a comprehensive list, it's purposefully selective. I did not include all the relevant or related books that I have read. Rather, I limited it to those books I found especially helpful and inspiring. The large percentage of books about writing is a reflection less of my personal interest than of the surfeit of readable material on the subject.

The Artist's Way, by Julia Cameron. Jeremy P. Tarcher/Perigree, 1992. A twelve-step program for creatively blocked artists of every ilk. Great psychological observations about the nature of the creative act and all the ways we rail against it.

Becoming a Writer, by Dorothea Brande. Harcourt Brace, 1934. One of the first and most eloquent accounts of the invisible psychological work necessary for becoming a writer.

Creativity in Business, by Michael Ray and Rochelle Myers. Doubleday, 1989. A spotty but often engaging application of self-help and spiritual techniques for the businessperson seeking new ways to think creatively.

CVJ: Nicknames of Maître D's and Other Excerpts from Life, by Julian Schnabel. Random House, 1987. A very personal account of the author's early years as a struggling painter in New York in the seventies and eighties, accompanied by full-color prints of his work.

Finding Your Writer's Voice, by Thaisa Frank and Dorothy Wall. St. Martin's, 1994. A book of wonderful exercises and short essays geared to help you discover your writing voice.

Impro, by Keith Johnstone. Theatre Arts, 1979. Though it is primarily geared toward theater artists and creative teachers, it remains one of the best books about the creative process ever written.

Meditation, by Eknath Easwaran. Nilgiri Press, 1979. The only spiritual self-help book I've read from cover to cover. A practical, often funny guide to becoming an enlightened being.

Terpsichore in Sneakers: Post-Modern Dance, by Sally Banes, photos by Robert Alexander. Houghton Mifflin, 1980. A historical recounting of the postmodern dance movement, with fascinating interviews with various avant-garde choreographers like Yvonne Rainer, Anna Halprin, and Trisha Brown.

Silences, by Tillie Olsen. Virago, 1980. A powerful look at how sex, class, color, and history influence writers and their ability to create.

Voicing Our Visions, edited by Mara R. Witzling. Universe, 1991. Excerpts from the writings of female visual artists throughout Western history. Lots of anguishing over how one develops an artistic voice and enough self-confidence to persevere. Great company for miserable moods.

Wishcraft: How to Get What You Really Want, by Barbara Sher with Annie Gottlieb. Viking, 1979. A general self-help success guide with an upbeat, no-nonsense approach and lots of useful observations about the problems and solutions to pursuing your goals.

The Writing Life, by Annie Dillard. Harper & Row, 1989. Gorgeous, pensive essays about the internal process of writing and, by extension, any creative act.

Index